PRAISE FOR *MAGIC AT THE CROSSROADS*

"*Magic at the Crossroads* tackles the taboo topic of the devil, an archetype as misjudged and maligned as that of the witch. Kate Freuler, through diligent research, leads readers down the lesser-known pathways of witchcraft to discover the devil as an icon of enlightenment and self-rule, not malevolence. Freuler invites readers to set aside entrenched dogmatic narratives and welcome these figures as symbols of challenge and emancipation, representing resistance to dominating and repressive forces. Her book goes beyond historical recounting, advocating for a witch's path marked by the magic of enlightenment, strength, autonomy, and metamorphosis for the audacious."

—**MAT AURYN,** author of *Psychic Witch* and *Mastering Magick*

"Kate Freuler provides an interesting examination of the devil as he appears in modern witchcraft and Satanism. Helping illuminate a topic once considered taboo, Freuler provides a valuable discourse that will simultaneously challenge preconceived notions and stir up sentiments of sorcerous rebellion."

—**KELDEN,** author of *The Crooked Path* and *The Witches' Sabbath*

"Kate Freuler takes us back to the origins of an age-old tale that is marked with taboo, transgression, and adversarial forces every step of the way, providing us with a witch's keen perspective.... Kate provides occult practices, plant lore, and regular self-check-ins to empower the reader with the tools necessary for this journey of inner illumination. Whether your path is to the left, to the right, or in between, *Magic at the Crossroads* is part of an important process of self-realization."

—**COBY MICHAEL,** author of *The Poison Path Herbal*

MAGIC
AT THE
CROSSROADS

ABOUT THE AUTHOR

Kate Freuler is the author of *Of Blood and Bones: Working with Shadow Magick & the Dark Moon* and has written articles for *Llewellyn's Magical Almanac*, *Llewellyn's Spell-A-Day Almanac*, and *Llewellyn's Sabbats Almanac*. She lives in Ontario, Canada, and can be found making art, wandering around in libraries, and writing. Visit her at www.katefreuler.com.

MAGIC AT THE CROSSROADS

KATE FREULER

THE DEVIL IN MODERN WITCHCRAFT

LLEWELLYN PUBLICATIONS · WOODBURY, MINNESOTA

FIRST EDITION
First Printing, 2024

Cover design by Shannon McKuhen
Interior art by the Llewellyn Art Department except for the following:
  Baphomet on page 187 is an Éliphas Lévi drawing and is in the public domain.
  Seal of Solomon on page 226 is in the public domain.
  Treatise on Man on page 195 is a René Descartes image and is in the public domain.

Llewellyn Publications is a registered trademark of Llewellyn Worldwide Ltd.

Library of Congress Cataloging-in-Publication Data

Names: Freuler, Kate, author.
Title: Magic at the crossroads : the devil in modern witchcraft / Kate
    Freuler.
Description: First edition. | Woodbury, Minnesota : Llewellyn Publications,
    [2024] | Includes bibliographical references and index. | Summary:
    "Through historical references, religious writings, and pop culture,
    this book explores the intersection between witchcraft and the devil"—
    Provided by publisher.
Identifiers: LCCN 2024009578 (print) | LCCN 2024009579 (ebook) | ISBN
    9780738776293 (paperback) | ISBN 9780738776385 (ebook)
Subjects: LCSH: Devil—History. | Witchcraft. | Satanism. | Magic. |
    Ritual.
Classification: LCC BF1531 F69 2024 (print) | LCC BF1531 (ebook) | DDC
    299/.94—dc23/eng/20240527
LC record available at https://lccn.loc.gov/2024009578
LC ebook record available at https://lccn.loc.gov/2024009579

Llewellyn Worldwide Ltd. does not participate in, endorse, or have any authority or responsibility concerning private business transactions between our authors and the public.
    All mail addressed to the author is forwarded but the publisher cannot, unless specifically instructed by the author, give out an address or phone number.
    Any internet references contained in this work are current at publication time, but the publisher cannot guarantee that a specific location will continue to be maintained. Please refer to the publisher's website for links to authors' websites and other sources.

Llewellyn Publications
A Division of Llewellyn Worldwide Ltd.
2143 Wooddale Drive
Woodbury, MN 55125-2989
www.llewellyn.com

Printed in the United States of America

ALSO BY KATE FREULER

Of Blood and Bones:
Working with Shadow Magick & the Dark Moon

DISCLAIMER

This book contains references to topics that may be upsetting for some readers, such as death, blood, and murder. This book also mentions the use of blood and bodily fluids in ritual. Should you choose to include these in your practice, please be absolutely certain to read the safety precautions provided.

Do not touch or ingest any poisonous or potentially poisonous plants. Do not handle any plant or flower unless you are 100 percent sure of its identity. The information in this book is not meant to replace any kind of professional medical care. Readers are advised to consult their doctors or other qualified healthcare professionals regarding the treatment of their medical or mental health concerns. Neither the publisher nor the author takes any responsibility for any possible consequences from any treatment to any person reading or following the information in this book.

ACKNOWLEDGMENTS

When I first started writing, something I didn't know about the publishing business was that a book takes years and a whole team of people to come to fruition. I spent my youth pouring over Llewellyn books with the crescent moon on the spine, so having my name on two of them is pretty cool. I'm very lucky to have had supportive, creative, and smart people on my journey as I've grown as a writer. A huge thank-you goes out to my editors, Heather Greene and Lauryn Heineman, without whom my writing would never make it to the shelves. Your guidance, patience, hard work, and faith in my work are priceless. I also give heartfelt gratitude to everyone at Llewellyn who is part of the process that makes my books possible. Llewellyn has given me opportunities that I always dreamed of.

Thank you to my husband for being a steady counterbalance to my chaos and supporting all my creative endeavors, even the failed ones.

Thank you to my two sisters for being my best friends and weathering life's storms with me. Three is better than one.

Thank you to everyone who has read my books, given feedback, and learned something. It's an amazing privilege to be part of your experience.

Thank you to the fellow authors who have inspired me, taught me, befriended me, and made me feel welcome.

Last but not least, thank you to the people in every area of my life who have encouraged and supported my creativity, knowingly or otherwise. I see every single one of you.

For Norm and Rosemary

CONTENTS

FOREWORD

The devil truly is in the details. Far too often, polite society suppresses the darkness that lies within us all. We build proverbial cages for our animalistic nature, but we come down to the human zoo to catch a glimpse of our shadow selves. As our animal spirits roar to be released, we may titter and squeal or draw back in horror of such a savage display. We retreat to the security of "normal behavior," and we feel relieved because those animalistic urges are safely locked away. However, dear reader, in picking up this book, you have come to the crossroads, and at these same crossroads you will find Kate Freuler. While she will not require you to sign away your soul, she will ask that you come with an open mind and a thirst for knowledge. Take a keen look at yourself and understand the ever-evolving devil within us all.

I grew up in the height of the satanic panic in the mid to late 1980s, which changed my life forever. I had been attending an Assemblies of God church with my parents when a guest minister came to preach a revival. He, being an "ex-Satanist," came to speak how his newly found faith had changed his life and given him purpose to expose the demonic influences of pop culture. Nothing was safe. My parents soon learned how demons were summoned to spread a satanic agenda in Saturday morning cartoons, in movies, in music, and even through toys. Suddenly, many things I loved were now considered "of the devil" and had somehow possessed some ancient, sentient, anthropomorphic evil hellbent on seducing as many souls as possible, with the solitary intent of dragging good Christian folk away from the church and into an abyss of eternal torture.

While Scooby Doo, He-Man, the Smurfs, and the music of Queen were all frowned upon as being latent tools of the devil, the foulest trick employed by Satan himself was the seemingly innocent celebration of Halloween. I was told that Satan used that day to mock Christ, to be exalted and celebrated before the advent of the King of Kings, in his late December holiday. To those in the budding Evangelical movement, Halloween was a day in which wealthy moguls venerated and welcomed the Dark Lord in exchange for profits on candy sales. Witches would look for children to sacrifice and would drink of the fat of the recently deceased. It was a day when devil worshippers would gather in dark robes to poison chocolate and listen to heavy metal. Of all the days in the year, Halloween was the one I feared the most. While other children donned homemade costumes or dressed as their favorite superhero and went door to door collecting candy, my siblings and I were huddled in the dark listening to a well-worn cassette recording of *Turmoil in the Toybox*. My parents, as kind and loving as they were, made certain that on that day, the drapes were closed tightly and the porch light was sensibly off, to detour any wayward trick-or-treaters who may inadvertently spread the message of Satan. (Not that we would have any visitors anyway on that evening because we lived in the woods a mile from town, but it was a risk my parents would rather not have taken.)

Though I grew up in a household where Halloween and the Care Bears were seen as evil, *The Addams Family* was not restricted. As a boy, my parents would take me to their doctor's appointments, where I would scour the *New Yorker* pages looking for Charles Addams cartoons, which always made me question not only how things work but how they could work. By 1989, I was addicted—nay, obsessed—with the 1960s reruns of the television show depicting the family that bore the Addams name. When the 1991 film came out on video, to the chagrin of my parents, I would beg to stay home from church and watch it on TV, regardless of how many times I had seen it. I admired that the Addamses were bold enough to be different. That even though the world did not understand them, they were happy being themselves. To this day, one of my favorite scenes is when Gomez sits watching daytime television. On screen is Sally Jessy Raphael, aping both her own show and the now-infamous Geraldo Rivera and his exposé on Satanism: "You claim your son was kidnapped by Voodoo witch doctors and forced to recruit others. Let's take a call."

The camera turns to Addams, who with excited eyes and a devious smile says, "Hello, Sally!"

She abruptly cuts him off, saying, "Mister Addams! Please stop calling! We do not know where they meet!"

The year 1991 was too close to the terror of the satanic panic and the misinformation spread by the aforementioned Geraldo Rivera to have a film's lead be too closely aligned with Satan. At the time, it was understood that when the word *Voodoo* was used, it meant "in league with the devil." Though often conflated in media, Voodoo and Satanism are not the same thing, but both are othered.

After over thirty years, *The Addams Family* still stands as a satanic film. So many Satanists see themselves in *The Addams Family* and pattern their lives to look much like the famed family of ghouls. In the 2019 animated rendition, all the Addams cousins gather in the mansion. In a final scene, a bald man sporting a goatee and horns walks in and greets Gomez, a direct reference to Anton Szandor LaVey, founder of the Church of Satan.

Though there is no mention of *The Addams Family* in this book, I felt it was appropriate here. One of the most endearing traits of those little *New Yorker* cartoons, the television shows, and the many films they inspired was how accepting and welcoming of the outsider they were, regardless of what society may have had to say about it. This book challenges you to be the outsider, to welcome the outsider, to understand the outsider. In this book, you will find magic that can be adopted into your own life and adapted to suit your own magical practices. Whether you are a follower of the left-hand path or are referred to as light worker, whether you are theistic, atheistic, nontheistic, monotheistic, pantheistic, or are simply a lover of history, you will find something in this book that will inspire you. Better the devil you know.

Kate Freuler fills this book with relatable knowledge and takes you on a journey from ancient times when horned gods were praised to modern witchcraft and cinema. She guides you through the perilous witch trials and the satanic panic and delves into conspiracy theories that have plagued the internet in more recent years. She takes you on a voyage but does not leave you adrift. She brings to light real magic and rituals that will help you heal, grow, and bring self-empowerment.

The symbol of the crossroads is a powerful one. Like the devil himself, crossroads bring you options. As a solitary practitioner myself, I find that I am often taking the road less traveled, but this book makes me feel less alone.

Hail Satan—but more importantly, hail thyself!

Richard-Lael Lillard

INTRODUCTION

It took me a long time to get the nerve to write this book. Satan is not often a welcome character in the world of modern witchcraft or anywhere else. After all, the word *witchcraft* has been dragged through the mud enough already without bringing the so-called personification of evil into it. At the same time, the visceral reaction people have at the mere mention of the devil, specifically those who are part of the witchcraft community, is precisely why it's worth taking a closer look at him.

More and more these days, people are drawn to Satan as they come to learn that the modern devil represents something quite different from what they've been taught. Many concerns are unique to a witch's perspective, and that's why I thought it was time someone wrote a book about our relationship with the devil. Because regardless of where you fall under the witchcraft umbrella, that relationship almost always exists.

When I first began fleshing out ideas for this book, to my dismay, it gave a rather flat explanation of modern Satanism, which wasn't what I wanted to create. While modern Satanism is certainly a big influence in my practice and daily life, the devil has so much more depth than his current form leads people to believe. It's true that when viewed solely as a Christian construct, he is quite young compared to Pagan gods and goddesses. But when thought of as a preexisting concept, he has been shape-shifting in and out of human life for ages in many forms: a force of nature, a deity, a symbol of rebellion, an inspiration, a scapegoat, and even as entertainment.

This book will dissect the overlap between witchcraft and the devil and attempt to explain their relationship. As you read this book, it may help to have a working knowledge of the basics of folk witchcraft, magic, Wicca, or a similar path, but it's not absolutely necessary. My intention is to encourage those within the community to consider various aspects of the devil and highlight the ways that his symbolism can enhance an existing witchcraft practice. To acknowledge the devil doesn't mean you must forgo your faith in the old gods or change your current beliefs.

Before delving deep into the topic at hand, I think it's important to share my own experiences with the devil to create context. While much of this book is based on research, it's also largely based on my own perspective, which naturally doesn't perfectly match that of others. I personally have spent my life in a mostly Christian society, so the majority of this book is written in relation to this experience. That being said, I think there are quite a few people out there who can relate to my story.

DEVIL ON MY SHOULDER

I have been fascinated by witchcraft, the occult, and mysticism since I was a child. Back then, information on the subject was hard to come by, so I had to make do with a handful of history books at the local library. These sources were filled with classic woodcuts and paintings of witches alongside the folkloric devil. Sometimes he was a beast with horns, cloven hoofs, claws, wings, and scales. Other times he was a dapper gentleman in black. Occasionally, he was a mixture of both. Almost always, he was a consort of witches.

My fascination with this character continued until I was around sixteen and finally got my hands on some modern books about witchcraft and Wicca. I discovered, to my dismay, that witches didn't believe in, or acknowledge, the devil and found the association insulting. Like many people still are, I was inundated with flawed history, taught that the devil was not real to witches but merely a current incarnation of the old horned gods—a concept that isn't quite accurate. The devil, *my* devil, appeared to be just as much an enemy of witches as he was of the church.

I was confused.

These new books told me that witchcraft had nothing at all to do with the devil. Yet at the same time, there were all these historical scripts and artworks depicting witches and the devil together, having a wonderful time, from what I could see.

I proceeded with the understanding that if I were to call myself a witch, I could no longer indulge in my fascination with the devil and must instead turn to older gods and goddesses. While my life and practice were certainly enriched by learning about various deities, I never could seem to replicate the connection that I had with Old Man Splitfoot.

Eventually, I got my hands on *The Satanic Bible* by Anton LaVey. At the time, it helped me understand the basic atheistic beliefs of Satanists. I found the book entertaining, at the time not understanding its more problematic elements (no internet back then!). I also discovered that LaVey and the Church of Satan were opposed to all kinds of mystical thinking, including all the witchy stuff I knew and loved.

There I was, stuck. On one side, I had the modern witch world rejecting Satan and, on the other side, the modern Satanist world rejecting witchcraft. I didn't fit anywhere.

Fast forward a decade or two, and my first book, *Of Blood and Bones: Working with Shadow Magick & the Dark Moon,* was published. This book doesn't involve the devil, but it does discuss some elements of witchcraft that are considered controversial. I found out through the grapevine that some people were reluctant to read it for fear of promoting evil magic. This showed me that even within our very open-minded community, there are wide-ranging opinions of what constitutes evil, which inspired me to contemplate its place in witchcraft.

That's how I found myself back where I began: with my good old misfit pal, the devil. I rediscovered not only my connection to him but also that there are growing numbers of witches and magical practitioners who feel the same way I do. I also found the modern satanic movement, which, while not mystical in nature, still attracts people who seem to share my worldview. Seeing the devil go mainstream has been both vindicating and entertaining.

All of this to say, I've never been able to fully separate witchcraft from the devil, and if I'm being completely honest, I don't really want to.

The reason I'm able to overlook the Christian aspects of the devil and include him in my witchcraft is because I see him as larger than what the church has reduced him to. He is many things at once. He represents a part of humanity that is older than biblical teachings and has always existed, but his current form is painted by Christian beliefs. I also view him as a powerful symbol that can bring meaning not just to my own witchcraft but to politics, social issues, and more.

After reading this book, you might too.

WITCH OR SATANIST?

Labels are handy. They tell us who someone is in one neat and tidy word and give us a sense of their values and beliefs. Choosing an identity for yourself can be empowering, particularly something like *witch*. It's natural to actively seek a category and put yourself safely in it. However, over the years, I've come to resent labels, as I have found them to be divisive, absolutist, and exclusive. For instance, someone who calls themselves a witch might be ridiculed if they also call themselves a Satanist. Labels are highly subjective, which means that there is always someone who wants to argue about your label and whether or not you deserve to bear it. Often, a label is chosen to satisfy others. For these reasons, I choose not to have one. People can call me a witch, a Satanist, or whatever they like. They will anyway.

We can be an amalgam of many things, even traits that contradict one another. Just as the devil has been depicted with both wings and hooves, which never occurs in nature, we too are a mix of complicated beliefs and experiences that don't always fit neatly in a box.

In the end, that's the beauty of it. You get to decide what your relationship with the devil is, whether it is symbolic, political, spiritual, or otherwise. You get to decide if you believe in magic or not. You get to choose your beliefs. You don't have to label yourself if you don't want to.

WHY WRITE THIS BOOK?

Considering the current state of the world, it's becoming clear that the real evil is not the devil but an imbalance of power and rampant corruption. When you learn the history, you might begin to understand that he's not really the bad guy after all but a powerful force against these monstrosities. Here are the goals of this book:

To Create Understanding: Sometimes polytheistic witchcraft, which is the veneration of multiple gods and goddesses, doesn't work for everyone. Going from one god to many or, as in my case, splitting the well-known devil into multiple deities doesn't always feel right. For your witchcraft practice to be authentic and meaningful, it has to resonate with *you*, not anyone else. The elements you include in your practice trigger emotions and raise energy. If you didn't grow up with multiple deities, they may not have this effect on you. You might wish to focus on one that is familiar.

To Dispel Myths and Broaden Viewpoints: I'd like to bridge the unexplained, unacknowledged gap that hangs in between the subject of modern witchcraft and the devil. If you're an experienced witch, then you know that witchcraft and Satanism are two very different things, but perhaps you have begun to wonder why, where they overlap, and where they don't. I urge you to read this entire book and not just skip to the rituals. You will need the background information to form a true understanding of what the devil stands for.

To Explore the Devil as a Macrocosm: I've attempted to gather up all the faces that the devil has had over time to show that he is a large phenomenon with many manifestations throughout history. The devil is so much more than a myth about a vicious ruler of hell. As we dig through all his facets and how they developed, we can better understand how to include him in the practice of witchcraft.

To Unify Witchcraft and the Devil: We'll explore the origins of the devil and his place in the history of witchcraft. The witch has always been the misfit, the outsider, and the scapegoat. To say that witchcraft has nothing in common with the devil seems willfully blind. Writing this book opens the conversation and hopefully addresses this confusion. The devil and the imagery associated with him hold meaning on a vast cultural level. Integrating him into your witchcraft practice can create a strong sense of purpose in your personal and spiritual life. Yes, the devil can be spiritual!

To Find Empowerment: I venerate the devil not as a theistic Satanist but as someone who resonates with his archetype. You might not be familiar with this archetype yet, but you will learn as you read. He is a divine rebel, a force against authority, and the right to be different. He symbolizes freedom of thought and expression. He is the light of imagination, creativity, and the courage to challenge what stands in your way.

The devil is not our enemy. Witches have been accused of cavorting with him for thousands of years. I propose we learn about this instead of shunning it. And maybe, just maybe, when the persecutors of the past said witches were in league with the devil … they were right.

PART I
THE DEVIL YOU KNOW

What do you think of when you hear the word *devil*?

The devil changes depending on who is looking at him, but no matter what, you know him well. He is the master of lies but also the serpent of knowledge. He's deemed the destroyer of humanity, yet he rules over earthly pleasures. He is the voice of revolt against tyranny for some and the personification of terror for others. He's depicted as a beautiful angel leading an army out of heaven but also a hideous beast from the bowels of the earth. He is inside every one of us but simultaneously cast out as the most shameful and foul parts of our humanness.

The history of the devil is a long and winding road of both light and darkness. What you see depends on where your heart lies and what you have been taught. Truth, however, overrides both. To get to the truth, we have to dig deep into the dirt of history. Grab a shovel—we're going to hell and back.

CHAPTER 1

IN DEFENSE OF THE DEVIL

As some of you probably know, venerating the devil raises a lot of confusing questions, and approaching the topic is complicated. One concern is that I'm dumping salt into a wound that witches and Pagans have had to live with for years. Another issue is that honoring the devil, whether as a Christian being, a societal construct, or a much older force, isn't the "right" way to practice witchcraft.

My response to these concerns is that history is ever evolving. The only constant is change. While neo-Pagans adamantly and justifiably denied association with the devil in the past for fear of persecution, I think this view is beginning to shift. To me, the devil appears to have grown beyond his biblical ties and developed his own set of values, beliefs, and attitudes. Most modern Satanists view the devil not as he is depicted in stories told to control and frighten people but as a symbol of the adversary, meaning one who stands in direct opposition to tyrannical forces. These forces are not necessarily religious but are behind systemic control today, just as they were behind the original witch hunts. The devil is not to blame for the trials and tribulations witches and Pagans have faced, for the satanic panic of the 1980s, nor for QAnon conspiracy theories. The human beings who participate are to blame. The devil, in these cases, is simply an ideological scapegoat for the ugliness and cruelty inside the hearts and minds of those involved.

CULTURAL CONDITIONING AND RELIGION

Some witches disdain organized religion and will not tolerate any trace of it in their practice. This is understandable, but in my experience, religion and its impact on us are almost unavoidable due to cultural conditioning.

As you go through life, your social environment impacts your internalized values, resulting in deeply programmed, unconscious beliefs. This includes things like judging right from wrong, social hierarchy, and more. We learn to behave in the approved ways and to expect certain behavior from others by collectively following what are called cultural norms. A cultural norm can be so deeply entrenched in our psyche that to go against it is uncomfortable and, in some cases, impossible. Some cultural conditioning is positive, such as the general rule that we all protect children. Other aspects of it are not so great. Much of it can be traced back through the generations before us to religion.

You don't need to be religious to understand the many outdated, harmful cultural norms in the West. Some are damaging yet so overreaching that we can't escape them. Take, for example, shame about the body, the concept of purity, and gender roles. Many of these things are rooted in monotheistic religion and are part of our life, even if we consider ourselves secular. Sometimes these views are so ingrained in people that they simply believe them, never questioning why.

I am an example of this cultural conditioning. As someone raised in a secular household, I used to think that I was uninfluenced by religion. However, over time I came to realize that despite having rarely set foot in a church, a lot of my unconscious perspectives were, in fact, shaped by Christianity: how I viewed myself; how I should think and act; where I, a woman, stood in relation to men; and what parts of my mind and body I should be ashamed of. Who decided these things? Because it wasn't me.

I am not free from Christian influence any more than I am free from the weather. It has surrounded me at every turn of my whole life. And whether I like it or not, it has permeated. Therefore, the devil is relevant to me.

In the last few generations, some people have stopped identifying their values as religious, but said values haven't changed. In this way, what was once a religious rule has become an unconscious cultural norm. For example, an atheist might be a bigoted misogynist, yet never wonder why they hold their beliefs. Acting against these beliefs was once considered evil or of the devil. Therefore, going against harmful societal norms can be considered the devil's work.

The power of conformity is monstrous, a constant pressure that all too often breaks people in such a way that they never fully experience their unique value or celebrate their true selves. In fact, many times, we're told that our uniqueness is bad, immoral, or silly because it is different.

In this respect, the devil is not just a religious figure. He is a presence within society and yourself who battles for freedom of expression and equality. He is the spark within that makes you chafe against ideologies handed down by your predecessors, telling you that you're innately flawed and that your natural self is shameful. He is the repository for all that is othered, cast out, or scapegoated. He is the collector of broken souls and the hero of misfits.

Reclaiming the devil is to embrace all the very natural things inside of you and fight back.

Historically, people who dared to question cultural norms were considered in cahoots with the devil. I say if the shoe fits, wear it!

THE SUBJECTIVE NATURE OF EVIL

Witchcraft is sometimes dubbed "evil" by those who don't understand it. The devil is subjected to the same treatment, keeping even the most curious of witches at a distance. But what is evil, really? It's generally something that inflicts harm, is offensive, or clashes with one's morals. It's also often a label that gets carelessly slapped onto unfamiliar things.

But there are many layers to it. Evil is difficult to define. What one person considers evil, another doesn't. It is shaped by context, perception, personal values, and social norms.

Some people believe that using witchcraft for cursing or love spells is evil. They're entitled to their opinion, but things are never as simple as they seem on the surface. What if a curse is done to protect oneself? Cursing an abuser to stop them from continuous harm doesn't sound evil to me. A witch trying to get a specific person's attention doesn't strike me as a terrible breach of free will, either. In the witchcraft world, what is considered evil is endlessly debated. There are no official rules, just opinions. My life experiences and values may be different from yours, and therefore, what we put into the "evil" category will not be the same.

Some things in history that were considered evil seem silly now, such as being born left-handed. This shows how the definition of *evil* shifts and how it will continue to do so. What you think is evil now might not be in a few hundred years.

Evil has often been used to make people behave in a desired way. While sometimes this helps maintain social order and prevents total chaos, it can and does become problematic when people's identities, authentic selves, and personal freedoms are unfairly villainized.

Evil was also often used to label anything that didn't conform to group standards or that challenged the existing power structure. So, to say that Satan himself is evil is not exactly accurate; Satan is merely that which was considered undesirable to the herd or group at any given time.

Nowadays, the act of standing up and fighting against oppressive norms is generally considered a positive thing. This further compounds the growing realization that the devil, with all his questioning, challenging behavior, just might be the good guy after all.

THE MANY FACES OF THEISM

Throughout this book, you'll see words like *monotheism*, *polytheism*, *atheism*, and more. To understand the different ways that the devil is perceived and to form your own opinions about him, it's important to know what these concepts are.

Theism is the belief in one or more divine or higher beings more powerful than humans, who create the universe, decide fate in some cases, and interact with people in their day-to-day lives. When someone is a theist, they believe that deities are real and that they can have a relationship with them. It also often involves belief in an afterlife, be it reincarnation or a place of reward. There are different kinds of theism. Monotheism is the belief in one supreme God. Religions like Christianity, Judaism, and Islam are monotheistic. Polytheism is the belief in multiple gods and goddesses. Pagans are polytheists, as are some witches. Duotheism is the belief in two complementary deities of equal power, such as the God and Goddess of Wicca.

Atheism is the rejection of all mystical and religious beliefs. Atheists do not believe in any gods at all, nor an afterlife or great creator. Instead, they look to science regarding creation and evolution. Atheists do not acknowledge the existence of spirits, psychism, or magic. Most modern Satanists are atheists. To take it one step further, there is the term *antitheist*, which includes people who, in addition to being rigidly opposed to any and all religions, have strongly negative views on those who follow one.

Nontheism is kind of a grey area. It's not quite atheist but not quite theist. I know. It's confusing. A nontheistic witch might be someone who believes in magic and spirits but not deities. This person might connect to nature, ancestors, or the spirit of place instead of gods and goddesses. They might also have beliefs about an afterlife but one that doesn't include deities. I myself fall into this category. I view deities as archetypal and created by humans, but I maintain my belief that there are unseen energies at play in the universe and within our minds that are very powerful and can be harnessed.

THREE KINDS OF DEVILS

Throughout this book, the devil shows up in three different ways: as the theological devil of biblical origins, the folkloric devil based on legends and superstitions, and the symbolic devil of atheistic Satanism.

The theological devil is the direct enemy of God in monotheistic religions. Early Christianity glorified intangible matters like the soul and the afterlife. The state of one's soul and devotion to divinity trumped corporeal experience. The theological devil was the antithesis of this. He represented all things earthly, such as survival and pleasures of the flesh, which were dubbed evil and dirty. This evil extended into all kinds of human behaviors, like emotions and instincts. The theological devil was at fault for all that was wrong in the world and all personal ills. Any action that was not in pursuit of the divine was the theological devil's territory. Additionally, this theological devil was at war with God and constantly trying to undermine him by tricking humans into straying from the divine path and dragging their souls to hell.

As Christianity took over Europe, there was a long period when Pagan and Christian beliefs overlapped, and this is where the folkloric devil was born.

The folkloric devil is a mishmash of stories, superstitions, and bits of old beliefs mixed with the Christian devil. The folkloric devil got many of his qualities from tales told by word of mouth, the witch trials, art, and literature. Some folk tales were lessons to warn against temptation. Others were to assuage fear by making the devil seem foolish. Some of his qualities were influenced by remnants of the old gods, while others originated in fairy tales and legends. This devil didn't always encompass pure evil like the theological devil. He could be clever, humorous, or silly. He was known to make pacts with those who dared, particularly witches. In 1643, the General Assembly of the Scottish Church declared that the causes for witchcraft are "found to be these especially—extremity of grief, malice, passion and desire of revenge, pinching poverty, solicitation of other witches, and charms; for in such cases the devil assails them, offers aid, and much prevails."[1] It would appear that those who questioned their place by pushing against poverty and suffering were the ones who were likely to be influenced by the devil. To me, this matches Satan's later incarnation as an adversary against authority and injustice.

---

1. Thomas Stephen, *The History of the Church of Scotland: From the Reformation to the Present Time*, vol. 2 (London: Longman, Brown, Green, and Longmans, 1848), 119.

This brings us to the symbolic devil of modern atheistic Satanism. This devil is not considered a real being at all but a symbol of revolt against tyranny. This symbol is based on mythology, literature, and art. In this context, Satan is the one who dared to thumb his nose at overreaching authority, use his intelligence to circumvent it, fight for his freedom, and challenge the rules. This version of Satan was embraced by Romantic-era revolutionaries of the 1800s as an icon of rebellion and is upheld as a representation of liberation and individualism in modern Satanism.

THE LEFT-HAND PATH

You may have heard the phrases *left-hand path* and *right-hand path* in discussions about spirituality. The right-hand path is distinguished by a belief in a higher being or beings who decide fate. Often this superior being makes judgment calls and can be communicated with or appeased. The left-hand path differentiates from these beliefs by turning instead toward the self. The right-hand path strives for goodness in its various forms, sometimes to the exclusion of all else, while the left-hand path welcomes the reality that there is value in destruction and darkness and aims to learn from them.

Witches who lean toward devilish doings are sometimes referred to as left-hand path practitioners.

The left side has always been considered different or even evil. The English word *sinister* comes from the Latin *sinister*, meaning "on the left side." There is a Bible story in Matthew 25:33–35 that portrays the left side as devilish. It says that at the end of the world, each person will be judged as either a sheep, which is good, or a goat, which is bad. Sheep will be placed on the right side and goats on the left. Those on the right will go to heaven, and those on the left will go to hell.[2]

To understand how these terms came to be used in discussions of magic and witchcraft, we can also look to the history behind left- and right-handedness. Being left-handed is rare, so it was once considered

---

2. Matthew 25:33–35 (King James Version).

a sign of witchery and something that needed to be eradicated. In centuries past, left-handed people were thought to be prone to demonic possession, and children were trained to use their right hands for fear of future deviancy.[3]

Defining the left-hand path is difficult, as it exists on a spectrum. On the tame end is a reasonable willingness to embrace both light and darkness in magical practice, acknowledging that destruction exists alongside creation and that both are equally important. At its most extreme, a practitioner embraces purely controlling practices aimed at harming others, considering themselves masters of the forbidden elements of magic. There aren't very many of these practitioners, and those that do exist tend to self-destruct, as this belief points to an inner problem.

The left-hand path embraces corporeal existence in tandem with varying levels of spirituality. For example, atheistic Satanists are considered of the left-hand path, but they don't believe in anything beyond the material. At the same time, Luciferians are of the left-hand path and some have a belief in magic. Then you have left-hand path witches, who are a mixture. Sometimes this means embracing magical practices that might be considered taboo by the larger community. It's a path of individuality that is not based on dogma or the morals of others and is frequently self-directed. The left-hand path often puts the self if not in place of gods, then at least on par with them.

So what does that mean for a witch interested in the devil? It means that you can combine beliefs that are corporeal and self-directed with spirituality. You don't have to be an atheist to include the devil in your practice, and you don't have to be devoted to deities to be a witch. You can find a balance. You can think for yourself.

---

3. Editors of Merriam-Webster, "The Left Hand of (Supposed) Darkness," *Merriam-Webster*, accessed November 3, 2023, https://www.merriam-webster.com/wordplay /sinister-left-dexter-right-history.

THE BLACK MASS AND THE WITCHES' SABBATH

Two of the many things that mix witchcraft with Satanism in confusing ways are the Black Mass and the witches' sabbath. Often the terms *Black Mass* and *witches' sabbath* are used interchangeably because there's a lot of overlapping lore about them. However, they are not exactly the same.

The witches' sabbath was a secret meeting of witches, whereas a Black Mass was an event held by alleged devil worshippers specifically to mock and pervert Christian rituals. The overlap occurs in that the devil was said to be in attendance at both, and some of the purported rites were similar. The details of the Black Mass were influenced by earlier descriptions of the witches' sabbath that were obtained under torture.

The Eucharist, a Christian holy rite sometimes called communion, is believed to manifest miracles by turning water into the blood of Christ and bread, called the host, into the body of Christ. It was thought, then, that a defrocked priest could perform the Eucharist backward to manifest the opposite of miracles, like curses. This rite was named the Black Mass.

In the 1300s, the Knights Templar, a wealthy military order in Jerusalem, were among the first groups accused of performing a Black Mass. They were said to destroy holy objects, worship decapitated human heads, and pray to the idol Baphomet. They also venerated the devil, who sometimes appeared in the shape of a cat.[4]

Satan-worshipping witches also held Black Masses, where they allegedly defiled the host by stomping and spitting on it. Urine was sprinkled on congregants instead of holy water, and the wine was replaced with brackish dirty liquid.[5] Leading all of this was an excommunicated priest wearing black or blood-colored robes embroidered with a goat, an inverted cross, and satanic symbols.[6]

---

4. Sean Martin, *The Knights Templar: The History and Myths of the Legendary Military Order* (Harpenden, UK: Pocket Essentials, 2004), 119.

5. Montague Summers, *The History of Witchcraft and Demonology* (London: Kegan, Paul, Trench, Trubner & Co., 1926), 154, 157.

6. Summers, *The History of Witchcraft and Demonology,* 154.

The Eucharist was intended to bring congregants closer to God, so the Black Mass aimed to do the opposite, causing people to become their most carnal, unholy selves. The Black Mass, or at least the description of it, was always leveraged at an "other" religion. It wasn't set aside for just witches and Satanists but anyone who wasn't Christian. Most groups who strayed even a little from Christian doctrine were deemed heretics and accused of performing a similar ceremony.[7]

While the purpose of a Black Mass was to worship Satan and pervert the Christian faith, the witches' sabbath was much more. While it was often described as involving blasphemy and rejecting God, it has taken on deeper meaning and details over time. It's understood today as something completely different than a Black Mass.

One of the earliest recorded mentions of the witches' sabbath was in France in 1335. Many were accused, but two confessions obtained under torture stood out when it came to describing the ritual. Two middle-aged women, Anne-Marie de Georgel and Catherine Delort, claimed to have belonged to the devil's army for twenty years. They had promised to serve him now and after death and attended the witches' sabbath every Friday night. Anne-Marie de Georgel said that a giant beast had appeared to her while she was doing the laundry, inviting her to worship him. She agreed in fear. The beast blew into her mouth, enabling her to magically transport herself to the sabbath at will. She claimed the devil took on the form of a goat and that participants had sex with him in exchange for magical powers and knowledge of baneful potions and ointments.[8] Catherine Delort claimed that a shepherd had taken her to a crossroads at midnight, where they burned human remains. She put some drops of her blood into the fire, and a demon named Berit appeared. From then on, she would fall asleep on certain nights only to find herself at the sabbath, where she too had sexual relations with the devil, participated in orgies,

---

7. Ruben van Luijk, *Children of Lucifer: The Origins of Modern Religious Satanism*, Oxford Studies in Western Esotericism (New York: Oxford University Press, 2016), 44.

8. Jeffrey Burton Russell, *Witchcraft in the Middle Ages* (Ithaca, NY: Cornell University Press, 1972), 182–83.

and engaged in cannibalism.[9] Both women were burned at the stake. Using torture to force victims to confess and accuse others of witchcraft set a horrifying precedent for how the witch trials would be carried out in the future.[10]

Accounts of the witches' sabbath spread across Europe with the witch hunts. The appearance of the devil at the sabbath seems to be cohesive across the board. He is usually described as ugly and foul and sometimes takes on the form of an animal. While a goat was often reported, he was also said to be a wolf, a dog, a bull, a cat, or a mixture of these.[11]

To get to the sabbath, witches reputedly rubbed themselves with flying ointments made from the lard of unbaptized babies and hallucinogenic plants. Then they mounted a broom, pitchfork, or occasionally an animal. They flew up through their chimney and away to a remote forest or crossroads where the sabbath took place.[12]

During the sabbath, various baneful workings were performed, like cursing the livestock of one's enemies. There was feasting, which in some accounts included human flesh and in others consisted of rotten, disgusting food. After feasting came dancing and an orgy that included humans, animals, demons, and other creatures.

While many of the accusers claimed the sabbaths literally took place, there was some suggestion that it was imaginary, a hallucination, or that it happened in the accused's sleep.[13] It's highly unlikely they ever occurred at all, as the confessions were given under torture.

Over time, details about the Black Mass and the witches' sabbath have bled into each other and become interchangeable to some.

---

9. Russell, *Witchcraft in the Middle Ages*, 184.

10. Russell, *Witchcraft in the Middle Ages*, 182.

11. Michael D. Bailey, *Origins of the Witches' Sabbath*, Magic in History Sourcebook Series (University Park: Pennsylvania State University Press, 2021), 91–92.

12. Bailey, *Origins of the Witches' Sabbath*, 94.

13. Rosemary Guiley, *The Encyclopedia of Demons and Demonology* (New York: Facts on File, 2009), 217–18.

The Black Mass and Witches' Sabbath Today

The witches' sabbath has been reclaimed by traditional witches, who do not conflate it with satanic activity or a Black Mass. For modern traditional witches, the sabbath is a spirit gathering accessed by entering another realm. The sabbath is where witches, familiars, animals, faeries, and otherworldly beings meet.

Some modern ideas of the witches' sabbath are inspired by a book by Charles Godfrey Leland called *Aradia, or The Gospel of Witches* (1889). This book details the rites of a coven in Italy, which venerated various pagan deities, including Aradia and Diana. According to Leland, Aradia was sent to Earth to teach witchcraft to those who had been oppressed by the ruling class.[14] According to Leland, participants first consecrate the food and drink to Diana and then feast naked, followed by dancing and making love in the darkness.[15] The book also contains spells for wealth and love. Leland elevated female deities to creators of the universe and encouraged the notion that a secret society of Pagan witches existed underground during the Christian revolution. Despite being deemed historically inaccurate, Leland's writing led to the modern Wheel of the Year, composed of eight sabbaths that occur on the equinoxes and solstices. These celebrations have become the modern version of the witches' sabbath.

Current ideas of the Black Mass are, like most things connected to the devil, also shaped by literature. Anton LaVey, the founder of the Church of Satan, declares the Black Mass purely fictional yet goes on to explain it in detail.[16] He describes a naked woman acting as an altar, with a candle made of baby's lard in each hand. On her abdomen is a chalice filled with the urine or the blood of a sex worker. Above it all hangs an inverted cross. A defrocked priest recites biblical passages backward, peppering them with swearing and profanity. This is much like what was described

---

14. Charles G. Leland, *Aradia, or The Gospel of Witches* (1899; repr., Custer, WA: Phoenix Publishing, 1996), 5.

15. Leland, *Aradia, or The Gospel of Witches*, 14.

16. Anton LaVey, *The Satanic Bible* (New York: Avon Books, 1969), 99.

throughout history during inquisitions and accusations of devil worship. LaVey considered enacting rituals based on this a form of psychodrama to evoke emotion in the participants, not as a service to an actual devil.

The Satanic Temple famously held what they called a "Pink Mass" in protest of the Westboro Baptist Church, a small fundamentalist group in Kansas founded by Fred Phelps. Phelps claimed that the tragic Boston Marathon bombings in 2013 were God's punishment for the legalization of same-sex marriage and abortion. This church threatened to picket the funerals of the victims to express their anti-LGBTQ+ stance. Disgusted by this and previous displays of hatred from the fundamentalist group, the Satanic Temple and some supporters went to Mississippi, where Phelps's mother was buried, and held a ritual. The event included LGBTQ+ couples kissing over her grave, with the implication that the act would make Phelps's mother a lesbian in the afterlife. The Satanic Temple declared that their belief in this ritual made it true and irrefutable.[17] This was not meant to be taken literally but to show the absurdity of the church's beliefs, to poke at their bigotry, to offend the founder, and to give them an eye for an eye, so to speak, by mirroring the church's irrational behavior and statements.

PACTS WITH THE DEVIL

An extremely popular notion is that witches have made a pact with Satan or sold their souls. Pact-making is another area that blends witchcraft with the devil. Pacts allegedly occurred not just at the witches' sabbath and the Black Mass but among regular people who turned to deals with the devil to manifest their desires. A pact is an official agreement between two parties that can't be broken without serious consequences. In a pact, the devil would grant someone what they needed in the here and now in exchange for their soul after they died, which would go to hell for eternity.

---

17. Russell Goldman, "Satanists Perform 'Gay Ritual' at Westboro Gravesite," ABC News, July 18, 2013, https://abcnews.go.com/blogs/headlines/2013/07/satanists-perform-gay -ritual-at-westboro-gravesite.

Stories of pacts with the devil first appeared in the fifth century in the writings of St. Jerome. St. Jerome's story is the inspiration for many others of its kind, which follow variations of the same plot.

The story is about a peasant who is lusting after a beautiful girl who doesn't return his affections. In desperation, he goes to a magician who says he must spurn the Christian faith in writing, go to a remote place, hold the letter in the air, and evoke the devil. When the man follows these directions, demons appear and take him to hell. There, he promises the devil his eternal soul in exchange for the girl's love. Sure enough, the beautiful girl falls in love with him, and they marry. After a while, people start to gossip and wonder why the husband never goes to church, suspecting he isn't a very good Christian. He ends up tearfully confessing to his young wife that he has a pact with the devil. In the end, good overcomes evil when a saint saves the man, and he is accepted back into the good graces of his wife and his community.

These pact stories became most popular in Europe during the witch trials. They all tended to follow a similar storyline: The devil would approach an unfortunate person who was pining for something sinful like money or sex and offer to fulfill their needs in exchange for their soul. Sometimes there was a timeframe allotted to the pact, and after a specific number of years, the devil would come to collect his due. In some cases, the victim would be saved just in time by a saint or other biblical figure. The lesson was that good would always triumph over evil. Sometimes in these stories, the person outwits the devil, making him seem like a fool and rendering him a little less scary. In many cases, the devil was a trickster, and those who made a pact with him were left with nothing or in worse shape than when they began.

During the time of the witch trials, it was believed that all forms of magic required a pact with the devil and that witches traded their souls specifically for the power to harm others with magic. The pact was said to be written in the witch's blood on virgin parchment, which was made with the skin of newborn lambs or cows.[18] The *Malleus Maleficarum* claimed that the devil approached a victim in the guise of someone they knew with an offer they couldn't refuse.[19]

A seventeenth-century priest by the name of Francesco-Maria Guazza (1570–1600s) wrote a book called the *Compendium Maleficarum* (1608). In it, he listed the steps taken to create a pact between a witch and the devil. It went like this:

First, a person must deny their faith. Then, they are baptized by the devil and given a new name. They must reject their godmothers and godfathers and be assigned new ones by the devil. They give the devil a piece of their clothing to symbolize his ownership of them. A circle is drawn on the ground, and from inside this circle, the person declares their loyalty to Satan. The devil then strikes their name out of the Book of Life and writes it instead into the Book of Death. The new devotee promises to sacrifice children to the devil regularly and to give annual gifts of black objects to his demons. Then the devil brands them with his mark, which varies in appearance: the footprint of a hare, the shape of a dog, or the shape of a spider. They swear to attend the witches' sabbath on appointed dates, and in return, the devil promises them a happy life and afterlife.[20] Despite all this, Guazza claimed, they didn't actually receive anything because the devil never keeps his word.[21]

In folk tales, pacts were sometimes made in odd ways. One method was to kill a black hen in the middle of a crossroads while chanting the proper words to make the devil appear.[22] There was also an age-old practice of soldiers writing a dedication to Satan, promising him their souls,

---

18. Antonio Del Rabina, *The Grand Grimoire* (1752), 28.

19. Heinrich Kramer and James Sprenger, *The Malleus Maleficarum of Heinrich Kramer and James Sprenger*, trans. Montague Summers (New York: Dover, 1971), 101.

20. Francesco Maria Guazzo, *Compendium Maleficarum: The Montague Summers Edition*, trans. E. A. Ashwin (Mineola, NY: Dover Publications, 1988), loc. 542–75, Kindle.

21. Guazzo, *Compendium Maleficarum*, loc. 596, Kindle.

22. Del Rabina, *The Grand Grimoire*, 44.

presumably in exchange for safety in battle. These letters were later found on their dead bodies in the 1866 Austro-Prussian war.[23]

It would seem that tales of pacts served several purposes. They were fables warning against dealings with the devil, and in the case of the soldiers, they were a desperate bid for survival. They provided entertainment and eased the fears of many because the devil was often tricked in the end.

One of the sources that popularized pacts was the writing of Margaret Murray (1863–1963), whose work has been hugely influential on witchcraft history. Murray claimed that the witches' sabbath was actually the meeting of an ancient cult that worshipped a horned god, who, like the devil, accepted pacts from participants, albeit in a less transactional way.

According to Murray, a pact was written on paper which the devil kept in a secret place. The devil did not trick people into making pacts. Instead, he would inquire if it was what the witch truly desired, and they would answer yes. If the witch couldn't write their name, as many people were illiterate at this time, they would sign with an X, or the devil would help by placing a guiding hand over theirs. Sometimes this pact was written in the witch's blood.[24] Murray also claimed that in Belgium, if you went to a crossroads after dark carrying a black hen, the devil would appear. He would grant your desires in exchange for the hen in a deal that lasted seven years.[25]

A Welsh witch could create a pact with the devil by pretending to eat the holy wafer during communion and secretly stashing it in their pocket. After the service, a dog would meet the witch at the church gate. They gave the stolen host to this dog and were then granted the powers of witchcraft in exchange for their soul.[26]

---

23. Van Luijk, *Children of Lucifer*, 65–66.
24. Margaret A. Murray, *The God of the Witches* (New York: Oxford University Press, 1970; repr., 1981), 103.
25. Murray, *The God of the Witches*, 104.
26. Murray, *The God of the Witches*, 104.

Murray had a theory that the devil had to sacrifice himself every seven or nine years, which was why some pacts lasted that length of time. For seven years, the witch could live a life of luxury, but when the time was up, the devil would sacrifice her in his place.[27]

Faust

By far, one of the most well-known stories of pacts with the devil is the play *Faust* (1808), written by German author Johann Wolfgang von Goethe (1749–1832). Faust is based on the legend of Theophilus, a church treasurer who sold his soul to the devil in exchange for becoming a bishop. It was rewritten and retold many times, so there are multiple variations of the tale.

In Goethe's writing, Faust is a religious and intelligent scientist who is disillusioned with the limits of the human experience. His curiosity leads him to indulge in many sinful things, such as lust and greed, and even an interest in magic. Faust summons the devil, called Mephistopheles, and makes a pact. In exchange for his soul, Faust will be provided with every single thing his heart desires while on Earth. Faust signs the agreement in blood, pledging to renounce his Catholic faith and be property of the devil from then on.

Mephistopheles fulfills all of Faust's desires, including the love of a specific woman. However, having every wish at one's fingertips can make a person easily bored, and Faust soon abandons the woman after impregnating her and killing her brother. Later, when Faust discovers that she's in prison, he feels remorse and tries to rescue her, but he is too late, as she's gone insane in her cell. Mephistopheles complains that humans are often too cowardly to carry out the consequences of their pact with the devil.

Mephistopheles takes Faust to consort with gods, fairies, and nymphs, while Faust soaks up as much knowledge as he can about the formation of the world, heaven, and hell. Never satisfied, he wants bigger and bigger things. The consequences of this all add up, and eventually, Faust dies. In

---

27. Murray, *The God of the Witches*, 105.

Goethe's version, however, he is saved by angels in the nick of time and goes to heaven.[28]

However, other variations of Faust end quite differently. In *Dr. Faustus* (c. 1592) by Christopher Marlowe (1564–93), the character meets his end when a host of devils enter his room and carry him away to hell, leaving nothing behind but his limbs.[29] This version taught a clear lesson about the dangers of making deals with the devil.

WITCHCRAFT AND PAGANISM

When I was very young, I wondered if witchcraft and Paganism were the same thing. The short answer is no. The long answer is it's complicated. This question is important because polytheistic witchcraft is often confused with Paganism, which lends even more credence to the erroneous theory that witches must venerate old gods and reject monotheistic teachings.

There was a time when if you called yourself a witch, it was assumed that you fell under the Pagan umbrella. You probably know that when a Pagan is asked if they worship the devil, they will say that their gods are much older than him. This was once a stock answer for modern witches as well.

In the fifties and sixties, *Paganism* and *witchcraft* became almost interchangeable words due to a lack of historical information. Old gods and goddesses were blended with ceremonial magic and modern occultism. Misinformation circulated about the witch hunts regarding how many people were killed and why, which at the time was taken as fact. Until quite recently, if someone were to claim the identity of *witch* while acknowledging Satan, they'd be booed out of the community. But this is changing.

---

28. Johann Wolfgang von Goethe, *Faust: Parts One and Two,* trans. George Madison Priest, Great Books of the Western World 47 (Chicago: University of Chicago and Encyclopaedia Britannica, 1952).

29. Christopher Marlowe, *Doctor Faustus*, ed. Sylvan Barnet (New York: Signet Classic, 1969).

The word *Paganism* describes a religion or spiritual path that is rooted in reverence for nature and the belief in multiple gods and goddesses, which predates the mainstream religions of Europe and nearby areas. Paganism is often deemed an umbrella term for many nature-based spiritualities, such as Wicca, Druidry, Heathenry, and some witchcraft traditions.

Witchcraft, on the other hand, is much harder to characterize. Nowadays, we know that there are many kinds of witchcraft from around the world that are not Pagan at all. Paganism is largely European and only represents a small slice of witchcraft beliefs. Unlike Paganism, witchcraft is not always classified as being older than monotheism and is not usually deemed a religion. Witchcraft is a practice that is so varied that it's difficult to give it just one definition.

To me, witchcraft is the act of harnessing life energy from the earth and the cosmos and directing it to shape reality. It's also an everyday way of living that integrates the spiritual with the mundane. It can include veneration of spirits and ancestors and the ritualization of daily tasks. Witchcraft can be practical folk magic, or it can be ceremonial and theatrical. It can be animistic, theistic, or neither.

This is why someone who calls themselves a witch doesn't necessarily have to believe in gods or follow an established tradition. Many witchcraft practices are a conglomeration of cultural conditioning, religious syncretism, and personal gnosis. On top of that, many people are self-taught, which makes witchcraft highly individualistic.

As a witch, you can base your practice on what resonates with you. If that happens to be sprawling pantheons of deities, great. If not, that's okay too. If you find the Virgin Mary figure comforting, that doesn't mean you are barred from practicing witchcraft; include her in your practice. I have. This is where cultural conditioning and religious syncretism come into play. I'm not Christian, but I understand that Mary is considered a mother figure who is loving, forgiving, and someone to whom people turn when in pain and trouble. My personal impression is that she is a current, socially acceptable form of older goddesses. She presents a pious, agreeable expression to the Christian world yet is actually hiding every other female archetype behind her mask, which is necessary to appease patriarchy. Anyone who has ever had to hide parts of themselves to survive can relate to this. I feel the Virgin Mary keeps secrets and protects others who must do the same. I understand this is not how Christians view her, so please know I mean no disrespect. But this illustrates the way the aforementioned variables play into a witchcraft practice and how personalized it can be. (It also illustrates that I have never been to church.)

WITCHCRAFT AND SATANISM

In all this history, we can see that witchcraft and the devil go hand in hand. So far, I hope I've conveyed that the devil, or Satan, is something larger than the religious understanding of him as an evil underground beast. Satan is a modern symbol representing the oppositional stance against things that interfere with your personal freedom.

It can be difficult to separate the devil from monotheistic religion, and understandably, it's undesirable for some witchcraft practitioners. But there are many ways to understand the devil outside of his place in Christianity.

The ethics of Satanism are in line with that of many witches. You've probably seen the memes saying, "Harm none but take no shit," and that just about sums it up. I've noticed a distinct increase in practitioners embracing the previously shunned parts of the craft. There's an emerging understanding of the necessity of balance and examining the shadow side of things. It's no longer encouraged to preach about the boomerang effect of magic. The Wiccan rede states, "An ye harm none, do what ye will." People once erroneously took that to mean you must never do a single magical working that is not strictly for good. Nowadays, the general sentiment is more like, "Harm none, unless you need to." I consider this a healthy progression.

Much of what falls into the "unless you need to" and "take no shit" categories are in line with the symbolism of the devil. The devil is that deep-seated anger you feel when you're treated unfairly, the smoldering coal in the pit of your stomach when you experience hatred, and that sharp flash of ire that emerges when you defend yourself. These are perfectly natural feelings and should be embraced. I'm not saying you should express your anger with violence, but you should honor the feeling at the very least. If you discover that anger is indeed warranted, then practical action should be taken. For those who practice witchcraft, this may look like cursing or hexing, or it might be sending bad energy back to its source. Both can be justified courses of action.

People often stumble down the path of the witch due to being an outsider of sorts. The witch is the archetypal fringe personality, rebellious even, which is why so many people love to take on the title. One cannot deny that this is also the devil's territory, for he is the ultimate outcast.

Satanism tells you that you are your own god, and you can directly create change in your life right now, on an earthly level. It teaches that you deserve to better your situation in any way you can within reasonable, logical limits. To me, that sounds like an invitation to cast a spell or two.

Satanism in its various forms is on the rise in popular media and culture, and while this happens, people in the occult community are softening toward it. In the current landscape of shifting paradigms and social unrest, people are challenging aging doctrines and outdated thinking. This is what the devil has always been about.

Even so, the devil is rarely discussed in depth through the lens of modern witchcraft. I think almost anyone with an interest in the occult or witchcraft has at least been curious about the devil at some point.

Due to history and culture, witches and the devil have become linked in the collective unconscious. Just look at all the famous paintings, woodcuts, and other art that can be found in so many history books. This link is worth learning about, even for witches who choose not to believe in or acknowledge the devil.

THE ROAD TO HELL

The devil has been used as a convenient trash bin for all of humanity's ills and evils. Some people actually still believe that Satanists engage in human sacrifice and cannibalism. It would seem that choosing to align yourself with such a misunderstood thing is a questionable choice. It really makes you wonder, what is it about the devil that charms people so?

In the Middle Ages, the devil could be asked for favors in times of desperation. The clergy and upper classes did not look kindly upon the average peasant and certainly weren't interested in helping them in times of need.[30] This led to the logical notion that if the church was not willing to help them, then perhaps the church's rival would. Sometimes people are drawn to the devil nowadays for a similar reason, although it is much more nuanced than that. It's not just money or basic survival people seek, but a sense of power when they're suppressed and unjustly treated by those in authority. Most people don't actually expect the devil to appear and give them special abilities, but by identifying with him, they take a stand against something larger than themselves.

These days, when people are inspired to do some digging about the devil, they're often pleasantly surprised by what they find. But to create that willingness to learn, there must have been something that piqued their curiosity in the first place. Everyone is different, of course, but there are a few themes that can be noted.

Religious Trauma

Religious trauma can occur when someone has been indoctrinated with spiritual beliefs that are weaponized against them. It is characterized by an authority figure using threats of punishment from a higher power to control and terrify a victim. It comes in the form of physical, mental, or verbal abuse that is blamed on an unseen, all-knowing force. Religious trauma can lead to unfounded guilt, extreme shame, fear of punishment,

---

30. Robin Artisson, *The Clovenstone Workings: A Manual of Early Modern Witchcraft* (Hancock County, ME: Black Malkin Press, 2020), 18–19.

paranoia of unseen forces, and self-hatred. Sometimes children are told omnipotent beings are watching them at all times, waiting to punish them for every misstep, if not now, then in the afterlife. Usually, the missteps that are deemed evil are perfectly natural, such as anger or pleasure, making it impossible to avoid the wrath of the higher power. This leaves the victim in a state of constant fear. Best-case scenario, a person will reach a stage in their life when they begin to not only question these teachings but to actively fight against them. Sometimes the logical way to do that is to turn to the devil and his symbols as a means of fighting the mental effects of this abuse.

Rebellion

What lies at the heart of rebellion is individuality. A person rebels when they disagree with what the group around them is doing or when they want to make it known that they refuse to bend under the authority of an unworthy leader(s). A smaller-scale example would be when an individual lashes out against an unhealthy family or group dynamic. Rebellion is often the healthy response to being pushed down by a person or system. Most people can only tolerate so much tyranny before they reach a breaking point and fight back. The devil is the ultimate rebel, thumbing his nose at what some consider to be the most powerful being of all.

Outsider Status

Everyone has felt like a misfit at some point in their lives, but for some people, it's a deeply ingrained, unshakable feeling. This can be a result of actual ostracism from the people around them, or it can be a result of trauma. When someone is perpetually pushed aside and excluded, they eventually stop trying to fit in. Instead, this feeling plants a seed of resentment for the group and causes the person to look inside themselves and gain power in their difference. Some become drawn to the most loved—and hated—misfit of all.

Declaration of Personal Power

If someone is raised in an environment that culturally conditions them to abide by restrictive morals, and they disagree with those teachings, they are likely to seek out an oppositional stance that backs up how they feel. The devil promotes freedom of thought and expression, individuality, and equality. If someone is treated poorly for being different, they will discover that the archetype of the devil represents embracing that difference, which can be a profound act of self-love.

Apotheosis

Apotheosis is to become a god. Sometimes this term is used to describe the deification of the self or spiritual enlightenment. It can also have a more material interpretation of reaching the pinnacle of your abilities, developing your strengths, learning, and being your absolute best self on Earth, right here and now, not in the afterlife. The devil teaches that the highest power is within you and that you have no gods to answer to but yourself, so become the highest self you can.

Disillusionment with Spirituality

It's taught in some spiritual practices that you can expect wonderful things if only you believe, pay money, or visualize enough. People are told that powers beyond their control decide their fate and can punish or reward them at will. This applies not only to theistic religions but to many metaphysical and magical teachings. Believers are assured they will be in direct contact with a higher power who will solve their problems or, at the very least, help them out a little. Lacking this, they might seek out spellcasting services or learn to do magic themselves. However, life on Earth can be tough despite prayers and petitions, and eventually, people lose faith and turn in the opposite direction. Instead of looking hopefully at the indifferent clouds above them, they look down at the real, tangible world at their feet. Rejecting the divine in favor of the material is the devil's territory.

The Call of the Old Gods

For some, the devil is not necessarily "Satan" and is considered much older. Some witches are drawn to the folkloric devil. Whether called the Horned One, the Witch Father, or a multitude of other names, this devil is the undercurrent of energy that calls to the witch, available to be molded by their will. These are the deities of the earth, the body, sensuality, and ecstasy. They rule over instinct, primal urges, and the hunt, but they are also often rulers of the afterlife. They embody life, death, and what lies in between.

◆ ◆ ◆ ◆ ◆

It goes without saying that not everyone who has these experiences turns to the devil or that you must experience any of them yourself to go down his path. Everyone has a unique story.

NOTHING IS BLACK OR WHITE

There are no absolutes in Satanism or in witchcraft. Both have some foundational philosophies, but there is no set-in-stone dogma for either. You have to decide what is right for you. Some people enjoy working in groups, so joining an organization or coven is the choice for them, while for others, solitary is the way to go.

While there are organized satanic groups one can identify with, it's worth remembering that they encompass one vision—their own. Some people will say, "To be a Satanist, you *must* be this, and you *must* be that," but the devil has always meant different things to different people over centuries. Why should that change now?

CHAPTER 2

THE ROOT OF ALL EVIL

We all have ideas about what the devil is, whether he exists, and what he might look like. But where did all these associations come from? In this chapter, I will trace the history of the devil back to his earliest possible origins and examine the ways he has morphed over thousands of years. In this history, you'll notice repeated patterns demonstrating that this frightening figure is as old as time and has had many names and shapes.

The devil as Satan, who is often understood as possessing strictly evil qualities, is a relatively modern take. Before Christianity, evil gods were not so one-dimensional. For example, the Mesopotamian demon-god Pazuzu ruled over drought and starvation but also protected pregnant people.[31]

Polytheistic societies didn't generally think within the binaries of good or evil the way some people do now. There were gods of war, for example, but war wasn't necessarily viewed as actively malicious. It was merely something that existed as part of life, like any force of nature. That's not to say that Pagan societies didn't have any ethics. They did. They had societal norms that shaped the dos and don'ts of behavior, but these were not necessarily linked to religious rules.

---

31. Jeremy Black and Anthony R. Green, *Gods, Demons, and Symbols of Ancient Mesopotamia: An Illustrated Dictionary*, 2nd ed. (1998; repr., London: The British Museum Press, 2004), 147–48.

EARLY HISTORY

The concept of an adversarial deity can be loosely traced to two sources.

One is the ancient Egyptian god Set. Originally, Set was revered as the protector of the sun, god of the desert, and ruler of foreign lands. During the Ramesside period (1650–1550 BCE), Egypt underwent profound changes in politics, wealth, and societal structure. During this shift, Set was praised as the *divine foreigner* by newcomers. However, as with any cultural upheaval, there were many people opposed to the changes. To them, Set came to represent oppressive, invasive rulers from outside lands and was soon known as "the lord of lies," a god of confusion who ruled over violence and storms.[32] The people even removed his image from monuments. Much like modern-day religious figures, Set was revered by some and shunned by others depending on where they stood societally, which shows that it was humans who attributed evil to Set based on their own opinions and experiences, not Set himself.

In Set, we see possibly the first instance of a god going from the good guy to a villain. It's all about perspective, similar to how some of us see the devil as positive while others do not.

The other earliest appearance of a good versus evil binary in gods was in the ancient Iranian religion of Zoroastrianism, in which everything in the world was believed to be polarized between good and evil. According to mythology, two opposing energies existed. Angra Mainyu embodied all that was bad, while Ahura Mazda contained all that was good.[33] All things in creation fell within these two categories, including people. People who were categorized as influenced by Angra Mainyu, for instance, were considered evil. It was said they met at night in secret and feasted upon decaying human flesh. These conflicting forces were engaged in an ongoing battle for supremacy. Ultimately, it was believed that Ahura Mazda would defeat the evil Angra Mainyu in battle, and all

---

32. Van Luijk, *Children of Lucifer*, 18.
33. Albert De Jong, *Traditions of the Magi: Zoroastrianism in Greek and Latin Literature*, Religions in the Graeco-Roman World 133 (Leiden, Netherlands: Brill, 1997), 13.

good would be restored.[34] These beliefs are thought to have influenced future monotheistic religions.

While both examples have a little dash of the devil to them, they were not, by definition, the same thing as modern-day Satan by a long shot.

BIBLICAL BEGINNINGS

In the holy writings of the three major monotheistic religions of Judaism, Christianity, and Islam, the devil has different names but similar characteristics.

The Holy Bible is made up of two sections: the Old Testament and the New Testament. The Old Testament is composed of writings from the Jewish Tanakh, dating back to roughly 400 BCE, while the New Testament emerged in the first century CE.[35] Jewish faith draws upon the Old Testament, while Christian belief is based on both the Old and New. When Christianity became widespread in the fourth century, elements of the New Testament were applied to the Old Testament retroactively, changing the way it is understood even now. This results in slightly different views on Satan in Judaism and Christianity.

In Hebrew, *Ha Satan* translates to "the adversary" or "an obstruction."[36] Contrary to popular belief, the Old Testament originally made no mention of the devil or Satan as an evil character. The word *Satan* appears twice in the Tanakh, which is sometimes called the Hebrew Bible, in the book of Numbers 22:23, when an "angel of the lord" appears in the story of Balaam.[37] Balaam, who is a seer, is asked by a king to curse the Jewish people. When Balaam attempts to carry out this task, God

---

34. De Jong, *Traditions of the Magi*, 178–80.

35. "When Was the Bible Written?" Biblica, accessed May 26, 2023, https://www.biblica .com/resources/bible-faqs/when-was-the-bible-written/.

36. Jeff A. Benner, "Definition of Hebrew Names," Ancient Hebrew Research Center, accessed May 28, 2023, https://www.ancient-hebrew.org/names/Satan.htm.

37. Isaac Leeser, trans., *Twenty-Four Books of the Holy Scriptures: Carefully Translated After the Best Jewish Authorities* (New York: Hebrew Publishing Company, 1853), Numbers 22:23.

places an angel in his path, "l'satan lo."[38] This being acts as an obstruction to Balaam, preventing him from cursing the Jews.

There are several other stories in the Old Testament that many people today believe include Satan, even though he wasn't originally named. For example, in Genesis 3:1, when the serpent enters the garden of Eden, it has no name. It is merely a snake who is punished by God to forever slither on its belly, eating dust (Genesis 3:13).[39] The figure who appears in the book of Job 1:6 to dole out torture and challenge Job's faith is referred to only as "the accuser," not Satan, and is acting with God's permission.[40]

If we are to believe that the accuser of the Old Testament is actually the devil, then his role is much different than in modern versions of the myth. The accuser existed as part of God's plan. His job was to put obstacles before people to test their faith. The accuser wasn't an enemy of God but a helper who attempted to weed out the disloyal.

It wasn't until around 400 BCE that evil beings came into the picture. Names of demons, based on Babylonian and Assyrian gods, emerged as people began to talk of the end of the world. It was around this time that the accuser in the Tanakh began to take on the first hints of his status as an evil being.[41]

Then came the first century and the New Testament. The New Testament was written by Jesus of Nazareth from Roman Palestine. In the New Testament, Satan became a prominent character, acting in direct opposition to God and all that was good. In the book of Matthew, which is the first book of the New Testament, we see the birth of Jesus Christ and the emergence of Satan within the first few passages. In Matthew 4:1, the devil appears to tempt Jesus away from his spiritual path. He is established as "the enemy" and "wicked one." In Corinthians, he is so deceptive that he "fashions himself into an angel of light." By the last book,

---

38. "Do Jews Believe in Satan?" My Jewish Learning, January 3, 2022. https://www.my jewishlearning.com/article/satan-the-adversary/.

39. Leeser, trans., *Twenty-Four Books of the Holy Scriptures*, Genesis 3:1, 3:13.

40. Leeser, trans., *Twenty-Four Books of the Holy Scriptures*, Job 1:6.

41. Van Luijk, *Children of Lucifer*, 20.

Revelation, he is "Satan, which deceiveth the whole world," and is cast down to Earth with his followers.[42]

Throughout the New Testament, it becomes abundantly clear that the devil exists not merely to test people but as a direct enemy. He is the cause of pain, suffering, and bad decisions and is well-established as the villain in the story of humanity. By the end of the New Testament, there is no question that a battle between good and evil ensues on Earth and that the devil is ready and waiting to scoop up anyone who might fall victim to his wiles.

In the Koran, the central holy book of Islam, *Iblis* is similar to the Christian devil when it comes to his role in the big picture of humanity. He is the leader of evil djinn called *Shaitan*, which are comparable to demons. In the Koran, it is Iblis who is cast out of heaven. Iblis refuses to obey the Lord's command to bow down before Adam because Adam is made of mud, and Iblis considers himself a higher being.[43] He is arrogant and vain, a betrayer and rebel, who leads people to temptation. The storyline of the Koran follows a trajectory similar to the Bible, but the three Abrahamic religions themselves have many differences.

While the devil is present in each of these religions, the focus of this book is on the Western view and mainly the Christian devil, as this is my area of experience. This isn't meant to ignore or discredit other religions but to focus on what I know rather than speaking for others about their beliefs.

The Birth of the Christian Devil

By the fourth century CE, who and what the Christian devil was had solidified. He had become an entity loaded with the burden of all that was bad on Earth and in the spiritual realm. Any human condition that

---

42. Matthew 4:1, Matthew 13:38–39, Corinthians 11:14, Revelation 12:9 (King James Version).

43. Muhammad Taqi-ud-Din al-Hilâli and Muhammad Muhsin Khân, trans., *Translations of the Meaning of the Noble Qur'ân in the English Language* (Madina, Saudi Arabia: King Fahd Complex for the Printing of the Holy Qur'ân, 2017), Al-Hijr 15:31.

was unpleasant or painful was his fault. After all, by messing around in the Garden of Eden, he had brought about the fall of humankind and opened the door to all suffering. This suffering, be it hunger, disease, or pain, could only be alleviated by one's obedience to divine law. This kind of thinking spread with the globalization of the Roman Empire, and before long, any belief other than Christianity was labeled evil, including Judaism, from which many of the scriptures in the Old Testament had originally come.

Paganism was, of course, included in this. Unlike some simplified stories about the history of the Pagan gods, this transition didn't happen suddenly. It took a long time for the Pagan deities to be fully integrated into the new Roman Empire. Additionally, the Pagan gods were not considered evil; they were not even considered real at all. They were deemed "false idols," empty vessels that contained Christian demons. These monsters resided in Pagan holy places, monuments, and statues that were destroyed or baptized by Christians. One of these was the Shrine of Aphrodite in Jerusalem, over which the Church of the Holy Sepulcher was built, which is said to be the site of Christ's crucifixion and burial.[44] The church didn't think the Pagans were knowingly worshipping the devil but were merely unaware of the demons residing within these idols.

Contrary to popular belief, Satan was not an amalgamation of old gods. He had already been invented by the time this occurred. The demons believed to reside in Pagan monuments took on some of the animal features of the old gods, like hooves and horns. This is likely where the devil got some of his more well-known physical traits over time.

Heretics

The earliest accusations of actual devil worship were leveraged not against Pagans but against various splinter groups of Christianity that strayed from the rules. These people were labeled *heretics*. A heretic was someone within the existing religion of Christianity who had new ideas or variations of the

---

44. Robin Lane Fox, *Pagans and Christians* (New York: Alfred A. Knopf, 1987), 671.

same faith. Most of the people commonly believed now to be burned as witches were actually heretics.

Jewish people were also especially demonized and othered. The description of Jewish people during the Middle Ages matches that of accused witches in disturbing ways. Jewish people were given characteristics similar to the devil, such as having claws for feet and horns hidden in their hair. The stories of what took place at a witches' sabbath, such as cannibalism and orgies, were first attributed to Jewish people. The word *Sabbath*, chosen to describe the witches' nefarious gatherings during the witch trials, comes from the Jewish words and practices *Sabbath*, *Shabbat*, and *synagogue*.[45]

Heretics were likewise accused of satanic-like rituals. Just like the people of the Zoroastrian Angra Mainyu, they were rumored to gather at night and do terrible things, including cannibalism and child murder. Interestingly enough, accounts like this mirrored accusations leveraged at early Christians by the Romans before their own takeover. *Christians* were the ones accused of rituals involving incest and drinking the blood of babies.[46] There is a clear and repetitive pattern here. These depraved rituals are repeatedly attributed to vilified groups right up to the modern day. It seems some things just never change.

Since religion and politics were intermingled even back then, usually accusations of heresy resulted in the death of the accused. The torture and murder of heretics and the act of religious othering became so normalized across Western culture by the fifteenth century that it opened the door for the infamous burning times: the seeking out, torturing, and murdering of witches.

WITCH HUNTS AND THE DEVIL

Heresy-related executions of Jewish people and those of some branches of Christianity, such as the Waldensians and Paulicians, were carried

45. Emma Shachat, "The Antisemitic History of Witches," Hey Alma, October 29, 2020, https://www.heyalma.com/the-antisemitic-history-of-witches/.

46. Russell, *Witchcraft in the Middle Ages*, 89.

out with ease and in great numbers. By the fifteenth century in Europe, Christians murdering people for their beliefs had become an accepted part of life. That's why when accusations of witchcraft started popping up, no one was surprised when the accused were killed. It was once said that millions of people were murdered as witches in the Middle Ages, but it's now estimated that it was more likely between 40,000 and 60,000 across different countries and over time.[47]

Many of our ideas about the devil originate in the witch trials and confessions, where the theological devil of the clergy merged with the folkloric devil of the commoners.[48] While the witch hunts were certainly spurred on by fear of actual forces of evil, there were other contributing factors, including class, profit, misogyny, and hysteria, to name just a few.

During this time, the devil was seen in several different ways. By the clergy, he was perceived as a terrifying force of evil whose sole mission was to corrupt humanity and who stood in opposition to the one real God. In folklore, on the other hand, this devil was shaped by the regional beliefs of wherever he happened to be. He was mixed with monsters, spirits, and other creatures of the land.[49] For example, in Scotland, he was blended with faeries.[50] In medieval Rome, he acquired dragon-like qualities.[51] In many cases, he appeared as different animals, including dogs, goats, and even a worm.[52]

Over time as the hysteria spread, booklets like the *Malleus Maleficarum* (1487) and *Compendium Maleficarum* (1608) were published and shared widely. They contained general lists of what to expect from a witch's confession. These manuals provided the accusers with lead-

---

47. *Encyclopaedia Britannica*, s.v. "Salem witch trials," by Jeff Wallenfeldt, last modified August 16, 2023, https://www.britannica.com/event/Salem-witch-trials.

48. Artisson, *The Clovenstone Workings*, 17.

49. Russell, *Lucifer*, 63.

50. James I, King of England, *Daemonologie: In Forme of a Dialogie* (Scotland: Robert Walde-graue, 1597; Project Gutenberg, 2008), chapter 5.

51. Hans A. Pohlsander, *The Emperor Constantine*, 2nd ed. (New York: Routledge, 2004), 27.

52. Russell, *Lucifer*, 67.

ing questions to subject people to under torture. Their wide publication accounts for the similarities in confessions across regions.

The question of who was targeted and why is complicated, involving social upheaval, politics, fear, and neighbors turning on one another in panic. In Europe, there was a battle between Catholics and Protestants to see who could capture the most witches, thus proving their supremacy and gaining converts and profit.[53] In the Salem witch hunts, anyone who strayed ever so slightly from the Puritan social construct could be targeted. People who were different in any way were exterminated by their community, whether it was because a woman was too ugly or too pretty or because they were past reproductive age. Sometimes it was because the person was outspoken and had offended someone, or they owned property that others wanted.[54]

The devil of the witch hunts still influences our imaginations today. He was described as being covered with coarse fur and having horns, claws, a long tongue, and bulging eyes that glowed like fire.[55] Other times he was described as a human form that did not cast a shadow.[56] He flickered between animal, human, and monster, like the shape-shifter we know him to be.

What was his role, specifically, at a witches' sabbath? Who was the devil to witches, and why did they supposedly worship him? Allegedly, it was the devil's job to initiate them, accept child sacrifices, and bestow worshippers with baneful magical powers. He led blasphemous rituals that denounced all things Christian. Witches would allow the devil to mark them with a brand, a claw mark, or other scars as a symbol of their devotion.[57]

---

53. Peter T. Leeson and Jacob W. Russ, "Witch Trials," *The Economic Journal* 128, no. 613 (August 2018): 2066–105, https://doi.org/10.1111/ecoj.12498.

54. Katie Brown, "Salvation and Scapegoating: What Caused the Early Modern Witch Hunts?" The Collector, April 20, 2023, https://www.thecollector.com/early-modern -witch-hunts/.

55. Bailey, *Origins of the Witches' Sabbath*, 91–92.

56. Bailey, *Origins of the Witches' Sabbath*, 12–13.

57. Clive Holmes, "Women, Witches and Witnesses," in *The Witchcraft Reader*, ed. Darren Oldridge, 2nd ed. (New York: Routledge, 2008), 279.

Some of the descriptions of the witches' sabbath included reciting prayers backward or enacting the whole Christian Mass in reverse. There was the desecration of holy objects in the most deviant of ways, often involving bodily fluids and sexual acts. Then witches would report to the devil what evils they'd unleashed upon the world since their last meeting.[58] An orgiastic feast followed, wild group sex involving both humans and demons and kissing the devil on the behind, as well as the eating of human flesh.[59]

Some of the confessions, which were tortured out of victims, support the accusers' points and paint a horrifying picture. The confessions were shaped according to the accusers' leading questions and personal beliefs.

Ultimately, the witches' sabbath was a collection of the sinful fantasies of the accusers. Their own imaginations created the witch and her relations with the devil. There's a good chance they relished it, for it would have been the only acceptable way to give vent to their less-than-pure ideas.

As is often the case, the devil of the witches' sabbath is the creation of humans trying to distance themselves from their true natures, in this case by pinning all sinful thoughts and ideas onto the alleged witch, reveling in the dirty grit of the forbidden without being implicated themselves.

THE AFFAIR OF THE POISONS

The devil's reputation up until the 1600s was mostly based on folklore, words of the clergy, and the writings of witch hunters. As the stories tell, people flew through the air, turned into animals, performed baneful magic, and had orgies with otherworldly creatures while the horned beast, who was in charge of it all, appeared regularly. What we haven't seen yet is an actual documented cult dedicated to Satan: the Satan of the Bible, the Satan who rules hell, the Satan that everyone fears the most.

---

58. Bailey, "Witchcraft and Reform in the Late Middle Ages," in *The Witchcraft Reader*, ed. Darren Oldridge, 2nd ed. (New York: Routledge, 2008), 37–38.

59. Russell, *Witchcraft in the Middle Ages*, 130–31; Kramer and Sprenger, *The Malleus Maleficarum*, 66.

That's where an incident known as the Affair of the Poisons comes in. The Affair of the Poisons is relevant in tracing the footsteps of the devil over time because the testimonies given may have influenced future stereotypes of satanic cults.

In 1679, a massive scandal involving aristocrats, magic, and poison swept through France. It was another trial involving witches and devil worship. However, it stood separate from other witchcraft trials for several reasons. First, because it was the earliest record of a "satanic cult" performing a Black Mass, not to be confused with a witches' sabbath. Second, it distinctly lacked supernatural elements. This lack of fantasy is important because it lends a scrap of credibility to the entire story. Since there were no fantastical claims, it's objectively possible that the satanic rituals occurred.

At this time in urban France, witch hunting had become passé, even though it was still occurring in other regions. Nonetheless, the Affair of the Poisons had many things in common with the witch trials: the finger-pointing and backstabbing, torture used to get confessions, and accounts of unimaginable violence.

Aristocratic women of the time frequently made secret trips among the commoners to seek out seers and magic workers for help with various things. Their problems, while varied, seemed to all hinge on the same thing: their relation to men and how to leverage it for survival. This was sometimes straightforward, like a spell to stop an abusive husband. Also very common was preventing or terminating unwanted pregnancies. Other times, a woman might seek out spells to sway a man into marriage since this was the key to any kind of security or safety. Sometimes they sought potions to cause illness or death to a rival or to make someone fall in love. Most noticeable, at least to me, was the markedly high number of requests to murder husbands.

The real action began when a well-known mystic and palm reader claimed that several high-ranking women—including King Louis XIV's mistress and affiliated chambermaids—had made pacts with the devil, promising their bodies and souls in exchange for various favors.

One particularly notable soothsayer was midwife Catherine Montvoisin, known as La Voisin (the neighbor). She attracted the attention of the chief of police because she was especially successful in business.[60] She independently earned enough money to support not just herself and her children but also her husband, who was known to be abusive.[61] Women of high standing often visited her in secret for magical things, from divination to spells for murder. And, of course, contraception and abortion.

La Voisin was no stranger to the problems women of all classes were facing, as she herself was said to have attempted to kill her own husband several times. Once, she and a lover by the name of Lesage cast a spell to bring about her husband's demise. They buried a sheep's heart in her garden as part of the spell, but at the last moment, La Voisin's conscience got the better of her, and she dug it up.[62] This was the same garden where she would later be accused of burying the remains of illegal abortions.[63]

Investigations into La Voisin allegedly unearthed an underground world of nefarious occultists, witches, and Satanists. Word spread, and the fear of poisoning and witchcraft exploded, fueled by a rumor that there was a plot to murder King Louis XIV with these methods.

The biggest scandal surrounded King Louis's mistress, Madame de Montespan, who supposedly sought out La Voisin and La Voisin's helper, who was a defrocked old priest named Guibourg. Madame de Montespan requested a Black Mass be held that would ensure the king's undying devotion to her. The king took this very seriously, resulting in a long and convoluted trial. He had a courtroom set aside specifically for this issue, called *la chambre ardent* (the burning room), which was lit by torches with the windows covered.

It was claimed that La Voisin and Guibourg performed a Black Mass over Montespan's sprawling naked body. On this human altar, they dese-

---

60. Anne Somerset, *The Affair of the Poisons: Murder, Infanticide, and Satanism at the Court of Louis XIV* (New York: St. Martin's Press, 2014), 151.

61. Somerset, *The Affair of the* Poisons, 152.

62. Somerset, *The Affair of the Poisons*, 153–55.

63. Somerset, *The Affair of the Poisons*, 156.

crated holy objects and sacrificed a child to the devil, and then everyone in attendance participated in an orgy. The remains of the sacrifice from this and other Black Masses were buried in the garden or burned in La Voisin's furnace.[64]

After these allegations, La Voisin was burned at the stake. That wasn't the end of it, though. The trial continued in the burning room, thanks to continued confessions from her daughter, her lover Lesage, and Guibourg.

Supposedly, they helped the king's maid make a pact with Satan in exchange for a deadly magical powder made with human bones and feces.[65] On another occasion, they allegedly had a client who was pregnant and desperate to be married, so Lesage made a mixture of the father's urine, bird's blood, and a sheep's heart that the woman was to keep in her basement. As part of this ritual, she kneeled before Guibourg while he invoked Lucifer, Beelzebub, and Astaroth. She was to keep this bottle in her cellar until her groom arrived.[66] Others claimed to witness births taking place in La Voisin's house, where the mother lay in a circle of candles spewing blasphemies. The newborn children were taken away as sacrifices.[67]

Guibourg became quite imaginative in his recollections. In addition to noting a naked woman acting as an altar, he described a cloth bearing a cross placed on her abdomen along with a chalice. Beneath the chalice was a list of requests for the devil, such as love, status, or the death of an enemy. A child sacrifice was always given in rituals, and in one case, the heart and entrails were dried and powdered, meant to be fed to the king.[68] This same priest told a tale of a chambermaid who had plans to kill King Louis with a magic potion. The recipe included her menstrual blood, a man's semen, flour, and the blood of a bat.[69]

---

64. Guiley, *The Encyclopedia of Demons and Demonology*, 30.

65. Somerset, *The Affair of the Poisons*, 246.

66. Somerset, *The Affair of the Poisons*, 172–73.

67. Van Luijk, *Children of Lucifer*, 47.

68. Somerset, *The Affair of the Poisons*, 271.

69. Van Luijk, *Children of Lucifer*, 48.

In the end, thirty-six people who were questioned and subjected to torture in court received death sentences.[70] Scholars disagree on whether or not La Voisin did what she was accused of because there is no concrete proof. She denied ever performing a child sacrifice or Black Mass right up until her death. No bodies were ever found.[71]

It echoes the witch hunts, with terror forcing people to turn on one another, tell lies, and give gruesome descriptions of the Black Mass.

Beneath this story and all the wild accusations, there is a familiar theme: people have always turned to magic, witchcraft, and the devil in desperate times.

The devil always serves a purpose. In this case, he represented women who were struggling to live in a brutal society that viewed their worth only in relation to men. The devil helped them secretly manipulate those around them. To those being manipulated, this was evil. To those doing the magic, it was agency.

LITERATURE AND THE DEVIL

A great deal of the devil's characteristics can be credited not to religious teachings but to the arts. The devil has been a muse for creatives since the beginning, cycling in and out of popular culture whenever his image is relevant.

One of the most important pieces of literature to shape the current secular views on the devil and Satan is the poem *Paradise Lost* (1667) by John Milton (1608–74), followed by the works of Romantic-era poets such as William Blake, Percy Bysshe Shelley, Vincent Hugo, and Lord Byron. Without examining this literature, we can't fully understand modern Satanism.

Milton's Paradise Lost

There's a very good chance you've heard the classic tale of Lucifer's fall from heaven. John Milton's poem expands upon this story, written in hopes of teaching a Christian lesson about the omnipotent power of

---

70. Somerset, *The Affair of the Poisons*, 306.
71. Van Luijk, *Children of Lucifer*, 55.

God. However, it had some unintended outcomes. Milton was extremely religious and didn't mean for his epic poem to be embraced by so-called Satanists for centuries to come, but unfortunately for him, that's exactly what happened. In *Paradise Lost,* he humanized Satan so well that readers developed sympathy for him, identified with his struggles, and cast him as a tragic hero. This led future writers to present him not as the supernatural face of evil but as a symbol of rebellion against oppression.[72]

According to the story, Satan began as Lucifer, one of God's favored and brightest angels. Lucifer became prideful and started to question God, thinking that he himself should have power and authority, but was denied. Enraged, he created his own army of other disgruntled angels. A battle ensued for several days, resulting in Lucifer's expulsion from heaven onto the earth. There, he was stripped of his angel name and dubbed Satan.

Milton's story then begins when Satan wakes up from his fall to find himself in a lake of fire. He and the other fallen angels set to work creating their own kingdom called Pandemonium, over which Satan rules. Throughout the story, he is reminded that he could come back to heaven at any time, but only if he agrees to submit to God's rules without question. Repeatedly, Satan finds this tempting but unacceptable, wondering why only God has such incontestable authority. Satan decides that even if he can't destroy God, he can at least get vengeance by ruining God's dearest creation, humankind. He hatches a plan to execute this destructive agenda via Adam and Eve, who live without sin in the Garden of Eden.

To enter the Garden of Eden, he has to get past the angel Uriel, who is standing guard. Satan takes on the form of a cherub to do so, which fools Uriel at first. But later, while watching this cherub, Uriel realizes its face is showing longing, regret, and conflict. This is alarming because cherubs are always blissfully joyful and ignorant of all unhappiness. That's when Uriel realizes his mistake. Once inside the Garden of Eden, Satan keenly feels the pain of being an outsider. Paradise is beautiful, and he longs to

---

72. Van Luijk, *Children of Lucifer,* 70.

be part of it, but he can't bear the idea of obeying God without question and living in ignorance under such inequality for the sake of peace and beauty. He decides it's "better to reign in hell than serve in heaven."[73]

Satan vows to fully enjoy his earthly state and sin to the fullest. He takes on the form of a snake, convinces Eve to eat from the forbidden tree of knowledge, and humanity is forever punished with shame and pain.

Back in Pandemonium, he finds a forest of trees with his fellow devils turned into snakes. Every time a snake tries to eat fruit from a tree, the fruit turns to ashes. The outcasts are in an eternal state of desire that will never, ever be satisfied. Still, Satan prefers this to an eternity of servitude.

This version of Satan is a charismatic character experiencing relatable human emotions of disappointment and jealousy. He also possesses admirable courage and determination. Some surmise Milton did this intentionally to seduce readers into sympathizing with Satan against their will, illustrating just how easy it is to unwittingly fall prey to temptation and evil.[74]

The poem intended to show that God and divine law would always rule no matter what. But future poets interpreted it differently.

The Romantics

Paradise Lost hammers on how God has absolute power and that anything other than blind obedience will bring suffering. This sentiment was reflected in oppressive political and religious structures in nineteenth-century France, which caused radicals of the era to draw parallels between the poem and the French Revolution. In July of 1789, citizens of Paris stormed the royal prison and executed their king, which allowed them to govern themselves.[75] In the poem, Satan is unswerving in his desire for justice and refuses to give up. He decides to make his own rules and build his own kingdom, much like the people of Paris.

---

73. John Milton, *Paradise Lost*, ed. James Robert Boyd (New York: Baker and Scribner, 1851), 31.

74. Thahiya Afzal, "Iconic Dualism: Satan in Paradise Lost," VIT University, March 14, 2016, https://www.academia.edu/23260187/Iconic_Dualism_Satan_in_Paradise_Lost.

75. Van Luijk, *Children of Lucifer*, 76.

Romantic writers of the mid-1800s, such as William Blake, Percy Bysshe Shelley, Victor Hugo, and Lord Byron, existed in a time of turbulent social change and secularization in France. Satan was the perfect symbol of their principles, which were democracy; freedom of thought, religion, and speech; and the support of minority groups.[76] Old ideas of the devil as an evil force dancing with witches were largely considered nonsense, particularly by freethinkers.[77]

Romantic-era revolutionaries viewed Milton's Satan as a hero: the only angel with enough courage to question the status quo, consider his own importance, and embrace his own worth rather than blindly obey an all-powerful being.[78] It was this interpretation of Milton's Satan about whom artists created plays, poems, and stories. He was discontented, just like people of the era. When rebuffed by God, he didn't back down, just as revolutionaries refused to buckle under authority. He built his own army and fearlessly fought for his beliefs, just as the people of France used their own power to dismantle the social structure. It helped that Satan just happened to be the enemy of the church, fitting with the writers' anticlerical views and their desire for the separation of church and state. Their work was widely read across Europe, showing the population a new way to view Satan: not as an evil religious figure but as a secular symbol of revolt, power, and a force against injustice.

It is from this symbolic devil that many modern atheistic Satanists derive their values, although the Romantics didn't call themselves Satanists. These artists integrated Satan *as a symbol* into their work to make a point about the power of the church, politics, and social justice.[79] The Romantics' views were considered controversial at the time. For example, Blake in particular took issue with the church's condemnation of physical pleasure. In his book *The Marriage of Heaven and Hell* (c. 1790), Blake challenges the religious rules of the times by flipping the

---

76. Van Luijk, *Children of Lucifer*, 77.

77. Asbjørn Dyrendal, James D. Lewis, and Jesper Petersen, *The Invention of Satanism* (New York: Oxford University Press, 2016), 29.

78. Van Luijk, *Children of Lucifer*, 69.

79. Dyrendal, Lewis, and Petersen, *The Invention of Satanism,* 31.

roles of God and the devil. He puts physical and material experience on the same level as divine experience, which is blasphemous. He describes hell as an energetic and exciting place, not a land of punishment. The book shows that life and progress are impossible without opposites, which means hell and the devil are just as necessary as God and heaven. Despite being Christian, Blake refers to God as a "jealous king" whose rules are stomped "to dust" by the devil.[80] In a section of the book called *Proverbs from Hell*, Blake writes, "The road of excess leads to the palace of wisdom. Prudence is a rich ugly old maid courted by Incapacity. He who desires, but acts not, breeds pestilence."[81] These lines point toward the importance of earthly experience over the superstition and self-denial taught by religion.

With a focus on creativity, science, and beauty, these creators helped the devil shape-shift once again into something new and positive: an advocate of revolution, individualism, and reason over fear.

THE HOAX OF LÉO TAXIL

The church remained overwhelmingly powerful, but by the nineteenth century, people had become emboldened, little by little, to chip away at its monstrous foundation. One way to do this was to make a mockery of the church on a large scale, luring in the very congregants who would be made fools of. The best way to do that was to appeal to their love of scandal and fear of evil while simultaneously emptying their pockets.

This is where Léo Taxil, a French former Freemason, stepped in. He had run out of money, but he had one thing: an idea. His shenanigans eventually caused a massive uproar in Catholic France.

Léo Taxil had pushed against the clergy for most of his life. He had a bookstore and publishing company dedicated to anticlerical material. One day in 1885, Taxil had a sudden change of heart while low on funds. Seemingly without explanation, he became a devout Roman Catholic,

---

80. William Blake, *The Marriage of Heaven and Hell* (Boston, MA: John W. Luce and Company, 1906), 45–46.
81. Blake, *The Marriage of Heaven and Hell*, 13.

publicly promising to redeem himself. He scrapped his original revolutionary business and instead began to write and publish books about the evils of Freemasonry. As a former Mason, he was in the unique position to be considered credible.[82] The church at this time condemned Freemasonry as Satan worship, so it was a timely and profitable endeavor.

Taxil knew a good opportunity when he saw one. He told the public that there were many dark doings among the Masons, some so wicked that only the highest-ranking members were involved. These primary members, according to Taxil, considered Lucifer to be the real god. An especially salacious twist was that there were secret Masonic lodges just for women who engaged in sexual rituals with prominent members.[83]

This development was irresistibly titillating to the public, being so taboo. Taxil described their strange and sexual initiation to a rapt audience. Watched over by a huge statue of Baphomet, an evil-looking, goat-headed humanoid creature, the female initiate was brought before a naked man who lay pretending to be dead. To a chorus of cheering women, the initiate had sex with the man, who then woke up and symbolically came back to life. This was followed by defiling the host and swearing to be a servant of Lucifer. After that, the initiate was known as a Templar Mistress.[84]

Taxil's imaginative narrative held the public captive. Supposedly, even the pope enjoyed his writing and invited him to the Vatican more than once. One could say he was a celebrity.

During his time as a Freemason, Taxil claimed to have witnessed other members walking through solid walls and to have known a Mason-adjacent person who had summoned a spirit that took the form of a crocodile playing the piano.[85]

---

82. W. G. Sibley, *The Story of Freemasonry*, 3rd ed. (Gallipolis, OH: The Lion's Paw Club, 1913), 29.

83. Van Luijk, *Children of Lucifer*, 208.

84. Van Luijk, *Children of Lucifer*, 210.

85. Arthur Edward Waite, *Devil-Worship in France or The Question of Lucifer: A Record of Things Seen and Heard in the Secret Societies According to the Evidence of Initiates* (London: George Redway, 1896; Project Gutenberg, 2007), 145–46.

Coincidentally, at just the right time to validate Taxil's claims, a 2,000-page book was published by a philosopher named Dr. Bataille in 1892. The book exposed a massive underground movement of satanic Freemasons. Dr. Bataille explained how he was called to the bedside of a dying Freemason who was desperate to save his own soul. The Mason told Dr. Bataille all the secrets of the satanic cult, knowledge that would grant Dr. Bataille access to the inner circles of the Freemasons.[86] Dr. Bataille then traveled the globe, infiltrating the world of Satan worship and recording all his findings in the tome, which pretty much declared many non-Christian groups around the world to be devil worshippers.[87] He claimed to be an eyewitness to many wild things, like women having sex with demons, entire schools just for Luciferian children, and a visit from the devil himself every Friday night.[88]

After this, there was a rash of anti-Masonic articles and booklets published, but one author who stood out most was the mysterious Diana Vaughan, who had been a Templar Mistress. It's important to note that, unlike the other Templar Mistresses, she did *not* engage in sexual activity at her initiation.[89] She happened to be engaged to a demon named Asmodeus, who forbade it, which kept Vaughan pure as the driven snow.[90] This was important because the public would not support her if she were not virtuous. She also gained favor among Catholics because it was said she refused to defile the host during initiation.[91] She, like Taxil, made a sudden switch to Roman Catholicism. Vaughan was especially beloved by the readers, being a source of scandalous material yet undefiled by the sin of sex and blasphemy. The public viewed her as an innocent woman who'd been misled down a dark path but was working to redeem herself. Vaughan, unfortunately, was never seen by the public because she was

---

86. Waite, *Devil-Worship in France,* 108–9.
87. Waite, *Devil-Worship in France*, 108–9, 120–21, 132–37.
88. Van Luijk, *Children of Lucifer*, 211–12.
89. Van Luijk, *Children of Lucifer,* 213.
90. Waite, *Devil-Worship in France,* 155–56.
91. Waite, *Devil-Worship in France,* 150.

living in hiding from Masonic assassins.[92] However, Taxil swore he knew her personally. He produced photos and letters to prove her existence. Some people questioned him, but Taxil pointed out that their doubt was exactly what Lucifer wanted, as their disbelief only made him more powerful.[93]

After some time, Diana Vaughan made an announcement. She would end the suspense and do a book tour of Europe. Best of all, she would be showing a picture of her demon lover, Asmodeus.[94] Naturally, everyone was dying to see it. On the date that Vaughan was supposed to make her debut, a huge crowd assembled in the Hall of the French Geographical Society to welcome her. But when it was time for her entrance, who should saunter onto the stage but Léo Taxil? To the horror of the hopeful spectators, Taxil revealed that he had made up every single thing: the satanic Freemasons, the Templar Mistresses, Dr. Bataille, and their beloved Diana Vaughan. Taxil had fooled them all. People were so enraged there was almost a riot.

So why did he do all of this? Much like some satanic groups today, he was making a point about blind faith, the public's willingness to believe nonsense, and what he saw as the stupidity of the church. This whole debacle shed an embarrassing light on the leaders of the time, making them seem gullible and foolish. Taxil's hoax endured for twelve years![95]

Even though everything that Taxil did was a farce, there is still a lingering belief that Freemasons are involved in Satan worship.

In this scenario, the devil took the form of a trickster, making a fool of those in power and exposing the stupidity of blind belief.

THE INFLUENCE OF WESTERN OCCULTISM

This is where things get complicated. Modern Satanists do not necessarily share the beliefs of the Western occultists discussed here, but there is

---

92. Van Luijk, *Children of Lucifer*, 214.
93. Van Luijk, *Children of Lucifer*, 215.
94. Van Luijk, *Children of Lucifer*, 215.
95. Sibley, *The Story of Freemasonry*, 36.

no denying the influence these occultists have had on them. Esotericists such as Éliphas Lévi, Helena P. Blavatsky, and Aleister Crowley didn't claim to worship the devil, but each of them contributed something to what modern Satanism has become. Some examples are the symbols they designed, such as Lévi's Baphomet, or general philosophies, such as a focus on the carnal, the rejection of convention, and Lucifer being a symbol of light.

Some of the people mentioned are problematic through today's lens, having done and said offensive or harmful things in their personal lives and beyond. While this cannot be ignored, the symbols, spiritual systems, and ceremonies they created left a mark. Their work has been recycled and rebranded throughout time, and much of it is still very prevalent, so it must be included. Knowledge is power, and understanding the facts doesn't imply support for the characters' wrongdoings.

Here, I'll share the ways that our current understanding of the devil was shaped by Western occultism, intentionally or not.

John Dee

One of the earliest Western mystics was John Dee (1527–c. 1608), an English astronomer, alchemist, ceremonial magician, and court adviser of Queen Elizabeth I. Although he was a Christian, he was also interested in magic. He received messages from angels and transcribed them into written form, creating the Enochian alphabet and language. The Enochian language is important in the context of this book, as are some of his symbols and ceremonies. John Dee's writings underlie some work of later occultists, and there are still traces of his ideas in Wicca, eclectic witchcraft, and Satanism.

Éliphas Lévi

Another influential occultist is Éliphas Lévi (1810–1875), a French author who was born Alphonse Louise Constant. He created the famous goat-headed figure known as Baphomet in his book *Dogma et Rituel de la Haute Magie* (c. 1854–1856) and was the first to explain the meanings of the upright and inverted pentagrams.[96] He was influenced by Kabbalah, which is a form of Jewish mysticism. Lévi's writings contributed to Theosophy, Thelema, Wicca, and LaVey's Satanism. Lévi believed all things were powered by an energy called the astral light, which encompassed both light and darkness and did not possess a moral code. He sometimes called this astral light Lucifer. The astral light could be turned into good, evil, and anything in between by humans, depending on how they chose to use it.

In *Dogma et Rituel de la Haute Magie,* he writes, "He who affirms the devil creates or makes the devil," meaning that invoking the devil made him real to the practitioner through creativity and the power of the mind.[97] Self-mastery was integral to his beliefs. Whether you're a witch who believes in spirits or a Satanist who doesn't, self-knowledge is probably important to you.

Lucifer, or the astral light, as an all-encompassing force, seems to be in line with the descriptions of the Witch Father and Horned God of traditional witchcraft, in that he contains all things both light and dark, life and death, and all the gray in between.

Perhaps most importantly, at least through the lens of modern Satanism, Lévi created Baphomet. This image was refurbished first by the Church of Satan into their own Sigil of Baphomet and later incorporated into The Satanic Temple's iconography.

Suffice it to say that Lévi, with his philosophies, his use of the name *Lucifer,* and his drawings and symbols, had a major lasting impact on our concept of the modern devil.

Helena P. Blavatsky

Influenced by Lévi, Helena P. Blavatsky (1831–1891) founded the Theosophical Society with Henry Olcott (1832–1907) in New York in 1875. While Theosophy is not the same as modern Satanism, Blavatsky and her philosophies did impact our understanding of the devil now, particularly

---

96. Éliphas Lévi, *The Doctrine and Ritual of High Magic: A New Translation*, trans. Mark Anthony Mikituk (New York: TarcherPerigree, 2017), 240.

97. Lévi, *The Doctrine and Ritual of High Magic*, 311.

in Luciferianism. She thought of Lucifer as a liberator and was the first Western occultist to openly praise the devil in a spiritual way, although she also admired him as a symbol like the Romantics did.[98] For this reason, some said her two books *Isis Unveiled* (1877) and *The Secret Doctrine* (1888) were satanic, although she didn't identify as such.

Theosophy is a complicated combination of spirituality, philosophy, and science. Blavatsky believed there was one universal religion rooted in ancient civilization from which all religions spawned and that Theosophy was an expression of this.[99]

Theosophy acquired a massive following with 227 sections around the world at one point and was one of the leading organizations of the nineteenth century's surge of alternative religions. It appealed to those aligned with radical social movements of the time and the growing pushback against the power of the church.[100] Being led by a woman, Theosophy was especially important to the growth of feminism.

Blavatsky herself was extremely unconventional for the times. She was openly anti-Christian; traveled the world all alone, which was unheard of for women; and had no interest whatsoever in marriage or conventional "ladylike" things and refused to pretend to.[101] She traveled the East, learning about different spiritualities, which she combined into her own religion.

Blavatsky believed that the devil, in addition to being an adversary, was a bringer of light and knowledge.[102] She didn't consider the devil, Lucifer, or Satan a deity but a blind force in nature and within people. This Satan was necessary for balance. Without the darkness of a devil,

---

98. Per Faxneld, *Satanic Feminism: Lucifer as the Liberator of Woman in Nineteenth-Century Culture*, Oxford Studies in Western Esotericism (New York: Oxford University Press, 2017), 123.

99. Faxneld, *Satanic Feminism*, 110.

100. Faxneld, *Satanic Feminism*, 111.

101. Faxneld, *Satanic Feminism*, 115.

102. Faxneld, *Satanic Feminism*. 117.

there could be no light of God, and so the two were actually one.[103] She rejected Darwin's theory of evolution and instead viewed human evolution as a spiritual journey that constantly moved forward and upward. Evil or destruction was simply a part of this, necessary for growth to occur.[104]

In 1887, Blavatsky published the first issue of a magazine entitled *Lucifer*. She chose the name not only for her own status as what some might call a "fallen woman" but because she considered Lucifer the bringer of liberation and freedom.[105] The title was also an affront to the church and provided shock value.

It's worth noting that in this magazine, Lucifer was sometimes referred to as "lady" and that all spiritual beings in Theosophy were androgynous.[106] The magazine published a poem called "The Lady of Light" by Gerald Massey, the lady being Lucifer. This points to the current understanding of the devil as nongendered, which is also displayed in Baphomet, who is all genders.[107]

Overall, although Blavatsky spoke much less about the devil than she did other gods, she was the first to publicly praise him in a spiritual context through her writing. In this way, she heralded the idea that the devil, Lucifer, and Satan could be part of a spiritual system.[108]

Aleister Crowley

Next comes the infamous Aleister Crowley (1875–1947), another occultist who was erroneously deemed a Satanist and, as such, influenced our

103. Helena P. Blavatsky, *The Secret Doctrine: The Synthesis of Science, Religion, and Philosophy,* vol. 1, *Cosmogenesis* (London: The Theological Publishing House, 1893), 572.

104. Faxneld, *Satanic Feminism,* 120.

105. Gary Lachman, *Madame Blavatsky: The Mother of Modern Spirituality* (New York: Penguin, 2012), 135.

106. Faxneld, *Satanic Feminism,* 127.

107. Helena P. Blavatsky and Mabel Collins, eds., *Lucifer: A Theosophical Magazine* 1, nos. 1–6 (1887–88; Project Gutenberg, 2019).

108. Faxneld, *Satanic Feminism,* 128.

current views of the devil. His work has also permeated many forms of witchcraft, from ceremonial rituals to folk practices.

Crowley did not worship the devil. Like Lévi and Blavatsky, he considered Lucifer the light bringer. But something he does share with modern Satanism is the sensationalist circus that the media created around him and a few elements of his beliefs, most notably his reverence of the flesh. Unfortunately, his terrible behavior in his personal life also contributed to some of the misconceptions about Satanism.

Crowley is perhaps most well-known for taking on the moniker *the Beast 666*, which he chose because, as a child, his deeply religious mother labeled him "the beast."[109] He added the 666 to the name later in life because of its significance in the Bible as the number of the Antichrist. He despised the strict religion of his upbringing and how it condemned all of his natural urges. Instead, he came to identify with all it forbade.

Crowley created Thelema, a religion that he hoped would take over the world. He, like many others mentioned, was anticlerical. He reveled in earthly pleasures as an affront to religion, especially as a bisexual person, which was illegal at the time.[110]

The press treated Crowley similarly to how tabloid talk shows of the 1980s treated Satanists. A collection of taboo fantasies were projected onto him by the public. That's not to say he didn't use it to his advantage. In 1947, Crowley was dubbed "The Wickedest Man in the World" in a very popular British tabloid called *John Bull*. The article calls his headquarters in Sicily a "cesspool of vice" and a "lust temple." It claims a drugged woman sacrificed a goat, that children were abused, and that Crowley forced female Thelemites into sex work to pay his debts.[111] These things may or may not be true. Over the years, the press dubbed Crowley a sex addict, a

109. Tobias Churton, *Aleister Crowley: The Biography* (Oxford: Watkins Publishing, 2011), 6.

110. Robert Garofalo, dir., *In Search of the Great Beast 666: Aleister Crowley, the Wickedest Man in the World* (Classic Pictures Productions, 2007), YouTube video, 00:31:00, https://www.youtube.com/watch?v=BEI_L35BzDU.

111. "The Wickedest Man in the World," *John Bull*, March 24, 1923, https://www.100thmonkeypress.com/biblio/acrowley/articles/1923_03_24_john_bull.pdf.

drug fiend, and a traitor to the people of his country. When Crowley died in 1947, the papers called his funeral a Black Mass.[112]

Due to this and other widely spread media coverage, which ignored the religion of Thelema, he became the face of the devil in the public mind and has occupied a place there ever since. Crowley is alleged to have done some problematic things, which contributed to how he came to be associated with Satan. Again, it's difficult to separate fact from fiction. For example, it was said that Crowley had a room in his apartment dedicated to dark magic, in which there was an altar bearing a human skeleton. He fed the skeleton blood and bone broth in an attempt to bring it back to life.[113]

For a time, he had a house in Scotland. The locals were afraid of him, believing that he sent out evil curses. Further adding to his bad reputation, he once led a mountain climbing expedition that ended with the death of four people. Some tabloids claimed he cannibalized two of them. He abandoned his team because he said he heard the voice of a demon.[114]

He had a well-known house in Sicily called the Sacred Abbey of the Thelemic Mysteries, where he lived with his partners and followers. They did lots of drugs, had lots of sex, and partook in rituals. The tabloids made many claims about this abbey, including speculation that human sacrifice was performed.

The abbey's undoing was when Oxford University student Raoul Loveday died from acute enteritis there. Rumor had it that his death was actually due to drinking a cat's blood in one of Crowley's rituals.[115] This

112. "Burial with Black Mass Alleged," *Birmingham Daily Gazette*, April 2, 1948, https://www.100thmonkeypress.com/biblio/acrowley/articles/1948_04_02_birmingham_gazette.pdf.

113. Garofalo, *In Search of the Great Beast 666*, 00:28:00.

114. Garofalo, *In Search of the Great Beast 666*, 00:57:00.

115. "Judgement for Defendants in Black Magic," *The Evening Post*, April 13, 1934, https://www.100thmonkeypress.com/biblio/acrowley/articles/1934_04_13_evening_news.pdf.

was unproven, but it attracted the attention of the press. Crowley was eventually kicked out of Italy.[116]

Beyond all of this was his work as the creator of Thelema, which still has practitioners today. The law of Thelema is "Do what thou wilt shall be the whole of the law."[117] The meaning of this statement is not to just do whatever you feel like but that the will can achieve perfect synchronicity with cosmic forces.

So, as we can see, Crowley's inclusion in this book isn't so much about a contribution to modern Satanism but rather an unfortunate association that leverages his negative qualities to further demonize it.

◆ ◆ ◆ ◆ ◆

The devil has taken on many forms over time. He's been a witches' consort, a terrifying monster, a bright light containing both good and evil, a tool for rebellion, a muse for poets, a political symbol, and fodder for tabloids. And that's just the beginning.

---

116. Garofalo, *In Search of the Great Beast 666*, 1:48:30.
117. Aleister Crowley, *The Book of the Law* (Berlin: Ordo Templi Orientis, 1938; repr., York Beach, ME: Weiser Books, 1976), 9.

CHAPTER 3

THE MODERN DEVIL

Over the centuries, people have utilized the devil in different ways and for different reasons, but one thing was always missing. Up until modern times, there had not yet been anyone of note to publicly and unapologetically embrace the title of Satanist. That all changed in the 1960s.

To understand modern Satanism, it's important to discuss the official organizations that exist since they are foundational in understanding the place the devil occupies today. The two most well-known currently functioning groups are The Satanic Temple and the Church of Satan. They are often confused with one another but are distinct and separate organizations. Many smaller independent satanic groups have come and gone, but these two are by far the biggest and most influential. I believe there are things to be learned from both, regardless of their differing views.

THE CHURCH OF SATAN

If you're at all interested in Satanism, chances are you've heard of the Church of Satan and its founder, Anton LaVey (1930–97). As with many historical figures, Anton LaVey is often viewed in two-dimensional absolutes. He is either praised as an idol or dismissed as a fool, with no trace of the complicated, multifaceted human being that he was. Some of LaVey's beliefs are considered problematic on many levels, causing some to dismiss him from the conversation about Satanism completely. To me, this is impossible. Regardless of his personal life, interests, or political views, he is the person who initially brought modern Satanism to life. Acknowledging this is not an attempt to endorse, erase, excuse, or minimize his controversial characteristics. It is possible to appreciate the work that a person has done in one area while also recognizing that you don't share all their beliefs. For the sake of learning about Satan and the devil, I'll focus on just that: LaVey's contribution to modern Satanism. You are free to make up your own mind about his character.

On Walpurgisnacht, April 30, 1966, LaVey and a circle of fellow occult enthusiasts performed a ritual officializing the first Church of Satan. This was to be, according to LaVey, Year One of the New Satanic Era.[118] LaVey registered the church with the state of California, thus legitimizing the very first religious organization dedicated to the devil.

Anton LaVey

Neither the Church of Satan nor the famous *Satanic Bible* can be discussed in any depth without getting a general understanding of Anton LaVey himself.

LaVey was a clever, creative, and opportunistic man, and he knew how to put on a show. Before becoming the face of Satanism, he wore many hats. He'd been a musician, a lion tamer, a crime-scene photographer, and more.[119] LaVey had an interest in the occult and, in the 1960s, began teaching lectures from his home in San Francisco. His home was the infamous Black House, which is exactly what it sounds like: a house in an otherwise ordinary neighborhood painted top to bottom in ominous, jarring black. He taught many of the typical things about magic and the paranormal, with some rather unusual exceptions. According to Blanche Barton, who was LaVey's partner and former high priestess of the Church of Satan, during one of these lectures, members all sampled

---

118. Peter H. Gilmore, "Anton Szandor LaVey," Church of Satan, 2003, https://www .churchofsatan.com/history-anton-szandor-lavey/.

119. Blanche Barton, *The Secret Life of a Satanist: The Authorized Biography of Anton Szandor LaVey*, rev. ed. (1980; repr., Port Townsend, WA: Feral House, 2014), 39, 32, 53.

grilled human flesh provided by a physician.[120] This certainly does hearken back to the witches' sabbath and Black Mass, which appear to have inspired his group activities to a degree.

LaVey was opposed to religion and hated restrictive moralist conformity so much that in his book *The Devil's Notebook* (1992), there is a chapter titled "Non-Conformity: Satanism's Greatest Weapon."[121] Conformity, to LaVey, included the so-called rebellious hippie lifestyle of drugs and free love that dominated the 1960s. The social upheaval of the era had many people questioning the teachings of their church-going elders, and there was an upsurge of interest in Eastern spirituality, Wicca, and Paganism, as well as a trend in starting new religions. LaVey disdained this fad, labeling the participants hypocrites.[122] However, there's no denying that the times provided him with the perfect conditions to start a religion of his own. Unlike some other leaders of the upstarts that emerged, LaVey was never a typical cult leader; he didn't expect members to revere him, he didn't proselytize, nor did he demand communal activities. In fact, all those things went against his new religion, which was, above all, focused on strength and self-preservation.[123] I imagine that if someone were to come groveling to him in supplication, LaVey would not have considered them a worthy member of the Church of Satan.

As a natural showman, LaVey quickly became a public figure. He was interviewed on television shows such as *The Joe Pyne Show* in 1966, and the Church of Satan was featured in popular publications, including *Time* magazine.[124] Since it was generally considered wicked to profit from or make a spectacle of religion, LaVey did exactly that. Doing so fit with his philosophy, which was to embrace the opposite of all religious teachings.

---

120. Barton, *The Secret Life of a Satanist*, 72.

121. Anton LaVey, *The Devil's Notebook* (Port Townsend, WA: Feral House, 1992), 63.

122. LaVey, *The Satanic Bible*, 51.

123. LaVey, *The Satanic Bible*, 33.

124. Richard RemembersJoePyne, "Anton LaVey Interviewed by Joe Pyne 1966 or 1967," October 13, 2009, YouTube video, 4:45, https://www.youtube.com/watch?v=8m3hHYtdegw; "The Occult Revival: A Substitute Faith," *Time*, June 19, 1972, https://content.time.com/time/subscriber/article/0,33009,877779-10,00.html.

Many people doubted his sincerity due to his shocking public persona, which probably helped him evade persecution. He wore a black cape and devil horns, rubbed elbows with celebrities, captivated the public with his subversive rituals in which he was surrounded by naked women, and was generally a charming person. The media loved him.

LaVey's Beliefs

Despite what some people thought, his work wasn't all for show. LaVey was sincere in his philosophy. He was an atheist who abhorred spirituality. Religion focused on the afterlife, so LaVey's Satanism focused on the here and now. Religion taught self-denial so, LaVey promoted indulgence. Religion spoke of the soul, LaVey posited that humans are equal to animals. Religion taught conformity, LaVey encouraged extreme individualism. Religion rewarded the meek, LaVey revered strength and domination. Religion taught selflessness, LaVey taught that the ego was the closest thing to a god that existed. LaVey championed freedom of thought and speech, sexual liberation, self-expression, and self-empowerment.

This raises the question of why someone who disdained religion so much would call their own philosophy a religion. For LaVey, this served multiple purposes. It offended and mocked the institutions he hated, displaying that anything could be dubbed "religion," which downplayed their power. Using words like *church* and *Bible* further shocked and offended older generations and fit into the counter-cultural attitude of the times. It elevated the oppositional values of the satanic movement to the same status as an organized religion. It also happened to be an excellent marketing tactic, as it targeted many peoples' identities as Christians, which garnered tons of attention. The Church of Satan is still in operation over fifty years after its inception. LaVey passed away in 1997, leaving behind a legacy of thought and practice that still applies to modern Satanists, even those who are not part of his church: a rejection of superstitious thinking, a refusal to bend beneath the authority of an imaginary god or unworthy leadership, and the dismissal of spiritual or religious rules in favor of an authentically enjoyable life.

Despite being progressive, LaVey despised the flower children scene. He was anti-drug and believed that people should try to thrive within society, not escape into a hallucinogen-induced fantasy land.[125] His ideology was not to rebel via love and peace but by fighting fire with fire. He believed humans are simply animals with the same needs and instincts as our feathered and furry friends. He thought it best, then, to be a predator and use all of one's natural abilities to get to the top, just like other animals in the food chain.

On the other end of the spectrum, one of LaVey's philosophies that many people disagree with was social Darwinism, which is survival of the fittest. This is the belief that people are not created equal and that those who rise to the top are simply better than others in intelligence and strength. This line of thinking may seem logical at first glance, but it completely ignores the systemic issues that create inequality and quickly careens into the dangerous territories of sexism, racism, classism, and eugenics. LaVey's focus on strength and social Darwinism has evolved among today's Satanists and has been rejected by many of them.

Anton LaVey, good, bad, and ugly, remains one of the most well-known Satanists in the world. He wrote *The Satanic Bible* in 1969, and it's been in circulation ever since.

The Satanic Bible

The Satanic Bible was the first book of its kind. LaVey went on to write numerous other works, but this one was and continues to be his most popular. It's not surprising that some of the history discussed in the last chapter can be found in the rituals of *The Satanic Bible*. For example, LaVey states that the altar should be a naked woman, just as in the Affair of the Poisons.[126] The Sigil of Baphomet, which is the logo for the Church of Satan, is based on the work of occultist Éliphas Lévi. LaVey also shared the Romantic writers' pursuit of knowledge, freedom, and science.

---

125. Van Luijk, *Children of Lucifer*, 298–99.
126. LaVey, *The Satanic Bible*, 135.

I think to properly educate yourself about Satanism, you need to read *The Satanic Bible,* even though you might be offended by some of what you find. Just because you read it doesn't mean you have to agree with it. Understand that his writing had a huge impact on Satanism's trajectory while bearing in mind that much of Satanism has grown with the times. There is also a glaring problem that cannot be ignored: a portion of *The Satanic Bible* was copied from the fascist manifesto *Might Is Right* (1896) by Ragnar Redbeard, a disturbingly ruthless, hate-fueled rant about social Darwinism.

Most of *The Satanic Bible* focuses heavily on LaVey's disdain for religion and the hypocrisy he perceived in it. To be fair, he disdained all religion and spirituality with equal venom, including occultism, despite his previous interests.[127] Much of LaVey's beliefs can be seen in the Nine Satanic Statements as written in *The Satanic Bible:*

1. Satan represents indulgence, instead of abstinence!
2. Satan represents vital existence, instead of spiritual pipe dreams!
3. Satan represents undefiled wisdom, instead of hypocritical self-deceit!
4. Satan represents kindness to those who deserve it, instead of love wasted on ingrates!
5. Satan represents vengeance, instead of turning the other cheek!
6. Satan represents responsibility to the responsible, instead of concern for psychic vampires!
7. Satan represents man as just another animal, sometimes better, more often worse than those that walk on all-fours, who, because of his "divine spiritual and intellectual development," has become the most vicious animal of all!
8. Satan represents all of the so-called sins, as they all lead to physical, mental, or emotional gratification!

---

127. LaVey, *The Devil's Notebook,* 29.

9. Satan has been the best friend the Church has ever had, as He has kept it in business all these years![128]

The Satanic Bible is mostly an anti-Christian tome but touches on modern witchcraft as well. To LaVey, new age practices were the same as the "white light religion" of the monotheistic kind, supporting the same old religious guilt.[129] He opined that the focus on healing, fear of repercussions via the rule of three, and pearl-clutching over baneful magic exposed self-titled witches as cowards who couldn't truly part ways with their Christian backgrounds.[130] Spiritualities of many kinds condemned or punished people for their natural feelings, like vengeance, anger, or pride, while Satanism aimed to embrace those things.

Interestingly enough, despite LaVey's rejection of mystical thinking, *The Satanic Bible* does include information on his version of magic. The "lesser magic" section of the book explains mundane means to gain power and achieve your goals, such as scent, sexual desire, and appearance. This type of magic exploits your natural assets to get what you want, much like animals do in the wild. He also includes ritual in his Satanism for psychological benefits, which he called psychodrama, using fantasy, atmosphere, and emotion to raise power.[131]

LaVey urged his followers to dive fully into pleasure, treating themselves as gods. He felt we should do what our animal selves truly wanted and that self-preservation and earthly existence were of utmost importance. This included destroying what stood in your way and fighting for what you wanted.[132]

Some other beliefs shared in the book were that you should fully express and embrace your own negative feelings, including hatred.[133] This is much like shadow work, a trend among today's witches, which is

128. LaVey, *The Satanic Bible*, 25.
129. LaVey, *The Satanic Bible*, 48.
130. LaVey, *The Satanic Bible*, 51.
131. LaVey, *The Satanic Bible*, 100.
132. LaVey, *The Satanic Bible*, 30–35.
133. LaVey, *The Satanic Bible*, 64.

to examine and embrace the parts of yourself that you have been taught to hide or ignore.

In the end, LaVey made the idea of Satanism mainstream, and for many years, his work has acted as a doorway into the devil's domain for those who wish to enter. It's important to remember that LaVey's version of Satanism is only one among many, that *The Satanic Bible* was written in a very different time, and that all the views expressed in it are not necessarily supported by modern Satanists or myself. It is, however, a mainstay for the Church of Satan.

LaVey and his word is still revered by many Satanists and contemporary members of the Church of Satan, which is currently run by high priest Peter H. Gilmore. The church's headquarters, which was originally the Black House in San Francisco, was sadly demolished in 2001. Now, members are encouraged to pursue their own satanic interests and find people who share their views if and how they choose. There is no official headquarters today, as members value individualism over congregation. They teach that each person's practice should be theirs alone and that the internet has replaced the need for in-person groups.

What About the Magic?

People often wonder if the Church of Satan practices magic, and if so, how is it possible for atheists? After all, *The Satanic Bible* contains lesser and greater magic with rituals for various ends, as noted. It also contains Enochian Keys, which are based on the ancient transcripts of John Dee, who recorded the Enochian alphabet from angels. So, the question of whether the Church of Satan believes in magic seems confusing on the surface.

The thing that sets LaVey's rituals apart from other magic is that the rituals are done in what he called the "intellectual decompression chamber," a state in which the Satanist knows they are performing and pretending, but in doing so they fully embrace their emotions and energy.[134]

---

134. LaVey, *The Satanic Bible*, 120.

Candles, chalices, swords, chants, and movements don't possess their own power but create an atmosphere where participants can suspend intellect and engage purely with the will and imagination needed for the ritual.[135]

Much like Lévi and Crowley, LaVey taught that orgasm was a means of producing and transmitting energy because it gathers power and culminates in a climax of release. Primal emotions like rage or attraction were also sources of energy in magic.[136] His magic employed visualization of a goal timed with the release of this energy. Ritual itself, with its atmosphere and props, could be intentionally employed to elicit a strong mental and emotional state. The energy from those emotions could be harnessed and directed toward a specific goal.

Last, in LaVey's *11 Satanic Rules of the Earth*, written in a 1967 publication for members, rule number seven reads, "Acknowledge the power of magic if you have employed it successfully to obtain your desires. If you deny the power of magic after having called upon it with success, you will lose all you have obtained."[137]

In the end, LaVey brought modern Satanism into popularity and continues to influence it even after his death. He had varying beliefs and interests over time, some good and some bad, and founded the first official satanic religion.

It is certainly not the last.

THE SATANIC TEMPLE

Founded in 2012 by Lucien Greaves (also known as Doug Mesner) and Malcolm Jarry, The Satanic Temple is currently the largest satanic organization in the world, with more than 700 thousand members.[138]

---

135. LaVey, *The Satanic Bible*, 125.

136. LaVey, *The Satanic Bible*, 88.

137. Anton LaVey, "The Eleven Satanic Rules of the Earth," Church of Satan, accessed June 30, 2023, https://www.churchofsatan.com/eleven-rules-of-earth/.

138. "New Milestone: Over 700,000 Members!" Satanic Temple, accessed October 6, 2023, https://thesatanictemple.com/blogs/news/new-milestone-over-700-000-members.

What started as a somewhat small affair exploded and continues to gain momentum, with congregations popping up around the globe. The Satanic Temple gained tax-exempt status from the IRS in 2019, making it a legitimate, recognized religious group.[139]

The Satanic Temple has headquarters in Salem, Massachusetts, a refurbished funeral parlor painted black. It doubles as an art gallery and a museum showcasing historical exhibits relevant to Satanism. They have amassed a huge online following and host many virtual and in-person events to bring the community together, like movie nights, lectures, and satanic-themed conventions.

Humble Beginnings

In 2012, Malcolm Jarry and Doug Mesner met at Harvard University, not knowing that they were the soon-to-be cofounders of The Satanic Temple. Jarry described his religion at the time as "atheistic Judaism," while Mesner was raised in a Catholic and Protestant home.[140] They bonded over their alarm at how Evangelicals had been allowed to infiltrate politics under George W. Bush's administration. Both had grown up during the satanic panic of the 1980s and had been affected by the moral terror that swept the nation. Mesner was intrigued by how the public responded to the panic and the allegations of satanic ritual abuse that came to the fore. These interests led him to learn about religious Satanism, and he eventually came to consider himself a Satanist.[141]

The Satanic Temple was born the following year when Florida Governor Rick Scott signed a bill allowing students to read "inspirational messages" at school events. Jarry and Mesner felt that this provided a platform for Christians to spread their religion, although Scott didn't come right out and say so. They decided to act against this development and planned a rally in Florida where Satanists would be thanking Rick

139. Joseph P. Laycock, *Speak of the Devil: How the Satanic Temple Is Changing the Way We Talk about Religion* (New York: Oxford University Press, 2020), 129.

140. Laycock, *Speak of the Devil*, 27–28.

141. Laycock, *Speak of the Devil*, 29–30.

Scott. By allowing students to give speeches about religion in schools, Scott opened the platform to *all* religions—including Satanism. This act of protest would give the religious majority a taste of their own medicine, so to speak, by making them experience the flip side of the bill first-hand. To gather attendants for the rally, they cast actors for the sake of anonymity. However, upon realizing that actors might jeopardize Satanism's integrity, Doug Mesner became the face of The Satanic Temple. He took on the name Lucien Greaves, which was originally a pseudonym used by the group for general correspondences.[142]

What began as a one-off experiment then gained momentum and grew faster than anyone involved could have expected.

Satan Becomes the Good Guy

The Satanic Temple has been accused of being trolls and pranksters who don't take Satanism seriously, but this is not true. While they do use humor in their efforts, that doesn't take away from the work they've done. They have forced America to look in the mirror at how rampant religious privilege is and the damage it can do. In fact, this sense of humor is what has attracted people from all walks of life to reconsider what modern Satanism actually is and its role in the bigger picture. The release of the documentary *Hail Satan?* in 2019 brought international attention to The Satanic Temple, along with many new members.[143]

The Satanic Temple is known for its media-savvy public demonstrations protesting religion in schools, theocracy, reproductive issues, and more. However, the organization is far more than a political group. Outsiders of all kinds have discovered a place of belonging there, virtually and in person. Some people who already had a grasp on modern Satanism followed. Others who were brand new to the idea were surprised to discover that there was no evil in sight and not a human sacrifice to be found. Instead, they discovered community.

---

142. Laycock, *Speak of the Devil*, 31–32.
143. Penny Lane, dir., *Hail Satan?* Hard Working Movies (Magnolia Pictures, 2019), 95 minutes.

An Atheist Religion?

One of the popular arguments against The Satanic Temple's legitimacy is the opinion that they cannot be a religion without theism, and at first glance, the term "atheist religion" does seem like an oxymoron. But The Satanic Temple isn't the first religion that doesn't emphasize deity. Other religions that don't center on deity include Confucianism, Jainism, and some forms of Buddhism. Religion doesn't have to involve the supernatural, contrary to what most people think.

A religion is a group of people who share values and beliefs; who abide by a collective set of standards; who have symbols, archetypes, or imagery that are central to their beliefs; and who have a community based on their principles. While The Satanic Temple doesn't view Satan as a god, they do view him as an inspirational symbol of their beliefs. The symbolism of Satan is just as important to The Satanic Temple as gods are in other religions, as is their iconography. Members feel a genuine connection to the archetype of the devil and all he represents.

As a religion, The Satanic Temple aims to obtain the same religious rights and advantages given to other religious groups, as stated in the American First Amendment, which promises freedom of religion, free speech, and the right to confront the government with grievances that interfere with these things. Like other religions, they have a ministry that can perform weddings and memorial ceremonies, a growing number of congregations, and in-person events for shared celebrations of Satan. The Satanic Temple celebrated its tenth anniversary in 2023 with the massive event *SatanCon*, which brought Satanists together for rituals, lectures, music, and revelry. The event was swarmed by Catholic protestors, who didn't do any research about the event beforehand.[144] If they had, they would have known there was nothing to be upset about.

After all, it's difficult for any rational person to argue against The Satanic Temple based on their seven guiding tenets, which are as follows:

---

144. Jacob Geanous, "Hundreds of Protesters Swarm Sold-Out SatanCon in Boston: 'Hellfire Awaits!'" *New York Post*, May 17, 2023, https://nypost.com/2023/04/29/hundreds-of-protesters-swarm-sold-out-satancon-in-boston/.

1. One should strive to act with compassion and empathy toward all creatures in accordance with reason.

2. The struggle for justice is an ongoing and necessary pursuit that should prevail over laws and institutions.

3. One's body is inviolable, subject to one's own will alone.

4. The freedoms of others should be respected, including the freedom to offend. To willfully and unjustly encroach upon the freedoms of another is to forgo one's own.

5. Beliefs should conform to one's best scientific understanding of the world. One should take care never to distort scientific facts to fit one's beliefs.

6. People are fallible. If one makes a mistake, one should do one's best to rectify it and resolve any harm that might have been caused.

7. Every tenet is a guiding principle designed to inspire nobility in action and thought. The spirit of compassion, wisdom, and justice should always prevail over the written or spoken word.[145]

Nowhere in there does it say to do evil, harm others, or commit child sacrifice. So now what? The Satanic Temple has been accused of using the devil for shock value, but this is not necessarily true. The Satanic Temple fights for the separation of church and state, for pluralism in the public sphere, and against the religious supremacy that creates inequality. They fight for bodily autonomy and reproductive rights, demanding that laws be made based on science and logic, not the religion of a chosen few. The Satanic Temple takes affirmative, genuine action in protest, in the American court system, and in day-to-day life to create real, measurable change.

---

145. La Carmina, *The Little Book of Satanism: A Guide to Satanic History, Culture & Wisdom* (Berkeley, CA: Ulysses Press, 2022), 112.

Baphomet Comes to Town

Wherever Christianity pops up in American places that are meant to be secular, so does the devil in the form of The Satanic Temple. This acts as a reminder of religious privilege and causes many to reevaluate what it really means to allow it in public places. For example, The Satanic Temple created the After School Satan Club to counter-balance religious groups operating in public schools.[146] Many of The Satanic Temple's activities follow a similar trajectory and purpose as these after-school clubs. Bringing the devil into public spaces in ways that mirror Christian activities achieves multiple goals. One, it provides an alternative to the majority religion. Two, it reminds people that if one religion is allowed in a public space, all religions must be allowed—including the ones they don't like. Three, often the mere presence of The Satanic Temple practicing their First Amendment rights is enough to cause the religious program in question to shut down completely; it seems most people would rather have no religion at all than have the devil hanging around.[147] All these things culminate in the end goal, which is to have religion kept out of secular spaces.

A similar situation occurred in Arkansas in 2015. Oklahoma City State Representative Mike Ritze donated a large monument bearing the Ten Commandments to the state. It was to be installed at the state capital, which is on public grounds.[148] Public grounds are property owned by the city. Public grounds are meant for everyone, *not* for a single religious group, which was why The Satanic Temple took issue with a religious monument being erected there. They decided to have their own monument put alongside the Ten Commandments in the spirit of plu-

---

146. Laycock, *Speak of the Devil,* 50–51.

147. Nick Wing, "Phoenix City Council Votes to End Prayer Rather Than Let Satanists Lead It," HuffPost, February 5, 2016, https://www.huffpost.com/entry/phoenix -satanists_n_56b4e2b2e4b04f9b57d9639f.

148. Hannah Grabenstein, "Satanic Temple Unveils Baphomet Statue at Arkansas Capitol," *Associated Press,* August 16, 2018, https://apnews.com/article/religion-arkansas -state-governments-1dfef6715487416eadfd08f36c7dbb4b.

ralism and their freedom of religious expression.[149] They commissioned a gigantic bronze statue of Baphomet, featuring the winged, goat-headed creature seated in front of an inverted pentagram with two children gazing adoringly up at it.[150] Members went through all the legalities, red tape, and bureaucracy required to get Baphomet legally erected. If one religion could do it, so could all the others, according to the rules.

Strangely, the state didn't agree. They even created an emergency act to prevent the statue from being installed.[151] Eventually, the Christian monument was displayed, but Baphomet was not. This decision sent a very clear message to the public about which religious group is actually in charge, regardless of what the Constitution says. So even though Baphomet didn't make it onto public grounds and now resides at The Satanic Temple headquarters, the mission was still a success. Those in charge had shown their true colors.

Here we see the devil manifesting as a trickster, exposing the ugly, foolish truth about the way things work in society and religion. The Satanic Temple repeatedly forces people to see the blatant hypocrisy at play in government. The Satanic Temple stands against religious discrimination in ways that cannot be ignored, forcing people to see things they would perhaps rather deny.

Flipping Evil on Its Head

As The Satanic Temple continues to grow and take action, something very interesting is occurring that just might permanently alter the way that Western culture views religion. By taking on the moniker of Satanists but acting in positive ways through advocacy, good deeds, and philanthropy, they have infiltrated American courts, politics, and the public forum in confounding and meaningful ways. The Satanic Temple takes on the positive attributes of the devil—equality, creativity, rationality, and empathy. They haven't broken laws, they haven't done any harm, and they're doing

---

149. Laycock, *Speak of the Devil*, 12.
150. Laycock, *Speak of the Devil*, 11.
151. Laycock, *Speak of the Devil*, 12–13.

charity work instead of sacrificing kittens. Could it be that by presenting the ever-dreaded father of evil in a positive light that they are a bigger threat than ever to organized religion? They're forcing a change in public perception about the big bad monster named Satan. In many ways, they take the fear out of the devil, leaving, instead, just another religious group minding their business having bake sales and hosting charitable events. Now the monster is … not a monster.

This presents an ideological problem. That monster is *needed* by those who wish to uphold Christian supremacy. That monster has kept oppressive religious systems going for centuries. He is a crucial tool of fear. Without him, what's left? The evil, soul-snatching, murdering devil provides the horrifying darkness needed to illuminate themselves while instilling just enough fear in their followers to ensure loyalty. The Satanic Temple is presenting them with their favorite weapon, claws and all, in ways that they are obligated to accept. His supporters are visible in the public sphere, doing all the things good citizens should. Without darkness, there can't be light. When the darkness is taken away, what does it mean for the good guys?

This work exposes the truth: that religious freedom and privilege in America are only for some.

As the saying goes, every story needs a villain. The Satanic Temple is changing the story and forcing a new one to be written. While it is certainly younger than the Church of Satan, I believe it will go down in history not only as the biggest satanic movement yet but as a political and social justice one as well.

LUCIFERIANISM

Sometimes the devil is referred to as Lucifer, whose veneration is called Luciferianism. There can be some confusion when it comes to Lucifer. Is he an angel? Are he and Satan the same being? What's the difference between Luciferianism and Satanism? As with most things, the answer to all these questions depends on who you ask. Some people use the names *Satan* and *Lucifer* interchangeably, while others consider them very different things. One consistency is that Lucifer is often considered a spiritual energy of sorts, whereas Satan is a representation of earthbound humanism and the rejection of superstition.

Luciferiansim is a belief system centered around Lucifer as a light bringer. Many Luciferians do not follow a specific leader and choose to go it alone, as treading one's own path is at the core of the philosophy.

History and Organizations

In 1906, a Danish man named Ben Kadosh (1872–1936) listed his religious affiliation as "Luciferian" in the Danish census. That same year, he published a pamphlet called *Den Ny Morgens Gry: Erdensbygmesterens Genkomst* (The Dawn of a New Morning: The Return of the World's Master Builder), in which he explained his Luciferian philosophy.[152]

While he didn't produce prolific amounts of writing, he was possibly the first to officially dub himself a Luciferian. In his pamphlet, Kadosh wrote that Lucifer was the sum of material nature. He claimed to venerate Baphomet and a goat god that he considered the creator.[153] He seemed to integrate Masonic lore into his beliefs, including the stories of Taxil, despite these sources being pure fiction.

Kadosh's writing probably would have fallen into obscurity if he hadn't been immortalized by several popular Danish novelists, who made him into a character in their books.[154]

The Neo-Luciferian Church, founded in 2005, was influenced by the work of Ben Kadosh, combined with other forms of Western occultism like that of Lévi and Crowley.[155] The church is currently active in Sweden and Denmark.

---

152. Van Luijk, *Children of Lucifer*, 287.
153. Per Faxneld, "'In Communication with the Powers of Darkness': Satanism in Turn-of-the-Century Denmark, and Its Use as a Legitimating Device in Present-Day Esotericism," in *Occultism in a Global Perspective*, ed. Henrik Bogdan and Gordan Djurdjevic (New York: Routledge, 2014), 57–78.
154. Per Faxneld, "'In Communication with the Powers of Darkness,'" 57–78.
155. Per Faxneld, "'In Communication with the Powers of Darkness,'" 57–78.

A more well-known Luciferian group is the Greater Church of Lucifer. In the 1960s, Charles Pace (1919–?) of Glasgow, England, dubbed himself a "Sethanic" or "Satanic Witch." He created the Luciferian and Sethanic teachings, which were based on ancient Egyptian mythology and rituals.[156] Pace equated Lucifer with the adversarial Egyptian Set(h), the god of storms and war, who challenged the rule of Osiris.[157] He wrote *The Necrominon: The Book of Shades* and *The Book of Tahuti*, neither of which were ever officially published. His Luciferianism wasn't just a means of defying monotheistic religion but taught that Luciferians were outside all natural hierarchies, both divine and earthly.[158]

Pace was in the military and stationed in Egypt during World War II, which is possibly where his interest in ancient Egyptian religion began. At this time, Aleister Crowley was a sensation in the press, and the Egyptian elements of his magic caught Pace's attention.[159]

Eventually, Pace's handwritten texts were accessed by Michael W. Ford, author and copresident of the Greater Church of Lucifer, which was founded in Old Town Spring, Texas, in 2013. Michael W. Ford expanded on these original manuscripts and brought them into circulation among modern Luciferians.

When the Greater Church of Lucifer opened its Texan headquarters on Halloween in 2015, it was met with angry Christian protesters and vandalism.[160] The church was forced to shut down one year later when the landlord refused to renew the lease after being doxed and bombarded with death threats.[161]

---

156. Michael W. Ford, *Apotheosis: The Ultimate Beginner's Guide to Luciferianism & the Left-Hand Path* (Houston, TX: Succubus Productions, 2019), 25.

157. Michael W. Ford, *Necrominon: Egyptian Sethanic Magick* (Houston, TX: Succubus Productions, 2013), loc. 221, Kindle.

158. Ford, *Necrominon: Egyptian Sethanic Magick*, loc. 231, Kindle.

159. Ford, *Necrominon: Egyptian Sethanic Magick,* loc. 172, Kindle.

160. "Protest and Prayer Fill Air Outside Greater Church of Lucifer," ABC13 Houston, October 31, 2015, https://abc13.com/church-of-lucifer-spring-protesters-protest/1060363/.

161. Niklas Göranssan, "Black Funeral Interview," *Bardo Methodology*, May 29, 2019, http://www.bardomethodology.com/articles/2019/05/29/black-funeral-interview/.

Ford's Luciferianism is far more complicated than modern Satanism, combining Pace's vast, intricate system of ancient Egyptian elements with Western occultism, modern Satanism, and Paganism.

Many modern Luciferians are solitary and do not identify with Ford's teachings or any specific group.

Last but not least is the mysterious German order, Fraternitas Saturnati, which means Brotherhood of Saturn. It is one of the longest-standing Luciferian groups, still functioning today. Founded between 1926 and 1928 by Grand Master Gregor A. Gregorius (1888–1964), also known as Eugene Grosch, the organization was born in Germany and then spread to Switzerland and Austria.[162] Despite its longevity and the large volume of written material it has produced, the order remains very secretive and mysterious.

The beliefs of the Fraternitas Saturnati are complex. Saturn, being the furthest from the sun in ancient cosmology, is considered representative of both Lucifer and Satan and is the "dark brother of the sun."[163] They believe that the higher power encompasses both light and darkness, putting Lucifer on the same level as God. Their practice is a combination of ceremonial magic, Hinduism, Rosicrucianism, and Thelema. In the beginning, they were interested in sex magic and drug use and looked favorably upon Satan, which garnered negative public attention. A good chunk of their writing was categorized as "satanic magic."

Fraternitas Saturnati embraces the Crowley-inspired "do what though wilt" philosophy, with the addition of "compassionless love," which is a reference to the harsh qualities of Saturn, such as responsibility, restraint, and rationality.

The Saturnian path is difficult, solitary, and full of suffering, and these things lead to nobility and independence. Gregorius Gregor said, "Become hard like a crystal. For a crystal is only formed through hardness."[164]

---

162. Hans Thomas Hakl, "The Magical Order of the Fraternitas Saturni," in *Occultism in a Global Perspective*, ed. Henrik Bogdan and Gordan Djurdjevic (New York: Routledge, 2014), chapter 3.
163. Hakl, "The Magical Order of the Fraternitas Saturni," chapter 3.
164. Hakl, "The Magical Order of the Fraternitas Saturni," chapter 3.

The beliefs of Fraternitas Saturnati are based on the mythology of engineer Hanns Hörbiger (1860–1931). His theory was that cosmic ice collided with a fiery star, causing an explosion that created the universe. The power of the sun, called Chrestros, brought light and, with it, life. Lucifer grabbed this light and ran away to Saturn. Saturn was the last visible planet before the void of darkness, so Lucifer was not only the bearer of light but a guardian of the threshold to the afterlife.[165]

Like other satanic and Luciferian beliefs, Fraternitas Saturnati teaches not divine faith nor intervention but a self-led path to one's own inner divinity.

Beliefs

There are different kinds of Luciferians, just as there are different kinds of Satanists and witches. Some believe in an afterlife, while others do not. Some lean very heavily into the angels-and-demons mythology, while others view Lucifer strictly as a symbol. Some associate Lucifer with the ancient sun, fire, and light gods like Prometheus, the Titan god of fire, and include older gods in rituals.

Some believe that Lucifer was not actually kicked out of heaven but that he willingly left so he could bring enlightenment and knowledge to humans as the next step in our evolution. Some practice ceremonial magic, and others have a combination of beliefs based on philosophies from around the world.

Beneath the multitudes of variables, Lucifer always shines. Luciferianism, at its core, is about the light of the self and actively bettering it through will, knowledge, and creativity.

How one views the parallels and differences between Satanism and Luciferianism is very individualistic. This makes it difficult to define but is on brand since both are about the path of the outsider. Neither is meant to be a singular, overarching system that is applied to all Lucife-

---

165. Hakl, "The Magical Order of the Fraternitas Saturni," chapter 3.

rians. The Luciferian path is not for those who are seeking a teacher or leader to tell them what to think.

The story of Lucifer and his fall from heaven has been told many times in many ways. For those of us on the left-hand path, the underlying theme is one of transformation and strength, not one of disgrace.

The Morning Star

Lucifer is often referred to as the Morning Star. *Morning Star* is a name the ancient Greeks gave to the planet Venus, which later became associated with Aphrodite, the Greek goddess of love. Venus is the brightest thing in the night sky aside from the moon. It is the first "star" to become visible as dusk falls and the last star to disappear at dawn.[166] For this reason, Lucifer is both the light-bringer and the night-bringer. He is a balance of light and dark. Destruction and growth are two sides of the same coin. Both forces come from the same source, and both live within us.[167]

Luciferian teachings can connect a person to their higher consciousness, which some might call a soul or spirit. In a physical sense, Luciferians know they are both creators and destroyers of their own reality on Earth and, if they believe in it, on other planes. Lucifer is all, he is everything within and without, above and below, and that's why he heralds both the morning and the night.

Lucifer's Light

Lucifer is the spark inside of each individual person that makes them unique. Apotheosis, which means to become a god, is the highest possible form of the self. Luciferianism teaches that everything you could ever desire can be provided, *not* by a god but by the light of your mind, will, and imagination.

---

166. Garry Hunt, "Why Venus Is Called the Morning Star or the Evening Star," *BBC Sky at Night Magazine*, February 2, 2023, https://www.skyatnightmagazine.com/space -science/venus-morning-star-evening-star/.

167. Ford, *Apotheosis*, 28.

Luciferians have some of the same values as Satanists and other left-hand path philosophies. They value nonconformity, freedom of thought for all, and respect for others, including those with different opinions. They also endorse reveling in the carnal joys of one's true nature. When it comes to morality, there is no list of rules; ruthlessly conquer your enemies and fight fire with fire if you wish.

Luciferianism splinters away from Satanism because it's a continuation of physical and earthly evolution into transcendence. It combines esotericism with the rationalism and carnality of Satanism. Some Luciferians adhere to the survival of the fittest theory, taking it one step further and applying it to spirituality, in that one's spirit must be among the strongest to be elevated to apotheosis. It's kind of like Satanism with a side of spirituality.

Luciferians don't worship or fear any god, nor Lucifer himself. Each individual utilizes their light in their own unique way. One who is unaware of this light within them, or who feels it's out of their reach, is not on the Luciferian path. The light is already in you. You just have to harness it. It is a self-liberating process that one must traverse alone.

OUTSIDERS OF THE OUTSIDERS

Modern Satanism has many other organized groups around the world beyond those already noted. It's generally expected that you identify with one or another, especially by people who don't understand the individualism of Satanism. However, some people don't click with an organization, and that is okay. I'm one of them.

The reasons for choosing to be a solitary Satanist and a solitary witch are similar.

Avoiding Group Dynamics

Individualism makes the demand to fall in with a group and adopt their ideas seem backward. That's not to say I don't value community. Finding a home among like-minded people is sometimes necessary. Many people need a sense of belonging within a group, be it a satanic organization or a witchcraft coven. Groups are also useful when it comes to creating large-scale change, as with The Satanic Temple, because many hands are needed to make an impact. But witches and Satanists often share a spirit of fierce individuality that doesn't always mesh well with group dynamics.

Satanic organizations aim to be nondogmatic, as do many witchcraft groups. They don't tend to operate with the goal of telling members what to think or how to behave. They are meant to be self-directed communities jelled by shared values and mutual respect, but unfortunately, that's not always what happens. There will always be people who don't grasp the importance of individualism and lean toward herd mentality. There is also a natural hierarchy that will form with leaders and followers no matter how hard one might try to avoid it. If you choose to distance yourself from all of that, you are considered solitary.

Theistic Ideology

Theistic Satanists believe the devil is a deity and commune with him as such. They do not fit in with any of the large established satanic organizations. There are not very many theistic Satanists around, but they do exist. While I don't share their belief, I feel they're free to practice as they please without ridicule or judgment.

Theism is far more accepted in the witchcraft world, but sometimes people will butt heads over what is right or wrong when it comes to different deities, leading many people to just go it alone.

Eclectic Practice

Some people, like me, just prefer to do our witchcraft in peace without being labeled or having to defend ourselves for what we think. I don't exactly match the criteria for any group. Many people disagree with my views on witchcraft, the devil, Satan, and Lucifer. That's okay. Since I am stable and grounded in my sense of self, I do not need to argue about it.

Outsider Satanists apply the basic elements of modern Satanism to their lives as they wish. At the risk of sounding unkind, if you're looking for a group that will direct you, hold your hand, and tell you what to believe, or if you're just searching for a cool social club, Satanism and devil-related witchcraft are probably not for you. Your relationship with the devil is yours alone. Satanism is about freedom and individuality, not parroting the beliefs of another person.

Other Reasons

Sometimes the decision to avoid groups and go solitary is simply practical:

SPIRITUAL SOLITUDE

Some people just can't concentrate when surrounded by others. When it comes to any kind of spiritual practice requiring mental focus, whether that's a simple ritual, meditation, or magic, it can be difficult to maintain concentration with others nearby. This might be a sensory issue because sounds interfere with your focus or social anxiety, which prevents you from fully immersing yourself in the experience. If being near others during these acts gets in the way, it's okay to just do them alone.

LIFESTYLE

Some witches keep themselves "in the broom closet," which means they do not tell anyone about their beliefs because it might interfere with their professional or social life. Some Satanists have similar reasons for being solitary. Not everyone in your life will understand your beliefs, and some may even judge harshly. This is especially true when it comes to religion, and if you might lose your job for being a witch or a satanist, you have every reason to keep it separate from your work life. The same goes for family and friends; if sharing your beliefs with them would cause discord, sometimes it's just easier to keep it to yourself.

FEAR OF JUDGMENT

I know I'm not the only one to have been ridiculed for my witchcraft practice, and it can be even worse when it comes to Satanism. A practice like ours is very personal, and not only is having outsiders judge and condemn us painful, but it can erode our confidence. There's no reason at all why these people need to know what you do in your private life. In some communities, outing oneself as a Satanist can even be dangerous due to misinformation and fear.

BELIEFS

When it comes to magic, some people believe that they should keep their workings private until they have manifested. There is a theory that when others know about your workings, their doubt can impede the effectiveness of your rituals and spells. Well-known, public-facing witches may have haters who will actually try to divert their workings via magic. For this reason, some people choose to keep their beliefs to themselves.

HAS THE DEVIL OUTGROWN RELIGION?

During the Romantic period, we saw revolutionaries create a split between the devil and religion by casting him not as an evil monster but as a symbol of rebellion and freedom. Since then, he's continued to be many things, often not religious at all.

The devil continues to act as a scapegoat in some religious groups, representing all that is evil and corrupt. He is still used as a tool to control through fear.

At the same time, many people don't view the devil as supernatural at all. He's a mythological figure in his own right, with songs, art, and culture centered around his many facets. It seems that the devil has been split into two for a long time, between folkloric and theological. Those of us who identify with the folkloric devil barely recognize the theological version of him at all.

Has he left his Christian origins in the dust? Not yet, but I believe eventually he will.

In many ways, he has become a secular character. For example, take the popularity of Krampus, the German Christmas devil-creature. Krampus was St. Nicholas's nasty, cloven-hoofed sidekick. With his scary horns and long ugly tongue, Krampus hit naughty children with birch sticks and carried them off to his lair in a sack. In recent years, the image of Krampus, once obscure, has become mainstream and is often viewed as funny and ironic. For most, there is little-to-no religious meaning to Krampus. He is a folkloric figure that appeals to those who perhaps have a dark sense of humor about the holidays. He even has his own movie.

The folkloric devil appears in our music, fashion, politics, and even home décor, all things that people don't consider religious. In this way, I feel that the devil has surpassed his origins and is now a new kind of symbol.

The act of embracing Satan began as a backlash against the authoritarian clergy. Over time, authority has come to describe many different things beyond religion. When I think of the devil as an adversary against tyranny, said tyranny is not limited to religion. It is any system or power structure that is oppressive and overreaching. Inequitable power takes many forms, like patriarchy, government, class, race, and on down the list. The force you are fighting against in your life is a personal thing. Everyone has some form of authority they want to overcome.

Satan has been so much more than a wee thorn in God's behind. Satan has spread into art, music, movies, and pop culture. He's a symbol of political revolt. He's a means of self-expression. He represents atheism, science, and intelligence. He is the deification of sex, drugs, and rock and roll and rejecting conformity. He is our animal desires and our deepest secrets.

It's for all these reasons that I think one can claim to be a Satanist or devil enthusiast without any religious context at all. While some adamant monotheists will never, ever accept this view, it appears to me that more people are coming to understand Satan not as an evil entity bent on destroying the earth but as something much more human and closer to home.

The devil has become such an integral part of our societal landscape that he has lost a lot of his unholy associations. Because of this, Satanism has become a philosophy free of religious trappings for many.

The devil picked up Pagan characteristics, then Christian ones, and is now continuing to grow into something else yet. He was here before monotheism, and he will be here after. I wonder what he'll be like five hundred years from now.

CHAPTER 4

THE OLD GODS AND THE DEVIL

You may have heard that the devil is just a vilified version of an old horned god or gods. Is it true? Sort of. Some witches, especially traditional witches, practice with the belief that today's devil is the same force that was once called by many other names. While there are certainly similarities, there are also disparities, the largest being that the Christian Satan is the epitome of evil and the old gods are not. There is also the fact that Satan is simply much younger.

But age isn't everything. A god doesn't have to be ancient to be real or powerful. Satan may be relatively new compared to Pagan deities, but the collective belief of billions has been feeding his power for over two thousand years. Today's devil is a modern creation, which means he's perfectly in sync with the times and energies of this moment.

To many modern Satanists, there is no meaningful correlation at all between Satan and Pagan deities. The mystical, magical undertones that the folkloric devil presents to witches aren't necessarily present for Satanists.

You'll find this folkloric devil bridging the gap between the Pagan gods and modern Satan, a shape-shifting being that embodies life itself. It is this version of him, what I call the witches' devil, that calls to so many of us.

While the old gods were not simply rolled into one ball of fur and horns and labeled "Satan" overnight, there are still many connections to be considered.

The devil is not a direct rebranding of Pagan gods as people once thought, but he was certainly influenced by some of their animal features and traits. This is likely because when Christians discovered the Roman, Greek, and Norse gods, they believed they were merely empty idols filled with demons. The characteristics of these idols became entwined with that of demons, which are strongly associated with the devil.

What these Pagan deities also share with the devil is the glorification of nature and all it has to offer. Carnality was considered a bad thing by the church, and many Greek and Roman gods certainly had a carnal side, especially those associated with fertility and the hunt. The church considered humans to be spiritually and intellectually superior to animals, which were viewed as lowly and unclean in comparison. The horns, scales, claws, and hoofs of the old gods embodied this carnality.

The most well-known characteristic of the devil is his horns. It's interesting to have a look at various horned deities and make a comparison. Many of these gods are known for their carnal aspects, such as the Greek god Pan and his sexual proclivities, Celtic Cernunnos and his association with the hunt, and Roman Bacchus with his love of music and revelry. That's not to say these gods didn't have spiritual elements because they did. They were associated with death and rebirth, fertility, the afterlife, and the soul. However, this is not the side of them that garnered attention.

To me, the old gods are something much larger than what many people think of as the devil. You can't look to a single book or person to understand them. You must look deep into the earth, the roots of the trees, and the darkness of the forest. To find these gods, you have to peer into the shadows of the self and the parts of you that are purely animal.

THE WITCH CULT HYPOTHESIS

There is a very popular story about the original Pagans of Europe, who venerated a horned god and were forced to take their practices underground during the witch hunts. Margaret Murray (1863–1963), a scholar, feminist, archaeologist, and Egyptologist, was most well-known for linking the horned gods to the devil in her book *The Witch Cult of Western Europe* (1921). The witch-cult hypothesis, which has been thoroughly debunked, was created by scholars before her, but she is the one most recognized for it. The hypothesis greatly influenced the future of Paganism and witchcraft, including the works of important people like Gerald Gardner (1884–1964), who is dubbed the father of modern witchcraft. Learning about these scholars' claims helps shed light upon our understanding of the devil in modern witchcraft.

Murray reworked the records of the witch hunts into a new narrative, in which the accused were not witches or devil worshippers at all but a misunderstood pre-Christian tribe.

Murray's story began with a cave painting in France that dates to the Paleolithic era. The painting depicts a mysterious figure that is a cross between a human and an antlered animal. The figure is positioned above several other animals as if to display its importance.

Murray dubbed this the original Horned God of the witches. She hypothesized that the early witch hunts were an attempt to actively exterminate Pagan people who venerated this antlered fertility god. They were forced to take their practices underground into caves and into the deep woods for fear of being murdered. For thousands of years, they kept their secret rites alive in remote places, passing their knowledge on to their descendants through word of mouth. Later, in modern times, this witch cult came out into the public, exposing their bloodlines, secrets, and practices, all of which centered around the Horned God.

Murray was considered an expert and wrote the definition of witch-craft for the *Encyclopaedia Britannica*, stating her theories as fact.[168] This definition of witchcraft remained in the encyclopedia until the 1960s.

Murray wrote about the witches' sabbath from a new angle, not as the frenzied evil described by witch-hunters, but as a misunderstood religious rite. She was the first one to say that a coven should be thirteen people. Murray wrote that children were initiated between the ages of nine and thirteen by lying at the feet of the "divine man" and making a public declaration of their faith. He asked, "Dost thou come of thy own free will?" and the child would answer yes. Then the initiate received a scar or tattoo to show they were a true member of the cult.[169]

Murray's version of the witches' sabbath included orgiastic rites, feasts, and dancing. Children were not usually sacrificed; instead, when a baby was born into the cult, they would be placed into the arms of the Horned God in a ceremony, wherein the mother promised that the baby would be a servant to him for life.[170]

She added some colorful details, such as the cross could ward off witches and the fae and that the more horns a god or goddess had, the higher their rank.[171] The devil could appear as a dog, goat, cat, sheep, bull, or stag, and he was a skilled fiddle and flute player.[172] These details are important because a lot of them can still be found in folklore about the devil and witches today.

Popular witchcraft books written between the 1950s and the 2000s are directly influenced by Margaret Murray's tale, presenting it as fact, mostly because that was the only historical material available to the authors of the time. Since the popular rise of this story, academics have discovered that it's incorrect in timeline and fact. While some Christians

---

168. *Encyclopaedia Britannica* (1947), vol. 23, vase to zygote, s.v. "witchcraft," by Margaret Alice Murray, 686–87.
169. Murray, *The God of the Witches*, 96.
170. Murray, *The God of the Witches*, 94.
171. Murray, *The God of the Witches*, 25.
172. Murray, *The God of the Witches*, 113.

in the Middle Ages certainly did demonize unfamiliar gods and goddesses, the witch-cult hypothesis is simply untrue.

That being said, to this day, our ideas about the Horned God(s) and his worship contain traces of the witch-cult hypothesis and probably always will.

CHRISTIANS AND PAGANS

Margaret Murray's take on the Christian overthrow of Paganism may be preferable to what actually happened. The idea of all the horned gods being conveniently balled together and called the devil is a nice, neat story. The real Christian conversion of Europe was far messier. There are many takes on how it happened, some of which tend to make it sound like an overnight process: Europe was full of happy Pagans one day, and then the next day, their religion was destroyed, their gods stolen, their holidays copied, their people exterminated—the end. That's not how it went.

Religious acculturation is when a dominant group causes a smaller one to convert to their teachings, pushing individuals to adapt to a new culture. It's not necessarily a pretty thing, but it's also not always fast and violent, either. Religious syncretism is when two separate cultures come together naturally due to various circumstances and overlap, resulting in a new type of practice containing elements from various origins. This refers to a more organic phenomenon than religious acculturation, which often forces one religion to relinquish its beliefs. Both have been happening since the beginning of human history, and both of these terms are relevant when discussing the Christian revolution in Europe.

The Pagan-to-Christian conversion was a long process spanning centuries. The Christian word spread along trade routes that carried the new religion far and wide. It's no wonder that during this time, a blend of beliefs among both sides emerged, particularly in rural areas that didn't have direct contact with the church, as they were receiving only bits and pieces of the new ideas, kind of like a game of telephone. In some cases, over time, Pagans and Christians adopted *each other's* beliefs and customs.

Originally, Pagan Rome didn't accept Christianity at all, and believe it or not, rumors circulated that *Christians* met in the night to commit evils very similar to the witches' sabbath, with the usual infanticide, incest, and cannibalism.[173] Around the fourth century, the tides turned, and accusations started flying the opposite way. People often depict the Pagans as victims of the Christians, but make no mistake: they put up one hell of a fight and did their share of slaughtering.

Emperor Constantine the Great (c. 272–337 CE) was an early adopter of Christianity in Rome. Constantine brought in a militaristic rule and was merciless in battle. His desire for power was unswerving. When vying for a position on the throne, Constantine had to figure out whom to appeal to—the Pagans or the Christians—to give him more power and better his political position.[174] It's said he celebrated the old gods for some time but eventually changed his views.[175] During a battle, Constantine allegedly received a vision from the Christian God, after which he triumphed. Since this new God had served him well, Constantine gave him allegiance.[176] This meant reallocating resources and money into Christian churches and endeavors, causing them to grow and attract more and more people.[177] Christianity was not largely embraced until Constantine legalized it in 313 and put Christians in government and other positions of power.

For several generations, Constantine's successors continued to endorse and financially support the church. Despite this, the struggle was not over yet: decades after Constantine's death, one of his distant cousins inherited the empire and went rogue, declaring the old gods once more in charge and

173. Kelden, *The Witches' Sabbath: An Exploration of History, Folklore & Modern Practice* (Woodbury, MN: Llewellyn Publications, 2022), 10.
174. James J. O'Donnell, *Pagans: The End of Traditional Religion and the Rise of Christianity* (New York: Ecco Press, 2016), 145.
175. O'Donnell, *Pagans*, 135–37.
176. O'Donnell, *Pagans*, 142.
177. O'Donnell, *Pagans*, 147.

revoking Christian privilege.[178] This cousin didn't rule for long, dying in battle on the Persian frontier in 363 CE. In the year 391, Roman Emperor Theodosius (347–395) created a ban on blood sacrifice and all Pagan rituals.[179] All of this shows that the Christian revolution was not a simple matter of conquering Pagans overnight but a lengthy tug-of-war.

It's not known if Constantine would measure up to our current idea of a truly converted Christian. Despite his shift in divine alliance, he didn't outlaw Paganism but allowed it to exist alongside Christianity. He was not baptized until he was on his deathbed; this meant he had a whole lifetime in which to sin and then cleanse it all away at the very end, ensuring his entry into heaven.[180]

Ultimately, Constantine's politics were probably far more important to him than religion. One might even say he used religion to leverage his influence, which would mean the Christian conversion was fueled by politics and a hunger for power, not genuine belief.

Another misconception is that all Christian holidays are stolen from Pagans. While it may look that way on the surface, it was probably more a result of syncretism. During the Christian conversion, it would have been impossible to avoid some mixing of beliefs and holidays as things evolved. For example, the Christmas tree is often referred to as Pagan, and you will see many a meme mocking non-Pagans for having one during the holidays. The story of the Christmas tree is a good example of how beliefs and traditions become blended through word of mouth, storytelling, and time.

While it is true that Pagan societies brought evergreens into the house around Yuletide as symbols of hope, there's little evidence that they decorated a whole tree. The Paradise Tree, however, was part of a Christian tradition in which evergreen trees were decorated with apples, holy wafers, and candles and included in plays about Bible stories. December 24 was a feast day of Adam and Eve, and trees were involved in

178. O'Donnell, *Pagans*, 14.
179. O'Donnell, *Pagans*, 195–96.
180. O'Donnell, *Pagans*, 143.

that celebration as well.[181] From this, we can deduce that there is a very good chance that Pagans and Christians influenced each other when it comes to Christmas trees and that the same can be said for many other traditions.

Often in witchy circles, you'll see some harsh words against biblical elements in witchcraft. I disagree wholeheartedly. The blending of Paganism and witchcraft with monotheistic religion can be a natural progression, sometimes done out of necessity and sometimes simply a result of the culture we live in.

THE HORNED GODS OF OLD

I'm going to share the ways that the horned gods have influenced the folkloric devil and modern Satan in appearance, personality, and associations. It's important to note and to respect that those people who venerate the Horned God don't typically consider him the devil or Satan in any way.

Gerald Gardner, the founder of Wicca, continues to influence Western practitioners decades after his passing and probably always will. He believed in a single Horned God who was a fertility deity, a protective father figure, and lord of the land and the woods. This Horned God is the very essence of nature itself, encompassing all its wild and unpredictable qualities, be they beautiful or frightening.

In some witchcraft practices, the Horned God is associated with sex and lust, drunkenness, feasting, and general earthly bliss. These carnal traits are part of the reason people link him to modern Satan. This, however, is only one aspect of him. The Horned God is also spiritual, as mentioned.

Some people venerate a single Horned God like Gardner, while others acknowledge many different antlered and horned deities individually.

Horned gods are often portrayed with erect phalluses to symbolize the fertility of the land, abundance, and sexual pleasure. Some witch-

---

181. Bruce C. Forbes, *Christmas: A Candid History* (Los Angeles: University of California Press, 2007), 49.

craft traditions keep a phallic symbol on their altar, as do some devil enthusiasts.

Monotheistic religion taught that earthly things in nature were evil and dirty. The Pagan horned gods embody nature, so here we see yet another way that they became associated with the devil.

The Sacrificial God

In some folklore, specifically the Margaret Murray variety, the devil had to sacrifice himself every seven to nine years. One of his favorite tricks was to find some poor human soul to replace him; that's why so many pacts with the devil involved a seven-year contract.[182]

One of the key things that separated Pagan practices from Christianity was the act of blood sacrifice. While animals, grains, and goods were offered to the gods, sometimes the gods themselves were the sacrifice.

Wiccans and some modern Pagans have coordinated this idea with their annual celebrations known as the Wheel of the Year. The wheel marks the eight solar events that occur each year and reflects the seasonal cycles of agriculture.

The Horned God was one with nature, so it makes sense that he was directly part of this cycle. The lore places the god and goddess in tandem with the Wheel of the Year to explain nature's cycle of death, conception, birth, and rebirth. Really, this cycle can be applied to much more than the seasons, as everything in our lives peaks, wanes, dies, and is transformed into something new.

This story of the Horned God and the Goddess is a bit of a turnoff for some, as it relies on gender binaries, excluding a whole lot of people. So while this myth may not fit perfectly into the modern world, it is a popular one, contributing to the general understanding of the Horned God. (My hope is that as you read on, you'll learn how the Horned God and the devil were actually non-binary shape-shifters).

The story goes like this:

---

182. Murray, *The Horned God of the Witches*, 105.

The Goddess gives birth to the Horned God on Yule (December 21–23), the longest night of the year, which marks the lengthening of days. The Horned God represents the return, or birth, of the sun. The goddess fades into the background at this time.

On Imbolc (February 1–2), candles are lit and fire is celebrated as a way to call the sun, and the God, toward the earth as winter continues. The Goddess takes on the form of her young self, meets the Horned God, and they begin courting.

At the spring equinox (March 21–23), day and night are of equal length, and the earth is starting to come back to life after winter. As the love between the God and Goddess blossoms, so do the flowers and trees.

At Beltane (May 1), a fertility celebration, the Goddess and God celebrate their physical union, and in some versions, the Goddess becomes impregnated by the God.

On the summer solstice (June 21–23), the sun is at its absolute strongest, and so is the Horned God. The God and Goddess are married, and in some stories, this is when the Goddess gets pregnant, ensuring that the Horned God will live on through her.

The sacrifice of the Horned God can take place at any of the remaining sabbats, as all three are harvest festivals: at Lammas (August 1), a celebration of the first crops; the fall equinox (September 21–23), when the second harvest takes place; or Samhain (October 31), which is the very final harvest before winter. As the vegetables were cut from the earth and gathered, the God's life is also cut.

After this sacrifice, the Horned God goes to the land of the dead until Yule, when the goddess gives birth to him again.

Yes, there are logistical issues with the story, but it is just a myth meant to help understand the larger picture, which is the cycles of the earth and life.

Since these things are symbolic, rituals performed in line with this myth can include people of all genders and don't have to be limited to strictly male/female participation. The Goddess and God, and what they represent, are in everyone.

Mistaken for the Devil

While there are many different horned deities with varying names over different time periods, some stand out as more devil-like than others.

The Greek god Pan, with his horns and cloven hoofs, is often mistaken for the devil. Sometimes, he's shown with a large phallus. The similarities don't end with his appearance. He's a god of sexuality, music, dancing, and general hedonism. At the same time, he's the god of shepherds and flocks and therefore associated with a certain degree of solitude, one might even say individualism. Even more interesting is that the word *panic* is rooted in the name Pan because he was known for causing humans to suddenly and inexplicably fly into frenzied chaos.[183]

It's easy to see how Pan is often confused with the folkloric devil, but he was most notably present in ancient Greece, which means there is a huge gap of time between his worship and the devil we now know.

During the Romantic and Victorian eras, Pan was highlighted in European literature, much like Satan and Lucifer. This version of Pan lacked some of his initial wildness and fervor. He represented the countryside and was a guardian of nature and a god of love. During this time, he also came to represent gay men.[184]

The Greek god Dionysus (Bacchus for the Romans) is another god who I feel shares characteristics with the devil. While he is generally shown with horns on coins and not statues or art in this time period, he has other similarities. He was associated with bulls, which were sacrificed to him, and his staff is topped by a pinecone dripping with honey, which is a phallic symbol.

Dionysus is sometimes a man and sometimes a genderless young figure. He's a god of ecstasy, fertility, and drunkenness. He was also one of the gods who traveled to the underworld. Dionysus possesses a dual nature, sometimes being a god of revelry and other times a god of rage, a polarity that is visible in people when they drink alcohol; some people

---

183. Jason Mankey, *The Horned God of the Witches* (Woodbury, MN: Llewellyn Publications, 2021), 55.
184. Mankey, *The Horned God of the Witches*, 149.

become happy-drunk while others are angry-drunk. Dionysus was followed by a group of women called *maenads,* who were said to be mad from wine. They danced, sang, and participated in orgies, after which they tore animals apart and ate them raw. This bloody frenzy is another thing attributed to the witches' sabbath. Dionysus could be described as a god of indulgence, and indulgence is one of the devil's known traits.

Last is Cernunnos, although he has antlers instead of horns. He is a Gaulish or Celtic god of the hunt, the wilderness, and beasts. The most popular image of Cernunnos shows him with the body of a man, an antlered head, a torc in one hand, and a serpent in the other. He's surrounded by animals and sometimes shown with a bag of coins. His ancient past remains somewhat mysterious, but he is sometimes seen as a protector, creator, and ruler of the cycles of death and rebirth.

Historically, the devil is not an amalgam of the old horned gods, but there has been a tenuous tie between them in our collective minds for a long time.

HELL AND THE UNDERWORLD

A logical connection between the devil and the old gods is the concept of hell and an underworld. Some people think that the Christian hell is synonymous with the underworld of older belief systems, but they aren't the same thing. Christianity teaches that bad people go to hell to be punished for eternity after death, whereas the underworld is not so cut and dry. What constitutes "bad" varies widely among all walks of life, but one could presumably expect it includes murderers and those who cause serious harm. However, hell has been a dumping ground for many things, some quite innocent, depending on who needs it and why. One way to use hell was for control, as shown in the Victorian-era book for children *The Sight of Hell* (1874) by Reverend J. Furniss. This book is full of grisly details that would strike terror into the hearts of even the most wicked adults, never mind its intended audience. It contains the most in-depth description of hell I've ever encountered, and since it was aimed at children, it also demonstrates how fear was mercilessly employed to promote obedience in that time period. The narrator leads children on a harrowing tour of hell, describing it as follows.[185]

Beneath a fiery mountain, deep in the very center of the earth, you will encounter a gate so wide, high, and strong that once inside, it is impossible to escape. Stretching out as far as the eye can see are red-hot stones and a constant hail of fire and brimstone. All that can be heard are the tortured screams of millions of creatures, and in every breath is the smell of rotting corpses. Across a river of human tears, you'll find the core of hell, where Satan is bound in chains. He is gigantic, horned, and hideous beyond description. This beast decides how each soul will be tortured and where exactly in hell they will be located, as it's split into three levels, the lowermost being the worst.[186] Residents of hell have a brand on their forehead stating which sin they've committed so everyone will know their shame. These sins can be blasphemy, stealing, impurity, drunkenness, or even skipping Mass on Sunday.[187] The prisoner is confined to a burning hot area, their flesh riddled with worms, with a devil placed on each side of them. One is the "striking devil," who doles out physical punishment such as sores, ulcers, and disease. The other is the "mocking devil," who relentlessly verbally assaults the soul, berating them for their missteps in life and reminding them that they will never be rescued, not even by their parents. The book graphically describes having one's blood boiled, children being kept in ovens, and more. This all sounds awfully harsh, particularly for children, but the book states, "The same law which is for others is also for children. If children, knowingly and willingly, break God's commandments, they also must be punished like others."[188] Variations of this description of hell are widespread.

The underworlds of various ancient societies are different from hell but do share some elements. For example, many versions of the underworld

---

185. J. Furniss, *The Sight of Hell*, Books for Children and Young Persons 10 (Dublin, Ireland: James Duffy and Co., 1874).
186. Furniss, *The Sight of Hell*, 9–10.
187. Furniss, *The Sight of Hell*, 11–12.
188. Furniss, *The Sight of Hell*, 21.

are gated and contain at least one river that must be crossed, such as the River Styx in Greek mythology and the River of Night in Egyptian stories. Most present arduous ordeals to endure and have various levels of punishment and reward. Unlike hell, the underworld isn't usually described as pure punishment for bad people. Typically, it is where all of the dead go, regardless of their behavior while alive.

While the Greek and Egyptian underworlds are filled with the dead, they are also places of regeneration and fertility. Sometimes they're associated with agriculture and crops because of their literal earthiness, and other times with wealth because metal and gems are mined there. Some myths involve a trickster god like the Greek Hermes, who can freely traverse between the earth and the underworld, but no mortals can do the same.

Gods of Death and the Underworld

While some underworld gods and goddesses are described as frightening or even cruel, they aren't typically one dimensional. In looking at some of these deities, we can draw some parallels with the modern devil while noting considerable differences.

The Greek Hades (Roman Pluto) is infamous for his mercilessness and lack of sympathy. He rules over the underworld, which is also called Hades. He is a frightening and uncompromising god of death, but he also represents the fertility of the earth and the regenerative cycle of nature. As such, Hades is a god of death but also a giver of life. Hades kidnaps his wife Persephone, imprisoning her in the underworld for half of the year. Hades wears a helmet and holds a two-pronged staff called a bident, which may be one of the reasons that the devil is sometimes shown wielding a pitchfork. The pitchfork is also similar to the trident carried by Poseidon, the Greek god of the sea.

Another well-known ruler of the underworld is the Egyptian god Osiris, who leads a double life as a god of the underworld and a god of fertility. In the underworld, he passes judgment on the dead while also ruling agriculture and the floods of the Nile River. Osiris is described with a green upper body, like vegetation, and his bottom half mummified like the dead. He carries a hook and flail.

Some rulers of the underworld don't seem to have anything in common with the modern devil, such as Hel, the Norse goddess of the dead, whose name was the same as her abode. Hel is depicted as terrifying to gaze upon, her body being half rotten like a corpse. She is considered uncaring for the plights of both the living and dead and wears an angry or sorrowful face. Aside from her name, there is little to connect her to the modern devil, and she is an example of an underworld ruler who perhaps escaped the association.

Baron Samedi of Haitian Voudou is a lwa who rules the dead and connection to ancestors. Baron Samedi is sometimes said to be the first male buried in every cemetery. He wears a top hat and sunglasses with one lens missing, symbolizing that he is watching both the land of the living and the land of the dead. Baron Samedi is part of a legion of lwa that is said to manifest in ritual as flashy, lewd, and sneaky.[189] Sometimes he is considered a force of justice for criminals.[190] While he bears no appreciative similarities to the Western devil aside from a mischievous streak, he was among the many entities of African Traditional Religions to be dubbed satanic and evil during the enslavement era and European colonization of the Americas.

Trickster Gods

Satan is often associated with trickery and manipulation. He's known for tempting people into doing his bidding. In the Bible, he manipulates Eve into eating from the Tree of Knowledge and challenges Jesus in devious ways. Something interesting to note here is that his trickery is never foolish but clever and calculated.

Trickster gods have appeared in myths from around the world, their role being to challenge people or cause them to fall victim to the error

---

189. Lilith Dorsey, *Voodoo and African Traditional Religion* (New Orleans, LA: Warlock Press, 2021), loc. 1024, Kindle.

190. Dorsey, *Voodoo and African Traditional Religion*, loc. 1043, Kindle.

of their ways. They are often in charge of passages, roads, gateways, and portals where realms intersect. Trickster gods are bearers of secret knowledge and are usually shape-shifters, taking on different forms and genders as needed, moving between the worlds of the living and the dead.

Greek Hermes (Roman Mercury) is a renowned thief and liar. He is a messenger for the gods, aids travelers crossing borders, and, like many tricksters, can come and go from the underworld as he pleases. Hermes is known for playing tricks on the gods to amuse himself and for having a scandalous love life. Clever and cunning, Hermes is the father to Pan, the half-goat god so often confused with the devil. Hermes is often shown as an attractive young person with wings on his feet, looking nothing like the hideous modern devil. However, he does share Satan's lying, stealing, and devious personality traits.

Another infamous trickster is the Norse Loki, who is part giant, part god. Loki is known to be sneaky and underhanded, yet sometimes, under the right circumstances, he uses his guile to help others. In mythology, he is disloyal and secretly converses with the enemies of the gods behind their backs. It is always unclear whose side he is on and whether he is good or evil. He often gets himself into trouble with the gods and escapes at the last minute by changing his form. In one story he turns himself into a salmon, and in another he becomes a horse. As a mare, he gives birth to Odin's eight-legged horse, showing that he can change gender too.

The orisha Eshú is the trickster who guards the crossroads and liminal spaces in Yoruba practice. He exists in between worlds, neither human nor divine. Eshú can be in many different places at one time and can multiply at will. Like many trickster gods, he acts as a messenger between mortals and divinity.[191] In the 1820s, Christian missionaries in Nigeria translated Bibles into Yoruba and used the name *Eshú* in place of Satan.[192] This created a link between him and the modern devil.

---

191. Dorsey, *Voodoo and African Traditional* Religion, loc. 678, 688, Kindle.

192. Deli Meiji, "Esu Is Not the Devil: How a Yoruba Deity Got Rebranded," OkayAfrica, December 15, 2017, https://www.okayafrica.com/yoruba-esu-is-not-the-devil/.

Last but not least is the Egyptian god Set, who has come up several times. As a betrayer, liar, god of storms, and killer of Osiris, he falls into the category of a trickster. As we saw in chapter 2, Set is possibly one of the first gods to shape the modern devil.

THE EGREGORE

The word *egregore* comes from the Greek word "wakeful." Inspired by the *tulpa* of Tibetan Buddhism, Western occultists defined an egregore as an energetic being birthed by collective thought, intentionally or otherwise. An egregore can also be created by one person. I include egregores in this chapter because I think they are a valid way to think about spirits, gods, and divinity.

The premise is that when belief and emotion are poured into an idea, this forms an energetic mass that can be tapped into at will. Basically, the more people believe in something, the more real it becomes. Sometimes people call this a thoughtform or collective group mind. While the concept of an egregore isn't usually included in discussions about the devil, I think it fits here because it helps explain some nontheistic approaches to Satanism.

A lot of emotion, energy, and belief has gone into the concept of gods and the devil, and to me, that makes them real in a sense. This doesn't mean I think there is an actual devil under the ground with a pitchfork, but that collective beliefs over centuries have created an energetic devil.

There is great power in belief. Emotions are energy. This is observable on a smaller scale when a group of people are all simultaneously struck with feelings. For instance, while watching an emotionally moving event like a concert, the energy stirred up in the audience is almost palpable. This can happen in any emotionally charged situation, such as at a rousing protest or when participating in rituals. Consider, then, the amount of emotion directed toward any given deity over time and how powerful, old, and strong it must be.

The theological devil egregore contains all the things that religion casts aside as shameful, unclean, undesirable, or unwanted. Everything that is deemed "bad" is dumped into this shadowy monster and rejected.

However, "bad" is a matter of opinion. Sometimes creativity is considered "bad" because it challenges the norm, and a creative person will be shamed into muting it. Sometimes curiosity, intelligence, and wonder are "bad" for the same reason. Our basic carnal desires are also deemed unacceptable, and simply having the gall to question authority in any way is often considered evil.

It is these conflicting and diverse traits that make up the devil's many personalities, just as bits and pieces of different gods may have influenced his physical appearance.

While there are more differences than similarities between the old gods and the modern devil, there is an ongoing link between them in the human mind that has perhaps created a new, different version of the devil altogether. This version is still growing and changing every day and will continue to do so far into the future.

CHAPTER 5

THE DEVIL MADE ME DO IT

Thus far, you've learned that the devil has not always been the bad guy. You've seen, instead, that, in contemporary society, he often represents autonomy, freedom, creativity, and self-respect. Something like the witch hunts couldn't possibly happen again in modern times, right?

One might think that by the 1980s, supernatural beliefs about the devil would be laid to rest and that reason would prevail. Unfortunately, the opposite happened.

Terror spread across the United States, Canada, the United Kingdom, and Australia because the worst had finally occurred. The devil was back. He was in every community, with cults festering behind every door. It was believed that Satan was hidden in plain sight and taking over. And this time, he was coming for the children.

In the 1980s, a phenomenon called the "satanic panic" swept the Western world, fueled by a perfect storm of politics, religion, and shifting societal norms. There was only one thing missing: an actual devil.

MORAL PANIC

To understand the satanic panic of the 1980s and early 1990s, the term *moral panic* must be defined, a phrase coined by criminologist Stanley

Cohen.[193] A moral panic occurs when accusations are leveraged against a specific group whose behavior, real or imagined, is viewed as a threat to the values and safety of the majority.

The recipe for a moral panic has several key ingredients:

1. A group of people that the media portrays as exclusively bad, which often plays on stereotypes and stirs up the public's existing biases and fears.

2. A large part of society that feels their values and safety are threatened by said group.

3. The involvement of authoritative figures like the law or government to lend credibility to the outrage.

4. A person, group, or system that benefits from the panic.

These things combine to spread terror, often without tangible proof of a problem, eventually culminating in disaster.

A prime example of moral panic was the Salem witch trials in the 1600s when fear of evil witchcraft took over the common sense of an entire town, ending in the execution of twenty people.[194] More recently was the 1950s McCarthy-era panic over communism in the United States; the HIV and AIDS scare of the 1980s, which demonized the LGBTQ+ community; the war on drugs, which intentionally incited fear and hatred for low-income people and people of color; and even the 2020 COVID-19 pandemic, which spawned conspiracy theories and had everyone at war over vaccines and masks. All these outrages were fueled by fear, targeting or othering a specific group of people. They were hyped by the media, the government and law enforcement were involved, and people were upset on such deep levels that they abandoned reason.

---

193. Mia Belle Frothingham, "Moral Panic and Folk Devils," Simply Psychology, last modified August 31, 2023, https://simplypsychology.org/folk-devils-and-moral-panics-cohen-1972.html.

194. Jess Blumberg, "A Brief History of the Salem Witch Trials," Smithsonian Magazine, October 24, 2022, https://www.smithsonianmag.com/history/a-brief-history-of-the-salem-witch-trials-175162489/.

When I first heard the phrase *satanic panic* many years ago, I thought it was a joke. It rhymes, it's catchy, and it would make a good name for a band.

But it wasn't a joke. In fact, I vividly remember it. In my very early teens, I read alleged true accounts of people who suffered ritualistic abuse at the hands of Satanists. Some of the survivors had suppressed the memory until adulthood, when it was brought back through hypnotism and therapy, while others had developed a condition called multiple personality disorder. I even saw reruns of the infamous *Geraldo* episode from 1988 called "Devil Worship: Exposing Satan's Underground," which showcased Satanists and purported victims of cults describing unthinkably gruesome things.[195] Apparently, there were underground satanic cults absolutely everywhere, abusing and murdering children, among other evils. Even though I was young, I remember thinking, *None of this can be true, can it?* The stories were more creatively depraved than the worst horror movie and just too disgusting and farfetched to seem real.

I was nowhere near as impacted by the satanic panic as those in religious communities. Utterly amazing in its fantasy elements, the panic swept people up and removed every shred of common sense they possessed. They can't really be blamed, as this is characteristic of moral panics. There were large systems at play, fueling their outrage and inflaming their deepest fears.

One might wonder now how so many people could possibly believe such outrageous claims without evidence, but when you combine all the contributing dynamics, it's easier to understand.

A delicate balance of factors was required for the satanic panic to occur: President Ronald Reagan's conservative rule, the rise of evangelism, the fear of serial killers and cults still present from the 1970s, shifting family structures, and psychiatric experiments. It's in this unsettled

---

195. Robert James, dir., "Devil Worship: Exposing Satan's Underground," *The Geraldo Rivera Special* (Tribune Entertainment Company and Investigative News Group, October 22, 1988), YouTube video, 1:31:50, https://www.youtube.com/watch?v=MjVpqMHrRpU.

societal climate that the satanic panic was able to flourish. In the follow-ing pages, we'll look at how each influence contributed to a landscape where the devil reigned supreme.

CULTS

There had been a building concern about Satanism and the occult begin-ning in the 1960s when hippies were turning to alternative religions. Many of these spiritualities were demonized by those who didn't under-stand them, including witchcraft, paganism, and Wicca. Some people began to identify openly as witches, while others embraced a wide mix of spiritual practices, seemingly from whatever was convenient at the moment. An extreme example of this mishmash of mysticism was in October 1967 when 35,000 protestors gathered in a circle around the Pentagon. They planned to end the Vietnam War by using their com-bined mental powers to levitate the building ten feet off of the ground. It was also supposed to turn orange and spin in circles. They shouted exor-cisms in Aramaic, expecting all the evil to vibrate out of the building.[196] While this bizarre attempt at magic didn't succeed, it certainly illustrates the mindset of the times. Misguided and probably drug-fueled as this particular incident was, there were many serious witchcraft groups to emerge around this time, such as Zsuzsanna Budapest's Dianic Wicca and the Pagan organization Circle Sanctuary founded by Selena Fox.

The popularity of the witch merged with second-wave feminism in America to create women-led Goddess-worshipping groups, inspired by a mix of Gerald Gardner's writing, Margaret Murray's research, the book *Aradia, or The Gospel of Witches* by Charles Godfrey Leland and the re-release of *The White Goddess* (1961) by Robert Graves. A lot of hippies were also experimenting with Eastern religions like Buddhism and Hin-duism, which were dubbed devilish by devout churchgoers. The cherry on top was Anton LaVey and the formation of the Church of Satan, which, unlike other groups, wholeheartedly endorsed Satan outright.

---

196. Michael M. Hughes, *Magic for the Resistance: Rituals and Spells for Change* (Wood-bury, MN: Llewellyn Publications, 2018), loc. 33, Kindle.

Alongside new religions, communal living became trendy in the 1960s, and with that came something much more sinister: cults.

In 1969, the Summer of Love ended with a media storm surrounding the Manson family cult, who murdered eight innocent people, including actress Sharon Tate, the wife of Roman Polanski. Polanski happens to be the director of the film *Rosemary's Baby* (1968), one of the most famous movies about satanic witchcraft. Evidence from the crime scenes included devilish-seeming writing and symbols smeared on the walls in blood, and the perpetrators displayed a lack of remorse that chilled the nation. While the Manson family didn't actually partake in Satan worship, these widespread details made the public believe they did and suggested that other communal groups may as well. To make matters worse, there was an unprecedented uptick in violent crime in the '70s, including serial killers who were loosely linked to Satanism, like David Berkowitz and the Zodiac killer.[197] Television sensationalized these crimes more than ever before, making them seem very close to home.

In the 1970s, people continued to seek spiritual enlightenment and form independent religious cults. Some of these were deadly, such as the People's Temple, run by Jim Jones. Jim Jones was a faith healer and a mind reader, but he was also Evangelical, which is perhaps why he was initially respected by the press and politicians. Jones amassed thousands of diverse devotees, and the People's Temple became known for unifying folks of all races and backgrounds. It was also a doomsday cult, which means they were preparing for the end of the world and ensuring they would be saved by God. Jones's followers viewed him as the personification of God and were completely obedient to him. In 1974, a portion of the cult relocated to Guyana in South America, where their commune became known as Jonestown. Reports of deplorable living conditions and abuse prompted a visit from Congressman Leo Ryan in 1978. Cult members believed his presence was the beginning of the apocalypse.

---

197. "Death Rate for Homicide in the U.S. 1950–2019," Statista, accessed June 30, 2023, https://www.statista.com/statistics/187592/death-rate-from-homicide-in-the-us -since-1950/.

In a panic, they shot and killed him. That same day, Jones ordered all the people of Jonestown to consume a grape drink mixed with cyanide, resulting in the mass death of over 900 people. Jones convinced them that if they didn't drink the concoction, the military was coming to take their children away. These people had been subjected to years of brainwashing and psychological abuse, making them genuinely believe the apocalypse was upon them. This tragedy has been called a mass suicide. However, it's been reported that many of the deaths occurred unwillingly under force from Jones's armed guards.[198] Also among the victims were children who couldn't consent and were likely killed by their own parents.

Other infamous cults of the 1970s were the communist Children of God, which encouraged the sexual abuse of minors, and Heaven's Gate, which taught that aliens would arrive and carry members to the afterlife. Heaven's Gate resulted in tragedy when in 1997, thirty-nine members committed mass suicide in conjunction with the arrival of the Hale-Bopp comet. They believed the comet contained the alien spacecraft that would take them to heaven, leaving their mortal shells behind.[199]

Regardless of denomination, these cults left an understandably horrified nation in their wake, with citizens living in fear of the evil that seemed to be everywhere.

FUNDAMENTALISM

In the late 1970s, there was a surge of growth in Evangelical Christianity and Fundamentalism, both of which are particularly concerned with supernatural things like demonic possession. They were expecting the end times, but not before the Antichrist brought unspeakable evil to Earth. The Evangelicals were large in number and possessed great political influence. Many of them were followers of Ronald Reagan, who

198. Alison Eldridge, "Inside Jonestown: How Jim Jones Trapped Followers and Forced 'Suicides,'" History, November 13, 2018, https://www.history.com/news/jonestown -jim-jones-mass-murder-suicide.

199. "March 26, 1997: Heaven's Gate Cult Members Found Dead," History, last modified September 26, 2023, https://www.history.com/this-day-in-history/heavens-gate-cult -members-found-dead.

became president of the United States in 1981. Reagan was anti-abortion and wanted Christian prayer in public schools, which tells you a little something about where his interests lie.

Reagan and his supporters openly opposed feminism and LGBTQ+ rights. They televised these hateful views and insinuated that these two things were a threat to the traditional white Christian family. Official news outlets reported tales of evil taking over, while the more sensational stories about Satanism were grabbed by tabloids and talk shows, spreading the message to every household.

Televangelism allowed churches to raise millions in funding for their religions, increasing their power. The existence of these organizations and their huge number of supporters goes to show how many people had existing fears about the devil.

Evangelicals disapproved of changes in the ideal traditional family. With increased numbers of women in the workplace, children had less supervision or were going to commercial daycare centers, which went against conventional values. The most famous manifestation of the satanic panic, which also happens to be the most expensive trial in United States history, is that of McMartin preschool, where up to 400 children were coerced into telling false stories of satanic ritual abuse.[200] After ten years of court proceedings, there was no evidence, and no one was charged, although many lives were ruined. This case highlights the demonization of women who stepped outside of their assigned roles. It was the mother's fault that the nuclear family was going to hell in a handbasket because she was working instead of watching her children.

ENTERTAINMENT AND MEDIA

Before the internet, people relied on what they read or saw on TV for information. When you consider how limiting that was, it helps shed light on how people became convinced that the devil was invading their

---

200. Cynthia Gorney, "The Terrible Puzzle of McMartin Preschool," *Washington Post*, May 17, 1988, https://www.washingtonpost.com/archive/lifestyle/1988/05/17/the-terrible-puzzle-of-mcmartin-preschool/067b38f3-eff0-4548-a094-cf6bd955803f/.

home and town, particularly if they already believed in him. There was no way to fact-check claims, get outside perspectives, or dig deeper into the stories they were exposed to. Various forms of entertainment, including TV, tabloids, movies, and music, all contributed to the perceived presence of the devil in 1980s culture. Popular talk shows hosted by the likes of Geraldo Rivera and Oprah Winfrey latched greedily onto the Satan scare and spun it in sensational ways. Heavy metal music hit the scene and horrified parents everywhere with its devilish screams and hellish visuals. Even cartoons and toys had a sinister dark side. If you looked for the devil hard enough, you were bound to find him.

Daytime Talk Shows and Cartoons

Daytime talk shows became huge in the 1980s. In each episode, the host interviewed sensational or controversial guests before a live studio audience able to ask questions and make comments. These shows were known as tabloid programs because the material was generally on par with the trashy print version of the same.

Geraldo Rivera hosted a two-hour episode called "Devil Worship: Exposing Satan's Underground," which was the highest-ranking NBC special aired to date, reaching more than two million households.[201] In other words, he went viral. You can still find clips of the episode online. An ad for the show said, "Geraldo reveals the many faces of Satanism: Human Sacrifices, Ritualistic Killings, Black Mass, Satanic Teenagers, Bizarre Cults! Tonight, learn what evil can do."[202] Pretty scary!

Geraldo had a range of guests, some of whom claimed to have witnessed abuse and murder as victims of satanic cults. The episode was a sideshow circus of misinformation about the dangers of devil worship and hammered into the viewer that evil was happening right now, in your house, in your town, and in your school. He included some dubi-

---

201. Kier-La Janisse and Paul Corupe, *Satanic Panic: Pop-Cultural Paranoia in the 1980s* (Surrey, UK: Fab Press, 2016), 149.

202. "Devil Worship: Exposing Satan's Underground," IMDb, accessed October 13, 2023, https://www.imdb.com/title/tt1136645/mediaviewer/rm365130240/?ref_=tt_ov_i.

ous "occult experts" alongside Anton LaVey's daughter Zeena Shrek (who barely got a word in) and Ozzy Osbourne of the heavy metal band Black Sabbath. At one point, there is a sudden, out-of-place clip of Geraldo attending a Haitian Voudou ritual. It's unclear what the ritual might be about, but that didn't matter to Geraldo: it posited Haitian ritual, and by association African religions and spiritualities, as satanic, adding even more fuel to the dumpster fire.

Talk shows of this kind were run and rerun, copycatted by different hosts, and viewed by millions, further spreading the word that Satan was swallowing up children by the thousands. For those parents whose teenagers were disillusioned, disobedient, or otherwise not conforming, there was a real fear that the devil already had them in his clutches.

But what could be causing this plague of devil worship among the youth of the 1980s? Concerned parents began to examine toys, music, and television shows for secret occult messages that may be corrupting the minds of their kids. The idea that violence on TV could cause youth to misbehave was a familiar one, and it logically followed that TV might also be to blame for occult activities.

Cartoons aimed at young children were especially suspect because they contained magic and fantasy. In his book *Turmoil in the Toybox* (1986), Evangelical author Phil Phillips says that occult practices were blatantly displayed in cartoons, many of them in direct opposition to scripture.[203] He explains that imagery in the cartoons, such as levitation, wands, spells, and magic, are impacting the brains of children by subconsciously placing satanic ideas in their heads. He claims that the cartoon *He-Man and the Masters of the Universe* not only contains witchcraft and necromancy but is blasphemous because the title implies that the action figure is on the same level as God.[204] Other shows on the list are *Smurfs* because Papa Smurf uses spells for problem-solving and *Care Bears* because their superpower is to zap evil with streams of positive

---

203. Phil Phillips, *Turmoil in the Toybox* (Lancaster, PA: Starburst Publishers, 1986), 14.
204. Phillips, *Turmoil in the Toybox*, 60.

emotions flowing from their stomachs. Phillips associates this detail of the Care Bears with Hinduism, which makes it evil according to Evangelical belief. Other cartoons believed to contain occult material are *Scooby-Doo, Spider-Man,* and *G. I. Joe.* In his other book *Saturday Morning Mind Control* (1991), Phillips warns parents that cartoons are teaching their children, step by step, how to summon demons.[205]

Music

The link between music and the occult began with the blues, long before the 1980s. The blues originated among descendants of enslaved African Americans in the southern United States after the Civil War. Blues musician Robert Johnson (1911–38) was said to have met the devil at the crossroads and sold his soul in exchange for his talent. Some churchgoers were concerned that the secular nature of blues music led listeners toward worldly concerns and matters of the flesh when they should be listening to songs about God and faith.[206] The blues shaped the sound of rock and roll, which was considered the devil's music because it encouraged teenagers to dance in a carnal fashion and behave rebelliously. Even Elvis Presley's music was dubbed sinful.[207]

Throughout the sixties and seventies, the relationship between rock and roll and the occult was cemented as devilish rumors began to surface in the music industry. The Rolling Stones released an album called *The Satanic Majesties Request* in 1967 and the song "Sympathy for the Devil" the following year. The cover of the Beatles album *Sergeant Pepper's Lonely Hearts Club Band* (1967) features a collage of famous faces. Peering out among them is none other than Aleister Crowley. The next year they released *The Beatles,* also known as *The White Album,* which became permanently linked to cult leader Charles Manson when he

---

205. Phil Phillips, *Saturday Morning Mind Control* (Nashville, TN: Oliver-Nelson Books, 1991), 131.
206. Peter Bebergal, *Season of the Witch: How the Occult Saved Rock and Roll* (New York: Jeremy P. Tarcher/Penguin, 2014), 7.
207. Bebergal, *Season of the Witch,* 11.

claimed the song *Helter Skelter* was heralding a race war.[208] The name of the song was written in blood at one of the crime scenes. This album also featured the song *Revolution 9*, which allegedly repeated the sinister phrase "Turn me on, dead man" when played backward.[209]

Aleister Crowley resurfaced when the band Led Zeppelin engraved the words "Do what thou wilt" on every vinyl copy of their album *Led Zeppelin III* (1970). Guitarist Jimmy Page was especially fascinated by Crowley, even living in Crowley's former residence, the Boleskine house, in Scotland in 1960.[210] The album *Led Zeppelin IV* features an image of a hermit holding a lamp that's extremely similar to the classic tarot card of the Rider-Waite deck. This album cover also has four mysterious symbols on it that became permanently associated with the band, although it's never been officially explained what the symbols mean.[211]

In the late sixties and early seventies, Ozzy Osbourne hit the scene with over-the-top stage performances that were famous for their satanic theatrics, like blazing fires and huge crucifixes. In one instance, Osbourne allegedly bit the head off of a bat while on stage.[212] Ozzy Osbourne and Black Sabbath would come to be known as the most satanic band of the times.

Heavy metal bands of the eighties embraced the theme, which garnered outrage, shock, and sales. Among them were Slayer, Venom, and the Misfits, who all had a menacing, sinister image. The bands themselves did not claim to be Satanists at all, and most of their fans understood it was all in good fun. Parents, however, didn't see it the same way. In 1985, the PMRC (Parents Music Resource Center) was formed by Tipper Gore, wife of former American vice president Al Gore. This group intended to

---

208. Bebergal, *Season of the Witch*, 61.

209. Christian Blauvelt, "'Paul Is Dead': A Beatles Secret Message in an Album Cover?" BBC Culture, February 24, 2022, https://www.bbc.com/culture/article/20180807-paul -is-dead-a-beatles-secret-message-in-an-album-cover.

210. Bebergal, *Season of the Witch*, 93.

211. Chris Huber, "The Four Led Zeppelin Symbols, Explained," Extra Chill, March 21, 2021, https://extrachill.com/led-zeppelin-symbols-meaning.

212. Bebergal, *Season of the Witch*, 105.

clean up the world of rock by warning parents which songs contained references to sex, violence, and the occult. They created a list called the "Filthy Fifteen," a selection of top offending songs by bands like Judas Priest, Mötley Crüe, and Prince. Most of the list focused on profane and violent content, but two bands made the list for being labeled "occult" (Mercyful Fate and Venom).[213] Some of you might remember the warning stickers on tapes and CDs that said "Parental Advisory: Explicit Lyrics." That was the work of the PMRC.

Between the sixties and the nineties, many musicians were accused of backmasking. Backmasking is when a subliminal message that can only be heard when played in reverse is placed into a song. The theory was that bands used this method to surreptitiously implant satanic thoughts into their fans' heads. Led Zeppelin's *Stairway to Heaven* supposedly included "Here's to my sweet Satan." Accusations of backmasking continued into the 1980s against bands like Slayer, Cheap Trick, and more.

Heavy metal didn't have to be played backward to be considered dangerous. In 1984, a nineteen-year-old man killed himself while listening to Ozzy Osbourne's song *Suicide Solution*. The family attempted to sue Osbourne, holding his music accountable for the death, but the case was thrown out. Osbourne was under the protection of the First Amendment.[214] In 1985, Judas Priest's cover of "Better by You, Better Than Me" inspired two young men to go to a church playground and shoot themselves. Only one survived but died three years later. His family blamed Judas Priest for the tragedy and took the band to court. This case was also thrown out because there was no proof of subliminal messaging.[215]

213. Kory Grow, "PMRC's 'Filthy 15': Where Are They Now?" *Rolling Stone*, September 19, 2020, https://www.rollingstone.com/music/music-lists/pmrcs-filthy-15-where-are -they-now-60601/.

214. Jonathan Wiederhorn, "36 Years Ago: Ozzy Osbourne Exonerated in 'Suicide Solution' Fan Death Lawsuit," Loudwire, last modified August 7, 2022, https://loudwire.com /ozzy-osbourne-exonerated-suicide-solution-fan-death-lawsuit-anniversary/.

215. "Judas Priest: The Lawsuit Over Better By You, Better Than Me That Shook The Metal World," Rock N' Roll True Stories, June 24, 2022, YouTube video, 13:48, https://www .youtube.com/watch?v=gHOFI5UNNck.

Eventually, the trend of occult imagery in music waned, and so did the concern surrounding it. However, there seems to be a bit of a revival creeping into recent music. Artist Lil Nas X released a controversial video for the song "Montero (Call Me By Your Name)" in 2021. In it, the artist descends into hell on a pole, where he gives Satan a lap dance. It ends with Lil Nas X crowning himself with the devil's horns. This video is a commentary on the demonization of homosexuality and how often LGBTQ+ people are threatened with hell. The video enraged some conservatives but was praised by the Church of Satan.[216] At the 2023 Grammy Awards, musicians Sam Smith and Kim Petra's performance of their song *Unholy* stirred controversy among conservatives and the Church of Satan again. This time, neither appreciated the flames, whips, horned people, and circle of hooded figures.[217]

Movies

Ira Levin's book *Rosemary's Baby* became a hit movie in 1968. A string of satanic movies followed, including *The Exorcist* (1973) and *The Omen* (1976). All these films are about the devil or witches hurting children and destroying families.

In her book *Lights, Camera, Witchcraft*, Heather Greene groups eighties witch films into two themes: "Sex and Satan" and "Save the Child." The "Sex and Satan" narrative plays on the witch and her terrifying sexual power. The "Save the Child" trope focuses on rescuing a child from the clutches of evil, which was especially relevant to the times.[218] Witch films of this era focused almost exclusively on women as villainous.[219] Sometimes witches

---

216. EJ Dickson, "We Asked Satanists What They Think of the New Lil Nas X Video," *Rolling Stone*, March 29, 2021, https://www.rollingstone.com/culture/culture-news/lil-nas-x-montero-call-me-by-your-name-video-church-of-satan-1147634/.

217. Dani Di Placido, "Sam Smith's Grammys Performance Criticized by Conservatives and Satanists," *Forbes*, February 10, 2023, https://www.forbes.com/sites/danidiplacido/2023/02/10/sam-smiths-grammys-performance-criticized-by-conservatives-and-satanists/?sh=5d875aff30b1.

218. Heather Greene, *Lights, Camera, Witchcraft: A Critical History of Witches in American Film and Television* (Woodbury, MN: Llewellyn Publications, 2021), 293.

219. Greene, *Lights, Camera, Witchcraft*, 279.

were hypersexualized vamps or, at the very least, engaged in sexual activity with the devil, like in the movie *The Witches of Eastwick* (1987), based on the book by John Updike. The three witches in the film are divorced, independent, and unconventional, instead of being traditional mothers and wives.[220] Other movies of the time played upon the fear of ritual child abuse in films like *Witchcraft* (1988), where a young mother must rescue her child from her 300-year-old mother-in-law who wants to make the baby leader of her coven. Another example is *To Save a Child* (1991), with a similar plot and in which the mother must keep her child safe from evil witches.[221]

In almost all of them, nontraditional women are the ones who open the door to the devil, reiterating that changing the traditional family structure can only lead to terrible things.

Dungeons and Dragons

Role-playing games have been around for a long time, but one of the most popular by far is Dungeons and Dragons (D&D), created in 1973 by Gary Gygax and Dave Arneson. D&D is a mixture of fantasy characters, medieval trappings, and wargaming. More importantly, it was one of the first toys to be linked to Satanism in teenagers.

Around the time that Christian evangelism swept the nation, D&D started to garner attention for allegedly having occult characteristics. What really set off the D&D scare was the 1979 disappearance of James Dallas Egbert, a University of Michigan student. Egbert was struggling with his sexuality and mental health and was abusing drugs. He disappeared in August 1979 and wasn't found until a month later by a private investigator hired by his family. Rumors spread that Egbert had gotten lost in the steam tunnels beneath the university. The investigator publicly stated that Egbert had disappeared while acting out a D&D fantasy, even though he was not known to be an avid player.

---

220. Greene, *Lights, Camera, Witchcraft*, 291.
221. Greene, *Lights, Camera, Witchcraft*, 292–94.

The game had already come under suspicion, so the media pounced on the suffering boy's story and twisted it into a tale about the dangers of D&D. Egbert became national news. He died from suicide roughly one year later. A bestselling novel based on the situation was quickly and tastelessly cobbled together and called *Mazes and Monsters* (1981) by Rona Jaffe. To make matters worse, the book became a TV movie. Even William Dear, the trusted investigator, exploited the situation by writing a salacious book about it.[222] In it, Dear recants his D&D theory, claiming he made it up because the young man requested it; Egbert had wanted to protect his family from embarrassment about his sexuality and drug use.[223] This speaks volumes about the attitudes of the time and the stigma and shame the young man was facing.

From this, a new scapegoat appeared. Any troubling or nonconforming behavior of teenagers could be pinned on the game … and the devil. In 1982, Irving "Bink" Pulling of Virginia used his parents' gun to take his own life. His mother said it was because he had been cursed while playing D&D. In 1983, she formed BADD—Bothered about Dungeons and Dragons. The group aimed to spread the word about the demonic nature of the game. They touted D&D as a doorway to Satan worship, blasphemy, witchcraft, murder, and rape. Pulling was one of many adults who built a career out of the satanic panic. She was consulted by police departments across the United States about the evils of role-playing games and was called upon in court cases as an expert witness about satanic activity. Her organization also gave expensive seminars.[224]

Respected television news shows further legitimized the crusade against D&D by having Pulling and other experts as guests. One expert

---

222. William Dear, *The Dungeon Master: The Disappearance of James Dallas Egbert III* (Boston, MA: Houghton Mifflin Company, 1984).

223. Dear, *The Dungeon Master*, 281.

224. Pat Pulling and Kathy Cawthon, *The Devil's Web: Who Is Stalking Your Children for Satan?* (Lafayette, LA: Huntington House, 1989), 179, 127.

claimed parents had actually witnessed their child summon a demon while playing the game.[225]

In the end, there were eight court cases that attempted to use D&D as a scapegoat for crimes including murder.[226] While none of them succeeded, they illustrate just how seriously people took the threat of demonic evil coming for their children.

Other Toys

Nothing was safe from the clutches of the devil's influence. Not even toys. What appeared to be cute, fun, and innocent playthings were also thought to be seething with satanic undertones. Usually, the toys on their own weren't the problem. It was the associated cartoons, as mentioned, that taught children to think in evil ways, according to Evangelical author Phil Phillips. The thing that triggered this realization for him was a plastic Skeletor toy from the He-Man franchise. The figure was holding a staff topped with a ram's head, which he felt was an occult symbol. Phillips soon received word from the Lord that toys like Skeletor allowed Satan to gain mind control over millions of kids. The Lord requested that Phillips do something about it.[227]

Phillips set out to investigate the playthings of the 1980s and was horrified by the evil he found lurking in the toy aisle: new age thought, Eastern religions, humanistic ideas, and magic.

Here are some of the evil things Phillips discovered. You might find some of your own favorite toys on his list. *My Little Pony* was satanic because some ponies were unicorns, and unicorns were a symbol of the Antichrist.[228] The Care Bears were a problem because they vanquished evil with their emotions instead of leaving it to the power of God, which

---

225. Ed Bradley, "Dungeons & Dragons," *60 Minutes* (CBS News, 1985), YouTube video, 15:01, https://www.youtube.com/watch?v=YFq5aci6CHA.

226. Janisse and Corupe, *Satanic Panic*, 59.

227. Phillips, *Turmoil in the Toybox*, 15–17.

228. Phillips, *Turmoil in the Toybox*, 79.

taught humanism.[229] Rainbow Brite, a doll who used rainbows to fight monsters, was evil because the rainbow symbolized the bridge between humans and Lucifer.[230] The Cabbage Patch Kids craze, which became an unprecedented fad among children and adults, was likened to idolatry. Cabbage Patch Kids also forced children to take on the responsibility of parents at too young an age.[231]

The list of nefarious toys also included Barbie, Transformers, and ThunderCats. If nothing else, we learn from Phil Phillips that if you try hard enough, you can find evil anywhere.

SHOCKING MEMOIRS

The satanic panic was profitable for some people. Fear often is. Once the ball got rolling, a lot of folks realized they could use it to their advantage and created entire careers riding the devil's coattails. One of these careers was writing memoirs. The book that is often credited with starting the panic is called *Michelle Remembers* (1980), written by Dr. Lawrence Pazder and Michelle Smith.

I cannot express how influential this book was and how horrible and unbelievable its claims are. To fully understand the perversity of it, you need to read it. It's not just the violent, twisted descriptions of what supposedly happened during satanic rituals but the inappropriate relationship between doctor and patient. The worst part is the power it, and others like it, held over the public.

Michelle Remembers is a lurid memoir recounting the therapy sessions between Pazder and his patient, in which he performed recovered memory therapy and age regression therapy. During their sessions, Smith supposedly recalled that her mother had subjected her to satanic cult rituals as a child. Allegedly, she endured years of physical and psychological torture, including surgery to give her horns and a tail and fetuses being

229. Phillips, *Turmoil in the Toybox*, 81–82.
230. Phillips, *Turmoil in the Toybox*, 83.
231. Phillips, *Turmoil in the Toybox*, 69–73.

rubbed all over her body.[232] The book describes incomprehensible things that could only be conjured by a truly deviant mind. The book continuously positions women as villains, reminding us again and again that women and mothers are to blame for what happened to Michelle Smith and other cases of satanic ritual abuse. This attitude aligned perfectly with the agenda of Reagan and his Evangelical friends. Near the end of the book, Pazder implies that Satan is going to come to Earth and make an appearance sometime soon.[233] This bestseller was believed to be a true story by many.

In the first edition, the authors claimed that Smith was a victim of the Church of Satan, but when LaVey threatened to sue, the mention was removed.[234]

With the publication of this book, Smith and Pazder became famous. They also got married, which makes the whole thing even more questionable. Together, they raked in cash from news outlets and talk shows, spoke at seminars, and became lauded experts on satanic ritual abuse. Pazder was consulted in future cases involving satanic cults, including the McMartin Preschool trial. His methods were imitated by other therapists working with alleged survivors, and the success of *Michelle Remembers* inspired others to write similar memoirs.

A woman by the assumed name Lauren Stratford claimed to have also discovered a past of satanic ritual abuse through recovered memory therapy and penned *Satan's Underground* (1991), detailing her harrowing experiences. One of her other books, *Stripped Naked* (1993), discusses her resulting multiple personality disorder.

Michelle Remembers was eventually denounced as a hoax, but not before the damage had been done. The copycat books it spawned further convinced readers that many people were holding on to a forgotten past of satanic cults. Its intangibility made it even scarier. What if you'd been

---

232. Janisse and Corupe, *Satanic Panic*, 162, 178, 179.
233. Michelle Smith and Lawrence Pazder, *Michelle Remembers* (New York: Pocket Books, 1980), 310.
234. Smith and Pazder, *Michelle Remembers*, 178.

in a cult and couldn't remember? After all, with such ambiguous symptoms, it could be happening to anyone—even you!

Even after this novel and others like it were debunked, the public continued to take them at face value for years to come.

SKETCHY PSYCHOTHERAPY

Exploitative psychotherapy was one of the biggest contributors to the satanic panic. In the seventies, two important psychological disorders hit the scene, both of which were popularized by memoirs of satanic ritual abuse and the satanic panic: multiple personality disorder (MPD) and repressed memory syndrome. Both were entered into the *DSM-III* in 1980 in a category of new dissociative disorders that were considered very rare. When the *DSM-III-R* was revised between 1984 and 1987, the doctors doing the research reported that the frequency of diagnoses of these disorders had increased significantly. In 1983, they founded the International Society for the Study of Multiple Personality and Dissociation, which had over 2,000 mental health professionals as members. In 1986, their conferences included discussions of satanic ritual abuse and cults.[235]

Current research on dissociative disorders now uses the term *dissociative identity disorder* and has a different description of symptoms than multiple personality disorder or repressed memory syndrome.[236]

In the 1980s, multiple personality disorder was described as a patient developing numerous separate identities and unknowingly switching between them. Repressed memory syndrome was described as a patient burying memories of traumatic events so deeply that they had no recollection of them. Therapists used hypnotism and age regression therapy to plumb the depths of a patient's memories, accessing these buried experiences and bringing them to the surface. Both illnesses are still debated by

---

235. Richard Noll, "Speak, Memory," *Psychiatric Times,* March 19, 2014, https://www
    .psychiatrictimes.com/view/speak-memory.
236. "Dissociative Identity Disorder (Multiple Personality Disorder)," *Psychology Today*,
    last modified September 21, 2021, https://www.psychologytoday.com/ca/conditions
    /dissociative-identity-disorder-multiple-personality-disorder.

the medical field today, and the techniques used to treat them are considered dubious at best. Some theorize that a patient in a vulnerable state is highly suggestible, and it's possible that memories can be implanted into their brains by their therapist.[237]

At the time, this new psychological technique was embraced and exploited. Some therapists may have truly believed in its efficacy, but when it comes to satanic ritual abuse, there's a good chance it was a means of achieving personal acclaim and making coin.

Recovered memory therapy produced a lot of sensational stories about satanic cult activity. Alleged victims went on television and wrote memoirs, sharing tales of murder and abuse at the hands of Satanists. Their claims were limited only by their own imaginations and that of their therapists.

When the courts and the public demanded evidence of the satanic cults, nothing could be found. There were no tunnels beneath daycare centers as described. There were no burial sites or missing children. The timelines of the allegations did not match up with the school and work records of the plaintiffs. In short, there was not a shred of proof.

Some argue that discrediting recovered memory therapy is a way to dismiss victims of abuse, but that is not the intention here. Here, we're speaking directly to claims of satanic ritual abuse in the 1980s, of which there was no evidence.

THE END OF THE PANIC

In this climate, almost every violent crime was blamed on satanic cults. Law enforcement created occult divisions to deal with the flood of calls coming in from the panicked public about cult activity. This only lent credibility to the situation.

It would be remiss not to mention the murders that have taken place over time that have been blamed on the devil, like those committed by

---

237. Joelle Hanson-Baiden, "The Debate on Repressed Memories," News-Medical.net, last modified December 23, 2021, https://www.news-medical.net/health/The-Debate-on -Repressed-Memories.aspx.

Richard Ramirez. It's important to note that the media and the perpetrators themselves brought Satan into the picture. Some murderers claimed that the devil made them do it or that they killed as a sacrifice to Satan.

Actual Satanists do not perform sacrifices or do tasks for the devil, so when you think about it, these heinous crimes are a result of misconceptions about Satanism. The killers enacted exactly what society told them devil worshippers would do. Their crimes gave form to the deep fears that powered the satanic panic. You could almost say that their deeds were just validating all the misinformation. It was never real Satanists who said the devil wanted blood sacrifice, crime, or assault. It was the people fueling the satanic panic.

This attitude led to many devastating false allegations, ruining innocent peoples' lives, as with the West Memphis Three. In 1993, three teenage boys were convicted for the murder of several children. They were accused based on nothing more than their interest in goth culture. Recent DNA evidence has finally proven they are innocent, but only after they spent a large chunk of their lives in prison. Between 1984 and 1986, in Bakersfield, California, twenty-six innocent people were jailed for participating in a nonexistent satanic child abuse ring. The allegations, which were based on claims from children, were later proven to have been coerced by social workers. There are still people sitting in prison today for satanic crimes that have never been proven.[238]

One has to wonder how this impacted the Pagan, Wiccan, and witch communities, who were all too often vilified for their beliefs and dubbed devil worshippers. Some important people stood up and fought back against the misinformation. Well-known Salem witch Laurie Cabot founded the Witches League for Public Awareness in 1986, and Selena Fox founded the Lady Liberty League in 1985. With the help of law enforcement, the media, and legal support, these organizations worked

---

238. Aja Romano, "Why Satanic Panic Never Really Ended," Vox, March 31, 2021, https://www.vox.com/culture/22358153/satanic-panic-ritual-abuse-history-conspiracy-theories-explained.

to differentiate the beliefs of Pagans, witches, and Wiccans from the satanic nonsense of the times.[239] We still benefit from their efforts today.

In 1992 the justice department publicly debunked the existence of satanic cults, and for the most part, the panic was laid to rest.

WHAT NOW?

The satanic panic included all the elements necessary to produce one of the most irrational moral panics since the McCarthy era of the 1950s.

We saw politicians mingling with powerful religious groups and manipulation of the media to sow seeds of fear. We saw trash media take the stories and blow them up into outrageous, salacious tales that the public couldn't resist. Mental health professionals capitalized on the scare and created new, frightening illnesses, while survivors came out of the dark to describe the unthinkable to a bloodthirsty, eager-eared public. There were allegations of crimes against humanity used to other a vague and intangible group threatening the safety and values of the public. To top it all off, law enforcement joined the fray with their own experts and cult divisions.

While there are still people around who think that Satan is real and holding court over various baby-eating cults via underground tunnels and pizza restaurants, they're not in the majority. Some things are still unfairly labeled evil by large groups of people, usually in support of beliefs that keep society in the past and uphold various oppressive paradigms. Categorizing new concepts as evil is an easy way to avoid challenging one's own experience. It's a convenient means of bypassing difficult discussions, avoiding the pain of growth, and keeping society as they wish it to be, with their chosen people in charge.

If we learned anything from the satanic panic, it's that when people fail to think for themselves, bad things happen. The worst part is that this type of moral panic will likely occur again. The only question is, who will be the scapegoat this time?

---

239. Greene, *Lights, Camera, Witchcraft*, 277.

CHAPTER 6

SATAN, WITCHES, AND WOMEN

Women have historically been considered especially susceptible to the devil's temptations. In the Bible story of Adam and Eve, Eve is blamed for the fall of humanity because the serpent easily convinces her to eat from the Tree of Knowledge. In the infamous *Malleus Maleficarum* (1486), a witch-hunting handbook that would influence generations to come, women are portrayed as weak, evil creatures who are devilish by nature. In early medicine, women were dubbed less intelligent than men, almost on par with animals, and their lack of intellect made it easy for Satan to fool them.

Women were shoved into a place of subordination by the church and scapegoated for the many ills of human experience because of their inherent evil. They bled, gave birth, tempted men into sex, and other base things. Their minds were certainly not holy or divine like that of their male counterparts. They could also be a force of destruction and must be controlled. After all, they held the power to give life, or not, with their bodies.

In the years after the witch hunts died down and Satan was lauded as a heroic outcast by artists of the Romantic period, the image of the witch was similarly embraced by the first wave of feminism. The connection of rebellious women to witchcraft has continued until the present, reclaimed repeatedly for different reasons.

LILITH: THE OFFENDING WOMAN

Lilith is an entity who has existed since the earliest civilizations and is sometimes known as Satan's consort. She started out as a sexually depraved, deadly demon. Today, she is viewed as a feminist icon. Going from demonic whore to feminist hero is quite a glow-up, not unlike the devil's travels through history.

The most well-known mythology of Lilith is that she was Adam's disobedient first wife. Adam was made from mud, and Lilith was made from filth and sediment. Lilith felt that since they were made of similar material, they should be equals. Adam disagreed and was annoyed that his female mate had opinions at all. They argued about sex because Lilith refused to lie beneath Adam, as she would not be considered submissive or below him. Adam wouldn't hear of it. So Lilith flew away to the sea, where she got into all kinds of trouble having sex with devils and spawning hundreds of demons. God sent some angels to confront her on Adam's behalf, asking that she return to her husband and behave herself. Lilith refused and swore that she would henceforth be a baby killer and murderer of mothers. Eventually, it was decided that Lilith would remain an evil destroyer of infants, but amulets bearing one of the angels' names would protect mothers and babies from her.[240]

This well-known story is not in the Bible but comes from a satirical Hebrew book from the Middle Ages called *The Alphabet of Ben Sira*.[241] Casting her as a man-hating baby killer hearkened back to her earlier roots. At the time of this publication, people had already been using the amulets described for centuries. This was because versions of Lilith had existed in various Eastern belief systems for ages, and she was eventually included in Jewish literature like the Zohar and the Talmud.

As mentioned, Lilith is actually a very old being. She may have come from the Mesopotamian Lamastu, which was a winged female demon

---

240. E. R. Vernor, *Lilith: The Mother of All Dark Creatures* (Fort Wayne, IN: Dark Moon Press, 2015), 29–33.

241. "Alphabet of Ben Sira 78: Lilith," Jewish Women's Archive, accessed June 16, 2023, https://jwa.org/media/alphabet-of-ben-sira-78-lilith.

who terrorized mothers and babies and caused miscarriages. She was believed to bring disease and evil. She had a lion's head and huge talons for feet, much like Lilith's current depiction.[242]

In Babylonia, there was a group of demons consisting of one male named Lily and two females named Lilitu and Ardat-Lili. Lily and Lilitu attacked infants and mothers, while Ardat-Lili rendered men impotent and women infertile.[243]

Once she was integrated into Jewish mythology, Lilith maintained her status as a succubus who had sex with sleeping men. She was said to have insatiable carnality and spread disease. Lilith was not just a harlot but pure evil, queen of the underworld, and consort of Samael (Satan).[244] Her sexual exploits provided an explanation for nocturnal emissions and a scapegoat for the sinful pleasures of the flesh. She also accounted for infant deaths and acted as a warning to women that they should be obedient and free of passion. Lilith represented all that was supposedly bad about women, setting the stage for future feminists and witches alike.

Over time, as women started to obtain autonomy, views on Lilith shifted, especially during the Romantic period, casting her in a new and powerful light. In modern times, Lilith is painted as independent and brave. She isn't a monster but a being who chooses her liberation and sexual freedom over Adam and God. It is this version of Lilith that people connect with today.

THE MALLEUS MALEFICARUM

In the 1400s, newsletters and books spread far and wide explaining how witches were responsible for misfortune. Crop failures, diseased livestock, bad weather, and illness were all caused by witchcraft. This propaganda contributed to the contagion of the witch hunts and was the

---

242. Black and Green, *Gods, Demons, and Symbols of Ancient Mesopotamia*, 115–16.

243. Guiley, *The Encyclopedia of Demons and Demonology*, 147.

244. Rebecca Lessis, "Lilith," Jewish Women's Archive, December 31, 1999, https://jwa.org
    /encyclopedia/article/lilith.

reason people in unconnected locations all seemed to be telling the same stories under torture.

One such publication was the *Malleus Maleficarum,* written by Heinrich Kramer (c. 1430–1505). The title translates to "The Hammer of Witches." This very popular publication was used to detect devil-worshipping witches while harping upon the evils of women in general. A section called *Question six* is titled "Concerning Witches who copulate with Devils. Why it is that Women are chiefly addicted to Evil Superstitions."[245] It explains that women "know no moderation in goodness or vice."[246] It contains other gems, calling women "an evil of nature, painted with fair colors!" and declaring "all wickedness is but little to the wickedness of a woman."[247]

This book, which, remember, was widely read and considered factual, describes women as utterly and completely without reason, expressing extreme highs and lows of pure good or evil, with nothing in between. Women are deemed a necessary torture in life, overflowing with sin. It says, "When a woman thinks alone, she thinks evil."[248] It reasons that women are generally less intelligent and more impressionable than men and, therefore, an easy target for the devil. It compares women's intellect to that of children and claims "the natural reason is that she is more carnal than a man, as is clear from her many carnal abominations."[249] When a man is impotent or loses attraction to a woman, it is because of witchcraft. Anything that prevents copulation or reproduction, like birth control or abortion, is "homicide."[250] Witches, apparently, can even trick a man into thinking his penis had disappeared![251]

---

245. Kramer and Sprenger, *The Malleus Maleficarum*, 41.
246. Kramer and Sprenger, *The Malleus Maleficarum*, 42.
247. Kramer and Sprenger, *The Malleus Maleficarum*, 43.
248. Kramer and Sprenger, *The Malleus Maleficarum*, 43.
249. Kramer and Sprenger, *The Malleus Maleficarum*, 43.
250. Kramer and Sprenger, *The Malleus Maleficarum*, 56.
251. Kramer and Sprenger, *The Malleus Maleficarum*, 58.

Midwives are especially evil, according to the author, who claims, "No one does more harm to the Catholic Faith than midwives. For when they do not kill children, then, as if for some other purpose, they take them out of the room and, raising them up in the air, offer them to devils."[252]

There is a chapter called "That Witches who are Midwives in Various Ways Kill the Child Conceived in the Womb, and Procure an Abortion; or if they do not this Offer New-born Children to Devils" and another titled "How Witch Midwives Commit most horrid Crimes when they either Kill Children or Offer them to Devils in most Accursed Wise."[253]

The book says that midwives are under obligation to kill as many children as possible for the devil and are also known to offer human women to incubi.[254]

All these things sound outrageous now, but it can't be stressed enough just how influential this book was and how it impacted the future of the witch hunts, women, and even women's health.

By the time the 1800s rolled around, fewer people believed in a literal devil, and medical science was hitting the scene, but neither of these things prevented the *Malleus Maleficarum*'s influence on women's health.

Midwives, Witches, and Doctors

Since all things sexual and female were considered the devil's business during the European witch trials, midwives in the fifteenth century were particularly evil. And powerful, which probably explains the desire to destroy them. Before the advent of traditional medicine, people depended on midwives for safe childbirth. Midwives also provided abortions, helped women through miscarriages, and advised them about contraceptives. These things allowed women to control, to an extent, whether they had babies or not and thus where they stood in society, since having a child out of wedlock or via adultery could result in ostracization or death. The descriptions of midwives as malicious child killers in the *Malleus*

252. Kramer and Sprenger, *The Malleus Maleficarum*, 66.
253. Kramer and Sprenger, *The Malleus Maleficarum*, 66, 140.
254. Kramer and Sprenger, *The Malleus Maleficarum*, 100, 114.

Maleficarum did not disappear but helped allow the male-dominated medical industry to take control of reproductive health across Europe and into North America.

Some midwives continued to aid with female ailments, but they were not on par with doctors and were not considered legitimate in the same way. Under pressure from the medical establishment, midwives were pushed out of obstetrics, and male doctors took over with their often unnecessary surgeries and innovations.[255]

Medicine and the church merged. Healers, or physicians, were now required to have a university education. The church declared, "If a woman dare to cure without having studied she is a witch and must die."[256] Bear in mind women were barred from such education, further pushing them out of medical practices.

While male doctors and priests were permitted to administer their prayers and healing to the upper crust, healers who looked after the poor were considered evil.[257] The suffering poor were told that their time on Earth was temporary, so they should just tolerate their hardship. It was okay for those who could afford it to seek healing from physicians and the clergy, but women administering to the poor's health was unacceptable. It was witchcraft, not medicine.[258]

The concern was that if these evil, devil-serving women were allowed to administer to the ill or pregnant, their satanic witchcraft powers would grow and lead them to use their magic against the church. When priests and the clergy provided healing, it was God working through them, but when women did the same, it was the devil.[259] Female superstition and male medicine were considered two disparate things, although they were quite similar in many ways.

---

255. Barbara Ehrenreich and Deidre English, *Witches, Midwives and Nurses: A History of Women Healers* 2nd ed. (Old Westbury, NY: The Feminist Press, 1973), 34.

256. Jules Michelet, *Satanism and Witchcraft: A Study in Medieval Superstition*, trans. A. R. Allinson, 5th ed. (New York: Citadel Press, 1965), xix.

257. Ehrenreich and English, *Witches, Midwives and Nurses*, 18.

258. Ehrenreich and English, *Witches, Midwives and Nurses*, 13.

259. Ehrenreich and English, *Witches, Midwives and Nurses*, 14.

During the witch hunts, doctors were considered an important authority in the detection of witches. Doctors served church and state and therefore were given respect.[260]

In the seventeenth and eighteenth centuries, male physicians were finally able to fully infiltrate the one remaining women's place in medicine: childbirth. The forceps were invented in England. They are a contraption that pulls a baby from the womb by its head. They were considered a surgical tool, superior to the techniques of a midwife. It was illegal for women to perform surgery, so this allowed physicians to take over the birth of babies, pushing women out of the picture with their so-called professional, scientific approach. Midwives attempted to fight the dangerous use of forceps and the commercialization of birth, but they were called superstitious and dismissed.[261]

A lack of bodily autonomy is, unfortunately, a familiar experience for many people still, particularly those who are genderfluid and those who have uteruses. With recent developments in the United States regarding reproductive rights and bodily autonomy, vulnerable people are seeing their freedoms go down the toilet. Currently, some Evangelicals in America believe that abortion is satanic, and the overturning of *Roe v. Wade* has caused people to feel robbed of their rights to govern their own bodies.

In contemporary society, Satan is still associated with reproductive issues, albeit in a new and interesting way. The Satanic Temple is leading a campaign for reproductive rights in keeping with their religious beliefs. They are attempting to obtain a religious exemption to antiabortion laws and are playing the long game in court. Bodily autonomy is one of the temple's core tenets. In this way, and many others, the devil continues to champion women's rights and be a symbol of power and solidarity.

---

260. Ehrenreich and English, *Witches, Midwives and Nurses*, 19.
261. Ehrenreich and English, *Witches, Midwives and Nurses*, 20.

HYSTERIA, DEMONIC POSSESSION, AND OTHER LADY TROUBLES

The church was once the source of healing for problems of the soul. Mental health was considered a spiritual matter. When psychiatry gained momentum in the early 1800s, approaching mental illness as science, it posed a real threat to the church's healing industry. Those shrinks were putting exorcisms out of business.

Female hysteria was one of the first mental illnesses attributed to women, and it was shaped by tales of witches and demonic possession. Psychiatrists studied artwork and literature about possession and likened it to the disorder. Hysterics were identified in much the same way that witches had been, including pricking women to see if they could feel pain.[262] This research development, unfortunately, went on to influence the medical profession.

What the church had considered demonic possession—seizures, speaking in tongues, having opinions—were reclassified as symptoms of a hysterical attack.[263] This made the church look very bad while cementing the link between women's health and the devil.

Female hysteria was a diagnosis given to a woman who behaved against the expected norms. They were supposed to be quiet, obedient, and chaste. To behave otherwise was a possible mental illness. While hysteria lacked the seizures and ravings of possession, some other symptoms were changes in sex drive, intensified emotions, increased appetite, swollen abdomen, chest pain, and increased heart rate. It could also appear as a desire to get an education or work for a living.[264]

The word *hysteria* comes from the Greek word for "womb," *hystera*. Female hysteria was sometimes blamed on the mysterious female sexual organs, specifically the uterus. Some doctors would perform a hysterectomy, which is the removal of the uterus, to cure women with the con-

---

262. Faxneld, *Satanic Feminism*, 211.

263. Faxneld, *Satanic Feminism*, 209.

264. Faxneld, *Satanic Feminism*, 212.

dition.[265] Hysterectomy is still performed today for legitimate medical reasons, but it's interesting to know where the name came from.

Among the first scientific sketches of skeletons, women's skeletons were intentionally drawn with smaller skulls and wider hips in an effort to compound the notion that they were merely physical beings, existing to give birth and fulfill bodily functions like reproduction—*not* thinking beings like their male counterparts.[266] This made them carnal and earthly, on par with animals, unlike men, who were supposed to be higher-minded, more evolved creatures. Due to their beauty and attractiveness, women were also considered a gateway to fleshly, degraded, devilish doings. Since women were reduced to sexual purposes only and sex was considered so sinful, women were closer to the devil.

WITCHES AND FEMINISTS

Women who stepped out of line or challenged the system were always likened to witches and the devil long after the witch hunts. This is especially true for well-known feminists throughout history, many of whom reclaimed the label of witch as an act of power.

In all four waves of feminism, the witch has been embraced as a symbol of rebellion and revolt, sometimes used to mock oppressors and certainly to make a statement.

In the nineteenth century, the suffragette movement emerged in the United States as women fought for the right to vote along with a rising interest in Spiritualism. Victoria Woodhull (1838–1927), a Spiritualist and medium, was a prominent early feminist and suffragette who advocated for women's equality, vegetarianism, legalization of sex work, and free love. She was called a witch and dubbed "Mrs. Satan" by *Harper's Weekly* (1872) in a mocking cartoon that summed up the role of women

265. Maria Cohut, "The Controversy of 'Female Hysteria,'" *Medical News Today*, October 13, 2020, https://www.medicalnewstoday.com/articles/the-controversy-of-female -hysteria.

266. Gabrielle Jackson, "The Female Problem: How Male Bias in Medical Trials Ruined Women's Health," *Guardian*, November 2, 2020, https://www.theguardian.com/life andstyle/2019/nov/13/the-female-problem-male-bias-in-medical-trials.

of the time quite well. Woodhull is shown with horns and devilish wings, holding a sign that says, "Be saved by free love." She is looking over her shoulder at a better-behaved woman who is trudging up a hill, struggling under the weight of a drunk husband and multiple children strapped to her back, refusing to be tempted despite her obvious misery.[267] When Woodhull and her sister started a business, the papers named them "bewitching brokers."[268] Woodhull's interest in occultism only fed the fire.

Another prominent first-wave feminist who was dubbed "witch" by the press was Sojourner Truth (c. 1797–1883), who escaped slavery and became an abolitionist, activist, and intersectional feminist. She is well known for her speech "Ain't I a Woman?" given at a women's convention in 1851, where she advocated for racial equality and women's right to vote.[269] She was the first black woman in the United States to win court cases against white men. Her first victory was when she fought to free her enslaved son. The second time she sued a newspaper for slander when they printed an article that called her "witch."[270] She was deeply religious and offended by the term. While Truth didn't embrace the term *witch*, this story shows how powerful the word was.

Matilda Joslyn Gage (1826–98), who happened to be a Theosophist, was happy to take on the moniker. She was among the first to reclaim the word *witch* as a feminist declaration of power and inspired future feminists to do the same. In her book *Woman, Church, and State* (1893), Gage challenges the misogyny of Christianity and the harmful overlap of church and state. She compared the sexism of the church to the witch trials of old, suggesting that the accused witches were victims of Christianity-inspired

---

267. Thomas Nast, "'Get Thee Behind Me, (Mrs.) Satan!' / Th. Nast," *Harper's Weekly* 16, February 17, 1872, 40, https://www.loc.gov/item/95512460/.

268. HarpWeek, "The Bewitching Brokers—Women on Change," *Harper's Weekly*, March 5, 1870, https://www.harpweek.com/09cartoon/BrowseByDateCartoon.asp?Month =March&Date=5.

269. "Sojourner Truth," National Park Service, last modified September 2, 2017, https:// www.nps.gov/wori/learn/historyculture/sojourner-truth.htm.

270. "Sojourner Truth," Library of Congress, December 9, 1998, https://www.loc.gov /exhibits/odyssey/educate/truth.html.

hatred for women. Gage places witches among the most scientifically minded people of the time.[271] She praises the witch as a wise woman, a symbol of knowledge, a healer, and a figure of power.

The church's rules placed women at the mercy of their husbands, stripped them of their rights, and turned them into property. In this way, feminists were in league with the devil because they stood in opposition to clerical rule, just as Satan did in literature, art, and mythology. For Gage, there couldn't be female equality *without* dismantling religion. Feminists had no choice but to be anticlerical.

When it came to the 1960s and second-wave feminism, there was no hesitation in reclaiming the name *witch*. As with past times of social upheaval, again, there was a surge of interest in occultism. A group called WITCH, which stands for Women's International Conspiracy from Hell, was formed on Halloween in 1968. WITCH made their feminist and anti-establishment demonstrations into outrageous public spectacles as a means of protest. A group of members dressed up as Halloween-style witches and publicly hexed Wall Street. They donned black veils and descended upon a bridal show, singing, "Here come the slaves, off to their graves," while releasing a bunch of mice into the crowd. This wasn't mere mischief but actions meant to protest the subjugation of women in society, particularly in marriage.[272] WITCH was not a spiritual or magical group, but they used the archetype of the wicked witch to make their point. A group called WITCH PDX reappeared in 2016 in Portland, performing similar protests. You may have seen the viral pictures of anonymous members at events, draped in black with pointed hats. They're holding black signs with slogans like "Hex the Patriarchy" and "Witches supporting other bitches." They stand for antiracism, antifascism, and LGBTQ+ rights.

With third-wave feminism of the 1990s and the emergence of riot grrrrl punk culture was another surge of interest in magic and occultism.

---

271. Matilda Joslyn Gage, *Woman, Church and State* (Amherst, NY: Humanity Books, 2002), 236.
272. Hughes, *Magic for the Resistance*, loc. 34–35, Kindle.

Once again, the witch and all her misbehaving female facets were at the helm of arts and entertainment with the explosion of screaming, furious, all-girl punk bands like Bikini Kill and movies about female power like *The Craft* (1996) and *Practical Magic* (1998). For the first time, information about real witchcraft was published in easily accessed books such as *To Ride a Silver Broomstick* by Silver RavenWolf and Scott Cunningham's plethora of magical correspondences. With these resources, people were able to claim the name of *witch* and create a personalized practice without having to seek out clandestine groups, resulting in an explosion of solitary practitioners that otherwise never could have been.

Today we're in a storm of social unrest once again as overt racism rears its head, hate is spreading from all sides regarding LGBTQ+ rights, and, yet again, the rights of women are under attack with the overturning of *Roe v. Wade* in 2022. Here, again, we see the witch emerging as the symbol of revolt. As in times past, the witch of today represents the power of the oppressed, either belonging to a marginalized group or acting as an ally of those who do. Many practitioners are very concerned with social issues and inequality regarding race, class, disability, gender, and more. Many witches today feel that by using the label *witch*, they're taking a stance that advocates for those on the margins. Beyond this, the witch aesthetic emerged on social media, and suddenly occultism was a trend in fashion and home décor. Many people can now openly call themselves a witch without fear of harsh judgment or persecution. As for calling yourself a Satanist? That's going to take more time.

What began as an insult to "bad women" like Woodhull has become a descriptor of someone powerful, magical, knowledgeable, and wild. The witch, with her forever consort, the devil, is front and center, stirring up trouble and demanding change.

SATAN AND WITCHES IN THE MARGINS

Many people with marginalized status are drawn to witchcraft and Satanism. Being marginalized means being pushed off to the outside of a ruling structure and deemed unimportant. Witchcraft gives a person agency, control, and a sense of power in their own right. When no one can hear your voice or your voice is ignored, it makes sense to turn to other methods. Sometimes, that's witchcraft.

The book *Aradia, or The Gospel of Witches* by Charles Godfrey Leland from 1899 tells the story of Diana, queen of the witches, and her daughter Aradia, who is fathered by Lucifer. Aradia teaches the poor to fight against the clergy and nobility using witchcraft and resistance. As mentioned, this book helped shape the understanding of witchcraft in the 1960s. Leland's message stuck: the witch continues to fight against various forms of injustice and champion the outcasts, generation after generation. Even when she goes out of style for a little while, we know she is always there in the background and that she will return.

Witches have often integrated their practice into politics. Gerald Gardner, the founder of Wicca, said that witches gathered and collectively cast a spell to prevent Hitler's army from invading allied troops.[273] Around the same time, Dion Fortune led a similar mass ritual, as did American Richard W. Tupper. These rituals of protest came back into the public eye on February 24, 2017. Under the waning moon at midnight, witches from all over the world, remotely and in person, collectively performed a binding spell on then-President Donald Trump. This phenomenon, led by author Michael W. Hughes, was the largest mass spell in history, made possible by social media.[274]

This joining of forces against political oppression is similar to what some modern Satanists value and consider part of their core mission. When it comes to feminism and gender equality, the devil is no stranger.

In some folktales, the devil takes the form of a woman. While many of us refer to the devil as "he," myself included, in truth, the devil is not strictly male. Early artworks of the Garden of Eden show the serpent with the head of a woman. Baphomet, one of the most popular symbols of the devil, is both male and female, having breasts and a caduceus, which

---

273. Gerald B. Gardner, *Witchcraft Today* (1954; repr., New York: Magickal Childe, 1982), 104.

274. Hughes, *Magic for the Resistance*, loc. 44, Kindle.

could be seen as a phallic symbol. Oftentimes angels, including Lucifer, were considered genderless.[275] Michelangelo's famous painting on the ceiling of the Sistine Chapel, called *Temptation and Expulsion*, portrays the devil as a snake with the head of a woman, handing the cursed apple to Eve.

Lucifer means "morning star," and the morning star is actually the planet Venus. Venus is Aphrodite, the goddess of love and beauty. This could mean that the devil and Lucifer are either nongendered or are all genders in one.

◆ ◆ ◆ ◆ ◆

Returning to Eve in the Garden of Eden, I don't believe she ate from the Tree of Knowledge because she was weak. One could argue convincingly that she was presented with new information and made a logical choice. The serpent was her ally. He led her to the truth, which, despite its flaws and pain, was also freedom from blind obedience to God and her husband.

From all of this, we see that Satan has always been in partnership with and in support of women and witches. He pointed Eve in the direction of knowledge, he championed reproductive freedom, and he caused women to challenge the patriarchal church as feminists. It's clear whose side he's on.

---

275. Faxneld, *Satanic Feminism*, 46.

PART II

IN LEAGUE WITH THE DEVIL

You've followed the devil's cloven footprints down the serpentine road of his history. You've looked into his different faces and discovered that he is legion. With his many incarnations and the multitude of purposes he has served, he has put his mark on all of us in one way or another.

In the following section of this book, you will get close to the devil through philosophy, everyday life, symbols, rituals, and lore. When you come face to face with the beast, you will realize that things are not always as they seem. The monster is brutal but also beautiful. Lucifer's light reveals all things equally, both the good and the bad, which offers us free will and choice.

The devil is within and without, above and below. He's the fire inside each individual and the revolt of many.

People have been warned for centuries that one day the devil will come for them, but we know the truth. He's already here. He's been here all along.

CHAPTER 7

MODERN SATANISM IN PRACTICE

All this brings us to modern Satanism. As explained, modern Satanism is mostly an atheist religion in which the devil is considered a symbol instead of an actual being, unlike in some monotheistic faiths. There are no sacrifices, murder, or other horrific crimes involved with real-life Satanism, and such tales are almost exclusively fictional, both in the past and present. There are organized satanic groups, but many Satanists consider themselves solitary. Satan, on the whole, is shaped by culture and the arts and by religion in equal measure.

In all this, there are some basic philosophies that most Satanists share. These strains of thought are seen in organizations and solitary practitioners. These philosophies do not include magical beliefs but are a way of approaching life in general. Adding witchcraft to it is your choice and, in my opinion, certainly doable.

ETHICS

The devil doesn't have rules. Perhaps this is why people fear him. If you are unwise in your use of freedom, you could become your own worst enemy with no one to blame. Such self-governance is scary to some because it includes great responsibility and the ability to truly trust oneself. Many people don't.

Organized satanic groups tend to have a set of statements outlining the keystones of their beliefs. These aren't rules but guiding principles.

The ideology of Satanism might vary from person to person or between groups, but they all share some underlying themes.

In attempting to sum up the basic ethics of modern Satanism, I've compiled a nonexhaustive list of universal values.

Free Will

Modern Satanism is based on free will. Free will means to do as you please and pursue your deepest desires without outside forces like religion, government, or even an overbearing family interfering with your choices. Each one of us is an independent, powerful being. But because Satanism and witchcraft hold free will in such high regard, it is unacceptable to violate that of others. Free will does not mean freedom from consequences.

This leads to a paradox. You have the free will to follow your desires, but you also have the free will to destroy yourself or others. Being self-governed belief systems, Satanism and witchcraft require intelligence and foresight. Just because you *can* do something doesn't mean you *should*, even if you really want to. Free will requires responsibility. There is a big difference between mindfully practicing free will and being a terrible human. You must be thoughtful enough to walk the line, which brings us to the next topic.

Knowledge

To seek knowledge is to question existing paradigms and to search for the truth. Healthy skepticism is a good thing. When someone possesses knowledge, they don't bend to the will of others without thought. As a seeker, they are always curious and look below the surface before jumping on any bandwagons. Those who seek knowledge rarely find themselves manipulated by others and are not typically vulnerable to controlling personalities. Those who ask questions are the ones who change the world.

With knowledge comes reason. To practice free will without either is a dangerous path. Common sense isn't off the table just because you call yourself a Satanist or witch. If you carelessly partake in a satanic prin-ciple such as indulgence without foresight, you might land yourself in some bad situations.

Emotional Intelligence

Emotional intelligence can lead to kindness, or it can be used as a weapon. An emotionally intelligent person has the power to empathize with, comfort, and help someone, but they have the equal capacity to destroy them. It's a double-edged sword. It takes a lot to push someone with true emotional intelligence into reacting with cruelty, as they tend to see the humanity in others, but this is not to be confused with being a doormat or being taken advantage of because you're "nice."

Those with emotional intelligence can see inside of people's hearts in a way. They understand the motives, fears, and insecurities that drive others. They can see when someone is lying to themselves, what brings them true joy, and what their biggest weakness is. This information can be used for good, but it can be used for vengeance when someone deserves it. Having a personal truth bomb thrown in your face tends to be more impactful than name-calling and deflecting. I'm not saying you should do something like this carelessly; hurting people for no reason is never okay. But if someone is hurting you, well, that's different.

Nature and Carnality

The devil represents all that is earthy and wild, us included. In direct opposition to the belief that our time on Earth is simply a step toward the afterlife, the devil reminds us that we ourselves are animals and should enjoy it. This is what's usually referred to as *carnality*, which means "the flesh." Embracing carnality is to enjoy corporeal experiences like lust, sensuality, and gluttony and to revel in all the wonderful things earthly existence has to offer. We are of the earth itself, and we're here to enjoy and cherish the experience.

Carnality includes sexual freedom without shame as long as there is consent between adults. There is no pressure to be pure or chaste since we are earthly beings with earthly desires. This open view on sexuality includes respecting the sexual choices of others, including those who abstain from it if that is their personal will.

Carnality is also the enjoyment of food, material luxuries, and beauty and cherishing connections to other people and animals. Corporeal pleasures are abundant and diverse, often the very things that constitute a happy life.

Self-Empowerment

Self-empowerment is sometimes called self-preservation or selfishness, but I find those terms have a negative feel to them. There is nothing wrong with prioritizing your well-being or even believing that you are your own god. The highest calling in your life is to be true to yourself. Do not sacrifice yourself to someone else's whims. If someone tries to squash your individuality, understand that they don't deserve to hold that power over you. Hold yourself in the highest regard, for when all is said and done, you have to live with yourself.

We're often encouraged to put the well-being of others above our own when in some cases, the very people we are bending over backward for would never return the favor. That perhaps sounds cynical, but it's true, nonetheless. Some Satanists' stance on the self is extreme, emphasizing dominance and survival of the fittest, with an every-person-for-themselves attitude. Some teach that as long as you have what you want, you needn't be too concerned about anyone else. I disagree with this, as I think self-empowerment involves connecting with others and practicing empathy. That seems contradictory, but empathy brings insight into the actions and behaviors of others, creating understanding. The more we connect authentically to one another, the stronger we become. When a bunch of self-empowered people work together, they can make great things happen.

Creativity

The light of Lucifer symbolizes the genius of having your own ideas and acting upon them. Each person is an individual with their own thoughts and inspirations. Creativity is crucial to individuality. It's through freedom of thought that creativity is born and wonderful things happen. With an open mind, fearlessness, and some confidence unhindered by negative outside influences, you might discover abilities and opportunities you didn't know existed. If a belief or person is blocking you from freedom of thought, push them out of the way and shine bright. You don't need anyone or anything dimming your light. Moreover, they don't have the right to do so. Certain special people may be so lucky as to bask in the warmth of your light as it spills outward like warmth from a fire, but they don't have the right to snatch the source for themselves.

Indulgence

Indulgence is to partake in activities purely for pleasure and not for a divine reason, free of shame. It doesn't matter if what you like is strange and bizarre or white-bread ordinary. Devote your life to fulfilling your deepest desires, not to a god or authority figure.

Sometimes when it comes to performing witchcraft, there is a specific goal in mind, like attracting money or finding a partner. Usually, these desires are connected to some form of indulgence like luxury, sex, or love. Witches don't typically avoid earthly pleasures or feel guilty about them. When we want something, we work magic and take practical action to get it.

The reason indulgence is on this list is that there are so many enjoyable things that are considered sinful, especially those that are perfectly natural. Some schools of thought teach that self-denial is a virtue. Why? The earth is a wonderful, interesting, enjoyable place, and we are going to have a good time!

Blasphemy

Blasphemy is the act of being profane toward or defacing what some consider sacred. In its most basic form, it means to use the Lord's name in vain or to vandalize a holy object. The idea of blasphemy can extend beyond religion into an act of rebellion. The sacred object can indeed be a holy item, but it can also be a rule, a person, a systemic issue, or a social norm. These may not be sacred in the spiritual sense, but they certainly are powerful and held in high regard or, at the very least, held over our heads for control. In a ritual designed to assert your autonomy, you are free to commit blasphemy against something that has harmed you or otherwise interfered with your well-being. Committing blasphemy can be an empowering act of offense and a way to destroy that which has stunted you or stood in your way. However, I'm not suggesting that you destroy other people's property. I'm referring to ritualized blasphemy in a private setting.

Radical Self-Acceptance

Many people are told all their lives that they *need* to fit in because there's something inherently shameful in not belonging. This creates a deep sense of humiliation in a person for being different. Many people drawn to Satanism and witchcraft have a feeling of being an outsider who is not accepted by the herd for a range of reasons. This can be a terrible feeling at first, but once you grow into yourself, you come to realize that you are an outcast because you are special and unique. That's a good thing! We outcasts are the ones who blaze trails, create change, and ask questions that lead to discovery.

In families, the black sheep gets cast out and used as a scapegoat. The black sheep are usually the same people who break generational cycles by casting light upon abuse or problematic dynamics that others don't have the courage to face.

There's something to be said for having the audacity to be alone in a world where fitting in is considered so vital. Someone able and willing to be independent has clearly made peace with themselves and is strong as a result. Sometimes people are wary of loners and outsiders, but not for the reason you think. Sometimes, they're intimidated by the courage it takes to stand alone.

Curiosity and Wonder

The world is an amazing place full of beauty and pain. There is so much going on down here on Earth that to spend life gazing into the unknown and wishing for an afterlife is a shame. Keep curious. Wonder and marvel at simple earthly things like a flower, an ocean, or the feeling of love. Celebrate what this earth and universe have to offer in tangible form. There is no need to whittle away the days worrying about what comes after death.

Engaging with your sense of wonder and giving in to your curiosity can lead to amazing revelations and joy. It's in our nature to question, investigate, and learn, so allow yourself to follow that instinct.

EVERYDAY SATAN

Currently, there are quite a few modern trends that reflect satanic ethos. I feel the mainstreaming of these things is just more evidence that the devil really isn't that strange or frightening anymore. I'm not suggesting that these seemingly unremarkable trends make any individual a secret devil worshipper. I put them here just to demonstrate how commonplace, nonthreatening, and positive satanic values can be and how they're often completely unrelated to religion.

Self-Care

This was once considered laziness and idleness. We now see a trend emerging that values the importance of taking time to rest, dream, and play rather than prioritizing work and money above our wellness. Self-care is allowing yourself to do what you enjoy, taking time to be alone, or spending a day looking after yourself. The self-care industry is booming like never before. It's becoming common knowledge that the constant push for productivity in the capitalist sense is harmful mentally and physically while destroying the planet. There's a saying that "idle hands are the devil's playground." If that means it is satanic to take time to nurture yourself, have leisure time, or check in with your mental state, so be it.

Boundary Setting

Setting boundaries is a term that comes up often in self-help circles. Setting a personal boundary is to actively communicate an inviolable condition for those who wish to have access to you, marking your comfort zone. Setting boundaries is usually done to preserve one's mental health, and doing so is not just a means of protecting yourself and your well-being but also an act of self-respect. You are listening to your own needs rather than being a doormat for those who may not deserve it. Boundaries are a deliberate declaration of your will.

Abundance Mindset

You often hear the ambiguous term *abundance* in spiritual spaces. When you remove the woo-woo, to most people, abundance means money. For some reason, many people don't want to admit this. Some ideology teaches that there is a wholesome, pure element to rejecting money, particularly when it comes to spirituality and religion. Centuries ago, people were told that by living in poverty, they were serving God through punishment and sacrifice, thus causing them to never question their station in life. This greatly benefitted those in charge.

An abundance mindset is just a soft way of saying it's okay to desire and try to get money and all it brings, removing the guilt of so-called greed. It's perfectly natural to want to live comfortably and to have at least some of the things your heart desires.

Personal Growth

Currently, people are being encouraged to explore their inner life. Therapy attendance is at an all-time high. Working on the self is to seek knowledge. Prioritizing mental health and working on interpersonal relationships is honoring the self in a wonderful way. Choosing to look inward, especially when it came to emotions, was once considered selfish in the negative sense, while at the same time, therapy was highly stigmatized. It's very fortunate how the conversation around therapy and mental health has shifted into the light. It's self-empowerment at its finest.

Body Positivity

In my lifetime, I've seen a huge shift in attitude toward body image. In my experience growing up, if you openly loved your body or found yourself beautiful, you were labeled vain, shallow, and prideful. For some reason, it was socially unacceptable to consider yourself attractive. One of Lucifer's key traits in mythology was that he was beautiful and knew it. The emergence of body positivity, which is teaching people to love their bodily form, is a literal celebration of the flesh.

Sexual Health and Expression

Throughout history, there have been some absolutely wild myths surrounding sexuality, and it was almost always considered the devil's business. It wasn't long ago that menstruating women were considered dangerous, and people believed masturbation would send you straight to hell. Fortunately, shame is slowly being removed from sexuality, and the taboos about discussing it are falling away. The harm of oppressing peoples' sexual orientation is better understood now as more and more people are beginning to view gender as fluid. Sexuality can be self-empowerment, indulgence, and carnality all rolled into one.

IS ANY OF THIS TRULY NOVEL?

It seems almost silly that any of these things could be considered satanic since most people do them without ever thinking of the devil. The question should be, why are these trends considered so novel rather than standard behavior? Why are such basic ideas—standing up for yourself, seeking profit, self-love—seemingly so new? It's because Western thinking has been heavily shaped by productivity-related guilt and self-denial, teaching us to put our own desires and actual *needs* on the back burner for fear of appearing selfish, vain, greedy, or disobedient. If you think about these actions in some Christian contexts, they're all things that were once illogically considered, if not a sin, at least very bad. These trends illustrate how social norms have shifted to the carnal, selfish side. In shedding old constraints, we're rejecting outdated ways of thinking in a way that is good for the self and for others.

Admittedly, in reducing Satanism to these terms, I'm really taking the teeth out of it. For old-school Satanists, it might even seem ridiculous.

But like I keep saying, Satanism has evolved along with society, and this growth is a good thing.

Throughout the following sections, I've included some bullet points of things to think or journal about. The purpose of this is to help you understand your true will, the ways you empower and disempower yourself, and to get you thinking about how to move forward and grow.

Self-Reflection

- Have you ever changed your opinion to match that of a certain group or person without thinking it through? Why? Look deep into yourself and be brutally honest about your motives for doing so. It could be fear, a desire to be accepted, or something else.

- Do you know someone who constantly changes who they are depending on their company? What do you honestly think about them and their behavior? Does it help or harm them?

- Has anyone ever disparaged you for taking care of yourself? What do you think their motivation was?

ANIMAL OPPORTUNISM

Nature and everything within it is opportunistic. Humans and animals are not that different, although some people like to think we are. As witches, we uphold the natural world and all within it as sacred. This includes the behaviors of plants and animals. It makes sense, then, that opportunism isn't always a bad thing but a natural thing. Just as a vine will climb a tree to get to the sunlight, we too take whatever opportunity we must to get where we need to be.

Often the word *opportunist* evokes images of people stomping on others to get ahead, not caring who they hurt as long as they get what they want. This certainly occurs, and while I don't necessarily approve of it, I suggest that there is such a thing as healthy, conscious opportunism.

Some forms of Satanism focus heavily on our animal instincts and traits. The theory, in this case, is that just as some animals have the advantage of claws and fangs, human beings have the advantage of intellect and manipulation. LaVeyan Satanism teaches that if you step on others in your quest for progress, it's simply social Darwinism in action. I don't personally share this view, as I care about people. Humans are, after all, social animals, and I'm sure some animal species also care for each other.

Opportunism doesn't always have to mean "every person for themselves." For instance, someone who is leading an important cause might see the chance to bring in help from people who can offer resources while benefitting them at the same time. This is climbing up collaboratively. Healthy opportunism can also mean that when you reach the top, you use your position to uplift deserving people for mutual gain.

While we should allow ourselves to follow our desires within reason, we must do so with foresight and wisdom. This often includes considering other people, especially if doing so benefits you. I know that sounds horribly manipulative, but it's not always. Think about how you benefit from treating your children well, or the sense of safety that comes from caring for others, or how good it can feel to participate in worthy causes. Almost everything we do, at its core, is for our own benefit. The same is true for animals.

While it would be nice if we were surrounded by conscientious, thoughtful moral people, we simply *aren't*. So if someone shows themselves to be an asshole, treat them like one.

Should you decide to manipulate your way into getting what you want—and you're free to make that choice—you need to make sure that it's a genuinely wise decision for your own sake. Are you absolutely sure that once you get to the top, you'll be able to live up to the role? Or will you be exposed as a fake? Are you actually worthy of that position? Because if not, chances are you're going to fail spectacularly.

Opportunism is the ability to see what is available to you, embrace it, and take risks. An animal will take an opportunity to get what it needs, but not at the risk of its survival. A wise opportunist understands the outcome of their choices.

Here is a timely little story about unwise opportunism that you may have witnessed yourself. Some opportunities, in the end, harm not only others but the self, even though it doesn't seem like it at first glance.

In today's toxic social media world, influence and follower count are everything. People desire popularity without truly thinking it through. They've simply been told it's what they should aspire to, and instead of thinking for themselves, they decide to go for it. An effective (and unfortunate) way to gain engagement is to make people angry. Our hypothetical person desires this and so targets others by accusing them of a social deviation that is trending and appeals to the morals of many. Drawn to the outrage and drama, people start feeding our viral friend with their interaction and approval. To keep their new supporters, this person must continue to peddle the same kind of outrage. After all, they've built an audience who enjoys seeing others torn to shreds, not funny cats. Without considering what kind of people are slavering for this type of content, our hypothetical person swells with power and incoming admiration. But there's a problem. They've put themselves in a very vulnerable position without realizing it. They must continue to wear the veneer of virtue by pointing out the evils of another, but underneath is insecurity and complete lack of self-knowledge. They're dependent on outside approval, and because they've built a career on pointing out the flaws of others, they better be squeaky clean themselves. One false move and their own followers will eat them alive.

Someone might argue that this person used an opportunity and their darkest traits to get ahead, so there's nothing wrong here. Sure. But Satan also represents individuality, intelligence, creativity, and wisdom, which our friend has omitted. They are a fool who will fall into the trap of their own making.

To truly be successful, look to your creativity and intelligence; don't steal them from another person. If you can't climb to the top by *actually* being the best at something, perhaps you shouldn't be there. Yet.

In the end, Satanism isn't about deviously clawing your way up. It's about shining a light on reality and your personal truth. A person not living in truth might use lowly, dirty means of reaching a goal, but it is a shaky tower they build, easily destroyed by others. While you can embrace opportunism like an animal, you must also be discerning and use the very thing that puts humans at the top of the food chain—your brain.

Self-Reflection

- Have you ever experienced positive animal opportunism? What about a time that it has turned out badly for you or someone else?
- Have you ever taken an opportunity and then felt guilty about it? Was your guilt truly warranted or the result of conditioning?
- Have you ever passed up an opportunity because it wasn't the "nice" thing to do? Reflect on whether or not you benefitted from this decision and if the overall result was worth it.

THE LIGHT OF LUCIFER

There are a lot of new age phrases making the rounds, like "protect your energy" and "don't let others ruin your vibe." Fluffy as it may seem, there's plenty of truth in some of these narratives. The light, in this case, is your individuality, creativity, and will. It's important to protect your personal energy, or light, from those who attempt to dim it or stop you from exploring life in all its glory. Some people will try to steal your light because they haven't discovered their own. They're often referred to as psychic vampires. Finding your light is work. Instead of doing that work, they try to suck it out of others through shame, guilt, bullying, or whatever methods suit them.

Some humans are mental and emotional predators seeking prey, constantly on the lookout for who they can use for their own gain. They're in a perpetual state of emptiness and will drain your energy to feed themselves. The thing is, those who keep you small and dim need you far more than you need them. What would they do without you? Where will they get their sense of power when they can't take yours? Often, just removing yourself is enough to exorcise the human leech. Let them starve. Denying them access to you is revenge in and of itself.

Like many empowered people who recognize their own worth, Lucifer was cast out, away from all that was familiar. When you come into your own power, there's a chance that you will lose those who try to dampen your flames and control you. Good riddance!

No matter where you are in life, there is always a spark burning deep inside you. No matter how small, it burns with the rage and power of hellfire, with a vengeance and will of a thousand devils. Once you find this flame and tend it, you will become unstoppable.

As someone who, for a large chunk of my life, thought that being nice, small, and silent was the best way to protect myself, I can testify from experience that it is not. Some people will see your attitude as weak and pounce on the chance to exploit it.

Satanism has taught me to trust myself, my ideas, and my own instincts. I have learned to recognize that I don't deserve to be pushed aside and that I'm not inherently less-than. I can recognize the vultures and the users when I see them. I can say no without guilt. I have autonomy over my own body. Satanism says to fight fire with fire, so when someone tries to take advantage of you, beat them down with the truth. When you are discerning and living your will, you can see their manipulation for what it is. When you become aware of the fire burning inside you, you are elevated in all you do.

Self-Reflection

- Pay attention to how you feel and with whom. Do you find yourself feeling insecure or doubting your judgment when you're around certain people?
- Think about something you loved doing as a child or young person but abandoned. Why did you stop? You might realize that the reason for giving it up was because someone dimmed your light and that you should take it back up.

- Think about a time that you did not stick up for yourself and how that felt. What stopped you? If it happened again, would it be worth defending yourself? What is the worst, and best, possible outcome?

HYPOCRISY

I wish that the world of witches was all loving and kind—and don't get me wrong, some of it is—but as with any group, problems can arise, particularly when it comes to strong and clashing opinions. In this crowd, Satan is a divisive subject that gets people pretty upset, so you will need to have a strong inner fire to deal with it.

We've all seen and read about how some witches and Pagans have a very strong stance against Christianity. There are many reasons for this, a lot of them legitimate.

Some witches will say they are anti-Christian because they don't believe in oppressing people for their beliefs or identities. The problem is some of these same witches then turn around and shun those of us who practice witchcraft differently than them. These people need to ask themselves why they're acting out the behavior they so vehemently protest on their social media. Witches claiming to be outcasts and rebels attacking other witches for being outcasts or rebels *the wrong way* is bizarre.

The nature of Satanism is to be adversarial, to question, to challenge, and to embrace your outsider status as a strength. The word *witch* has similar connotations. Many people use the renegade label of witch because it makes them feel rebellious but then behave like watered-down tyrants, throwing around dogma and rules.

The title of witch doesn't have pretty roots. A witch was someone who was shunned for being weird, deviant, or hideous. Being called a witch wasn't cute or trendy; it was a label that, if it didn't get you tortured and killed, would cause you a life of exile. Reclaiming the word *witch* has been important to many people leading the movement to legitimize their practices and, in many cases, decriminalize them. They were not looked upon kindly.

Those who claim this label need to understand its true meaning. It was a name for those who were rejected, people who lived on the fringes of society and were possibly considered dangerous. To call yourself a witch but then run away from those characteristics is hypocritical. If you can claim the title of witch, accept that some claim the label of Satanist in a similar manner.

In light of all the division and controversy already going on around us, witches and Satanists shouldn't be fighting with each other. The two indeed have some conflicting beliefs, but it's well time we started working together because, whether you like it or not, we are more alike than different.

Self-Reflection

- Considering what you've learned so far, what is your view on witches who venerate the devil? Has your opinion changed?
- If you view Satan as unacceptable within your own practice (which is perfectly okay), can you recall why you developed that opinion?
- Would you be comfortable including satanic imagery in your practice? Why or why not?

THE COMPLEXITY OF SELFISHNESS

Selflessness to the point of martyrdom is not natural to us or any animals. This pure, giving altruism that is so overvalued is actually often very draining and a means of hiding from confrontation. Some people believe that to get into heaven, you must always put others ahead of yourself. If you don't believe in heaven, why exhaust yourself serving others who don't deserve it?

On the surface, selfishness seems like a quality teetering on the edge of evil acts. However, once you begin to actually think this through, it is far more complicated than that because there are different kinds of selfishness.

Here's the thing. Even when we do things for others, we have our own selfish reasons for it. An example for me is that when my grandmother was living in long-term care, I always visited her regularly, even though I found the place horribly depressing and distressing. I could claim I was selflessly visiting entirely for her benefit, but the truth was that, in addition to genuinely caring about her, I couldn't live with my own conscience if I didn't visit. Ultimately, that is why I went. Because it made me feel better. At the same time, she did benefit from it. She had someone who checked on her regularly and brought the things she needed and a person to talk to. You could say it was mutually beneficial, which goes to show you that selfishness isn't necessarily bad.

Often people join charitable organizations and claim their actions are purely altruistic, but this is not necessarily the case. The real reason they participate is because it makes them feel good, and you know what? That's great! Science says that when you help others, dopamine is released in your brain.[276] Admitting this doesn't take away the benefit you've provided to a cause.

Then there is the other kind of selfishness, which is when your actions put people around you at risk or hurt them. Some might argue that if they stick around and tolerate it, they're weak and deserve it. I disagree. While you are free to do your will, even in this nasty way, be sure that you won't regret your actions later. You could lose people, or your impact on them might cause a ripple effect that gets you into trouble in innumerable ways. Make sure that your choices are noble. For every action, there's a reaction. It's usually best not to be an irresponsible jerk.

Selfishness is not always destructive to others. Doing things for your own pleasure and benefit can be positive for others. Many people spend their entire life in resentful, obligational servitude to others because it's hammered into their brains that selfishness is wrong. That is a life half lived.

---

276. Steve Siegle, "The Art of Kindness," Mayo Clinic Health System, August 17, 2023, https://www.mayoclinichealthsystem.org/hometown-health/speaking-of-health/the-art-of-kindness.

Self-Reflection

- Think about the last time you considered another person selfish. What exactly was the reason? Would you do the same as them, given the chance?

- Has anyone ever accused you of selfishness? Consider if your actions were harmful to anyone else. If not, is it still selfish?

- Recall a time that helping others made you feel good. Did you notice a ripple effect? Did helping one person spread to others in some beneficial way?

THE FIRE OF TRUTH

"Living in your truth" is a phrase thrown around so often that it might seem devoid of meaning. Phrasing it differently might help. Think of it as having a fire inside, burning bright. To live in your truth is to genuinely know yourself and live your will.

Often, what we *think* we want in life is very different than what we *truly* desire. Cultural influences tell us what we are *supposed* to aspire to, like the pressure to get married or have children, to attain certain beauty standards, or to have a bustling social life. Plenty of people don't genuinely want any of those socially dictated things but aspire to them anyway, not realizing they can choose a different path. They're not living in their truth.

Living in your truth is knowing that whatever you're doing right now is something you chose and genuinely wanted.

Heeding your inner fire can be challenging. It can mean cutting other people off or acting in a way that is considered unconventional to your community. It can bring backlash. But after the initial pain of expansion, you will find deep peace in all you do because your foundation is built on your choices, not the flimsy opinions of others. You'll also develop a very good BS detector and immediately sense inauthenticity.

What other people or society tell you is the right way to live may not be for you at all. The measure of success is not the same for everyone.

Most people think money equals success, and the more you make, the more successful you are. But perhaps you value freedom over money and would rather escape the grind and work for yourself, even though it means a smaller income. In this case, freedom is success. Success can be anything you choose. You must define it for yourself.

Many people devote their life to pursuing what others tell them to, saying what others want them to say, going along with the crowd, and protecting themselves by disappearing into the flock. Living in this way might bring temporary rewards, but it never leads to an overall satisfying life. You cannot look to anyone else to tell you what your authentic truth looks like.

When you are living in your truth, you understand that you cannot control other people or the chaos that is life. You *can* control how you react. Some people are frustrated by this advice, but don't underestimate its power because it will shape your future. If you neglect to focus on your inner world because you're desperately trying to control outside forces instead, you will be like a dog chasing its tail. Your peace depends solely on you.

No one can dictate how you feel or navigate your life for you. When you realize that your best defense against a situation or person is simply being your honest self, you will always win. The truth is one of your best weapons.

Self-Reflection

- We do a lot of lying, appeasing, and modifying to fit what others want. Pay attention to how many times per day you do it. The next time you start to say what someone wants to hear to your own detriment, try telling the truth instead. See what happens.
- Think of something that you are frequently angry or upset about. Is it within your power, in the moment, to take action and create measurable change? If not, can you channel your feelings in a constructive direction?

- Once a day, take a second to think about what you're doing at that moment and why. Are your actions aligned with your personal truth, or are you just doing what you're told? While it's not necessarily possible to change everything (we all need to work and make money, for example), this exercise will lead you to start making small changes that eventually add up to big ones.

CHAPTER 8
THE DEVIL AND THE SHADOW

The term *shadow work* has become commonplace in the witchcraft world, and although sometimes misunderstood, it has led lots of people to consider the nature of balance in their magical practice and mundane lives.

The shadow concept was created by psychologist Carl Jung, who described it as the unwanted parts of our personalities that we push back into the darkness or shadows.[277] We often deny these qualities, hiding and avoiding them because bringing them up can be uncomfortable. While someone is doing shadow work, they're usually going through a difficult time and dealing with the darkest parts of themselves. Shadow work can be done intentionally, or it can be forced upon a person by life's harsh circumstances. The good news is that on the other side of the darkness are strength and growth. Embracing the shadow self creates wholeness and a better understanding of all the things life throws at us.

Shadow magic and shadow work are not the same thing, although they are related. Shadow magic refers to baneful elements of witchcraft that are of the left-hand path or toeing the ethical line, like cursing and other workings that harness negative energy.

---

277. Carl G. Jung, *The Archetypes and the Collective Unconscious*, The Collected Works of C. G. Jung, vol. 9, trans. R. F. C. Hull, ed. Herbert Read, Michael Fordham, and Gerhard Adler (London: Routledge and Kegan Paul, 1959), 20.

The shadow self contains many suppressed emotions. Like the devil, this part of the self has been pushed away and banished to the darkness.

As a macrocosm, the devil is the collective shadow of those who believe he exists in the form of evil. The negativity inside of them, or the thoughts that are deemed bad, can be cast out instead of examined, reflected upon, and worked through. The devil is the shadow of humanity as a whole. He is the scapegoat, burdened with all that is shameful, sinful, or undesirable. The devil represents parts of human nature that people find socially unacceptable. He is blamed for the bigger issues at play in the world that scare us the most. These issues do not exist because of the devil. They are inside of and committed by human beings. Some are so unthinkable that people would rather blame an outside force than consider the true horrors that the human animal is capable of. Since we are all just human animals, we might have the same cruelties within us too.

As a microcosm, the devil is the shadow of each one of us. He can represent parts of yourself that you've denied so you can conform to family and community norms. Sometimes the shadow version of ourselves contains things that are not objectively negative or evil beyond our own circle of people. For example, if sex is forbidden before marriage, one might have learned that sexual desire is shameful and pushed it into their shadow. Looking deeply at your shadow self might reveal that some of your deepest fears are actually not that powerful.

When you really take a good long look at what lives in your shadow self, you can then understand your own behavior and why you do things, and you can question your own thoughts and habits, ultimately leading to growth.

Other times, what you find there might be truly troubling and require time to work through, in which case a therapist can be of help if you can afford one.

It's important to note here that shadow work is not meant to encourage anyone to blame themselves for abuse or harm inflicted upon them by others. It is meant to help you look at unconscious beliefs or behaviors that may be holding you back in life. This chapter is about accountability to the self and self-knowledge, not forgiving those who have done wrong.

If you've been taught that the devil is evil and contains all the ills of humanity, including your own, working with him in rituals can help you access these pain points and reframe how you view them—and yourself. When you are not tethered to unconscious feelings of shame, you can confront them and vanquish them. Then, you can begin to realize your own strength. Working with the devil encourages you to truly consider why you hide certain parts of yourself. Often the reason has nothing to do with evil at all.

TOXIC SPIRITUALITY

In witchcraft and shadow work, something that must be considered is whether or not you are engaging in self-delusion. Choosing delusion is tempting. Ignorance is bliss. If we can avoid real life and do magic instead, everything seems easier. As I write this, there is a massive trend in what some call "white light" spiritualities, particularly in people posing as life coaches. This includes things like certain so-called positive forms of witchcraft, angelic channeling, energy healing, Westernized chakra work, mediumship, crystal healing, and more.

While these things can genuinely enhance some peoples' witchcraft practice, they can be, and often are, used in harmful ways. They provide escapism for some and are monetized by "healers" for physical, mental, and spiritual sicknesses. Like anything, when taken to an extreme, they become toxic. For instance, someone who is ill might pay for energy healing instead of visiting a doctor and become seriously sick as a result. Sometimes people convince themselves that they're a mystical empath rather than dealing with what might very well be a trauma response or projection. I've witnessed people refuse to face their mental health issues by blaming their symptoms on the spirits of their dead relatives. People have gone into debt to purchase pretty rocks that promise to fix their financial problems instead of taking practical action.

The reason that Satanism uses an inverted pentagram, much to the chagrin of many witches, is because Satanism rejects the focus on the ethereal and intangible aspects of these spiritualities in favor of the here and now on earth. When upright, the topmost point of the pentagram represents spirit above matter. The upside-down pentagram is a rejection of those paths that teach us to focus on invisible realms, sometimes to our own detriment.

Being inundated with memes, inspirational quotes, and good-vibes-only content has encouraged people to neglect their earthly existence in favor of chasing the evasive concept of spirituality. Some abandon doing work on the physical plane and turn to prayer, chanting, and chasing a higher state of being. Often the self-proclaimed gurus offering their expensive services and courses claim that your problems—be they poverty, relationships, or even physical ailments—can all be remedied with meditation, breathwork, and light language. When their teachings fail to fix a student's life, they will blame the student for not being enlightened enough.

A blatant example of this is when a spiritual leader teaches that a student is experiencing poverty because of their mindset. This bypasses all the real-life issues the student is facing. To make it worse, the solution isn't even something that can be tangibly identified and worked on; rather, it's an amorphous, imaginary state that the lowly student is unable to reach without continuing to pay their teacher. The ideology that every problem or hardship you encounter is a spiritual one and can be solved by making image boards and performing daily mental gymnastics to repair your energy is rampant in the spiritual and witchcraft community. Toxic spirituality will tell you that if you simply learn to vibrate on a higher frequency, whatever that means, these problems will solve themselves. If they don't magically disappear, it's because you are being punished by karma, the three-fold law, or a past life. This keeps your head in the clouds instead of reality and drains your bank account.

When poverty, illness, or hardship have been handed down to you through multiple generations, your mindset is not to blame. To be told you're experiencing hardship because you haven't done the right spiritual work is insulting and ignorant.

Ignoring the here and now in favor of escaping into toxic spirituality will only worsen your current earthly affairs. Satanism rejects this illogical bypassing. While there's nothing wrong with engaging in these activities if they genuinely benefit you, there is definitely a line that can get crossed. If you're hiding within the white light movement instead of sorting out your life to the best of your ability right here on the earthly plane, things will not get better. We exist in the here and now, and we have to face our material life. This can involve some difficult and unpleasant work, but it's the only solution.

I've been practicing witchcraft for a long time and have fallen into the trap of toxic spirituality more than once, especially in the beginning. I wondered what I was doing wrong in my craft to bring about every misfortune and what I should change. However, the older I got and the more life experience I accumulated, the more I realized that there are systemic issues at play in this world that are far larger than my spiritual beliefs. With the facts glaring me in the face, I could no longer hide in a bubble of white light and pretend that there wasn't a ton of tangible work to be done.

Upon realizing that no amount of chanting and spellwork could ever dismantle these overwhelming problems, I had no choice but to admit that I sometimes immersed myself in witchcraft to hide from reality. If I wanted anything to change, I needed to go into action, not light more candles (although it never hurts).

Satanism puts immediacy and realistic thinking above escapist behaviors. It reminds a practitioner that you need to combine practical work with your spiritual endeavors. Satanism has taught me that not everything is magical or spiritual. Sometimes, life just happens. Not every falling leaf is an omen, and sometimes a black cat is just a black cat.

RETHINKING SIN

In light of all you've learned about the origins of Satan and the modern devil, you could conclude that Satanism values self-empowerment, pleasure, material profit, intelligence, and advocacy. However, since satanic ideology is self-governed, it can be misinterpreted as *anything goes* when there are certainly things that are discouraged in satanic belief. Some satanic groups have their own list of sins that go against the ethos of Satanism. In the spirit of this, I'll include my own here.

Self-Destruction

Self-destruction is the opposite of self-empowerment. In a practice that is open to indulgence, people can fall down a slippery slope into addiction and other forms of self-harm, claiming that to do so is their will. In truth, they have lost their will to a substance or behavior they can't control. If you're in a self-destructive state, seeking help is an honor to the self. While a person is free to imbibe in intoxicants if they like, to consume to the point of it negatively affecting their life is not in line with satanic thinking. You're here to enjoy the earth, take pleasure in life, and celebrate existence, not spend it suffering in servitude to an addiction. None of this is to say that addiction is a choice. It's not. If you find yourself at the bottom of the aforementioned slippery slope, I hope you will be open to help.

Self-Deceit

Deceiving the self is a coping mechanism that I think almost everyone has employed at least once. It takes many forms, such as telling yourself that everything is fine in your relationship when it is not, choosing to ignore problematic group dynamics, or even in the refusal to objectively look at yourself with an honest eye. Lying to yourself is to deny reality, which is not using your reason or intellect. While self-deceit may be rooted in hope or even a justified means of surviving at times, it's temporary and does nothing to solve a problem or improve your life long-term.

Worship

Satanists don't worship the devil. Instead, I prefer the word *celebrate*. To worship is to put oneself below, or in subservience to, an entity. This might include having to make payments, make confessions, or enact various rituals to appease a deity. This is not part of Satanism. Celebration, on the other hand, is a form of respect for a symbol or being, done willingly and without fear, and creates a connection between the mind of the practitioner and the entity (even if the entity is not real to the practitioner in the theistic sense). Even atheistic Satanists might include iconography in rituals or have an altar dedicated to the devil to benefit from the emotions they elicit. In celebrating, we're acknowledging the admirable qualities of the devil and enjoying how that makes us feel, which leads to further self-empowerment.

Apathy

There's a saying to "be the change you want to see in the world." While it's true that this may be something you've seen embroidered on a pillow, the sentiment is a powerful one. Fighting against dangerous, outdated tropes is something the devil has always done. That's why in modern Satanism you see so much activism. Corrupt and inequitable realities unfolding before our eyes are impossible to ignore. We have to practice what we preach. This can take the form of organized group activism, or it can be a smaller, everyday approach wherein your personal actions impact the whole.

Misanthropy

This is admittedly the toughest one for me. I choose not to seek out any organization or group to join regarding Satanism or witchcraft. I have to always remind myself that there's a difference between healthy independence and misanthropy. Misanthropy can become hatred for and fear of humankind, leading to isolation and losing touch with reality. If you're already dabbling in the occult, this can lead to some serious delusion.

I believe we're all connected and that having a support system of people is healthy, especially if there are larger-scale issues you'd like to confront. The danger of becoming misanthropic is somewhat pronounced in those of us who are already outsiders, but it's unlikely that rejecting all human contact will result in a fulfilling or successful life. It's okay to be a solitary person who likes their own company, but you are still connected to the whole of humanity.

Idolization

Idolization, not to be confused with idolatry, is the excessive adoration for another person, often a leader, public figure, or even an ideology. Idolization occurs when a person is held in such high regard that they almost take on the form of a god. They're stripped of their humanity and deified, and a cult of personality forms. Those who follow the leader lose their sense of self and depend on the leader to tell them what to think. They mold their personality according to what their idol says or does. No human being's beliefs should replace your own, and giving someone this god-like status is not in service to the self. All of this also applies to when certain ideas become dogma.

Herd Mentality

These days there's a real problem of herd mentality. When one slightly influential person shares an ill-researched quote or graphic online, thousands of people will immediately believe it without question and spread it. If anyone challenges them or expresses an opposing view, people will pile on the dissenter and destroy them for the sin of speaking out against the dominant opinion. This kind of behavior has no room for freedom of thought or curiosity, creates a culture of fear, and silences those who dare to think differently for terror of persecution or being cast out.

It's important to consider *why* you're joining a group should you choose to do so. If it's because you want to participate in works or rituals or just shared fun, great. But if you join a group because you feel lost, you're afraid of standing alone, or you have not formed your own opinions, you're in a vulnerable spot and are going to get hurt.

Destroying Someone's Light

This is also known as being a good old-fashioned hater. The story of Lucifer is one in which others try to destroy his creative light. Don't be a light-snuffer. Some people's light takes the form of being a dreamer, being kind, or having a genuine passion for something. In a sea of negativity, this is such a wholesome thing! Seeing people attempt to destroy this in others for no real reason breaks my heart. It's tragic when an innocent person is targeted, used, scapegoated, and then thrown in the trash. This world is a tough place.

Snuffing out someone else's light is a display of weakness and petty character. If you have light of your own—that is, self-confidence, knowledge, and truth—you wouldn't need to ridicule or ruin anyone else's. If you find yourself wanting to inflict harm on someone who hasn't actually wronged you, give some serious thought about why. Is their light outshining yours?

Rigidness in Thought

Refusing to tolerate the perspective of others or trying to quell their rights works against your own freedoms. You will not always agree with other people, and that's okay. However, to believe they should be absolutely silenced is to forgo your own freedoms.

There is a lot to be learned by interacting with people and material you disagree with. Sometimes, you are exposed to new ideologies that lead you in a surprising direction. The devil, particularly as Lucifer, is the light of the highest possible intelligence. Part of aspiring to this is to fully understand all points of view to form your own.

Healthy opposition is good. Debate is good. Respectful discussion about disagreements is good. When both parties go away having learned something new, even if they go away angry, they've gained something. It doesn't mean you must change your own opinions or values. Just let other people have theirs. From there, you're free to challenge them all you like.

DEALING WITH DELUSION

Being honest with oneself about the reality of any difficult situation can be challenging. I myself have fallen into self-delusion on more than one occasion, escaping into magical thinking to avoid some very harsh realities about myself, my mental health, and the life I was leading. This is a topic that I feel isn't discussed enough: witchcraft can be escapism and can be used as a crutch to avoid the truth. The devil, being carnal, can be the symbol that brings us back to earth, so to speak. Satan encompasses the opposite of mysticism. Sometimes this counterbalance is exactly what you need.

If you find yourself slipping into delusion and losing your grip on reality, which happens to the best of us, try the simple charm below. Remember, even if you don't believe in magic, something like this can act as a simple psychological tool to ground you and bring your thoughts back to the present.

Materials
Pinch of earth
Small piece of horn or antler
Small piece of black obsidian
3-by-3-inch square of black cloth
1 foot of red thread

The pinch of earth represents grounding. The piece of horn or antler is to represent the devil. However, if this is unavailable, you could use any small object that reminds you of Satan. Black obsidian comes from a once-live volcano and is included for its fiery, hellish connection. You can also personalize this charm in any way you see fit. You can add the petals of your favorite flower or a bit of an herb that is meaningful to you.

Place all the items in the center of the cloth, then tie it up with string to make a little bundle. Keep this charm in your bag or pocket. Any time you find your mind drifting off to unrealistic scenarios, rub it between your fingers and remember where you are right now.

UNPACKING DISDAIN

One interesting way to identify your own shadow is to consider what characteristics you disdain in others, especially if you can't pinpoint the reason. (I don't mean when a person has caused obvious, legitimate harm, in which case the reason you disdain them is clear and justified.) For example, if you were taught very young that asking for help was not acceptable, you may be annoyed when you witness someone else doing it and label them needy. If you learned that speaking up was rude, you might find those who self-advocate abrasive. Sometimes there is a reason that the traits of others bother you that can be found deep down inside the self. Once you identify it, you can pull it out and deal with it. Again, this is not in reference to people who have abused you in any way but to smaller interactions in life that leave you feeling negative.

Try this exercise as an experiment to gain some insight into yourself. It's especially helpful to do if you are repeatedly having a negative emotional reaction to the same minor things again and again. Please note that if the feelings you're dealing with are major, such as rage that interferes with your daily life, this ritual is not the answer, and you might consider professional assistance.

Before you begin, make a list of words describing the person or scenario.

Materials

Piece of paper cut into the shape of a person or a clay or cloth doll that
    resembles someone who annoys you
Markers or paint
Sewing pins

Write the descriptors from your list onto the figure with the marker or paint. Take a pin and poke it into one of the words you have written. Think hard about the ways this word affects you and whether or not you have felt this way at other points in your life. Be honest. Repeat this with each of the words, stabbing a pin into each one and contemplating whether or not you can identify it in your past. When you are finished, you may have gained some insight and even developed a bit of empathy for the person in question. This doesn't mean you have to forgive or befriend them. The point of the exercise is to seek self-knowledge.

Burn the figure or destroy it in some way and dispose of it.

PARASITES

When you are doing shadow work, it's common to gain a new perspective on existing relationships. Sadly, sometimes you'll realize that some are one-sided or unhealthy. One of the worst feelings in the world is the realization that someone is using you. Sometimes it's obvious because you only hear from them when they need money and favors. Other times it is more subtle and insidious, which in some ways makes it worse. Emotional users will cling to you like you're a life raft in a sea of their self-imposed drama. This kind of user is difficult to spot at first because they play on your empathy, making you feel a need to help, guide, or rescue them. Often they use up a lot of your energy. While at times it's appropriate to be a shoulder to cry on and offer support, it can cross into exhausting territory. It's hard to free yourself from this situation because of guilt and obligation, but at some point, you must ask yourself, what do they offer you? If the answer is nothing, it's time to build the courage to set them loose in their roiling ocean of theatrics. Don't worry; they'll latch on to the next person who comes along. On a sidenote, there is a big difference between a user and someone who is your responsibility or a dependent.

Materials
Black chime candle
Sharp object for carving the candle
Bowl of dirt and salt
3 drops of your choice of oil

Carve your name into the candle. This candle represents you. Rub the oil all over the outside of it and then roll it in the bowl of dirt and salt until it's completely covered. The dirt represents the user who clings to you. Notice how the dirt gathers in the carving of your name, much like the person has embedded themselves in your mental space. Contemplate this for a moment. Light the candle and place it in a holder. As the fire burns, it symbolizes you shedding the parasites that have clung to you.

Anytime you are feeling used and resentful or guilty, repeat this ritual to strengthen your resolve.

BUILDING AN ALTAR TO THE DEVIL

At this point in your exploration, it's a good time to start putting some action behind what you've learned. One way to do this is to build a simple altar to the devil. This will deepen your understanding of what he means to you and possibly lead you to try some of the rituals in this book. This includes the earlier workings in this chapter that are specifically related to looking within the shadow to create self-awareness, one of the keystones of Satanism.

There are three kinds of satanic or devilish altars in my mind. There is the traditional altar based on LaVey's Satanism, a slightly different altar of Luciferianism, and then the altar that you make up yourself. If you're new to altars and witchcraft, it's helpful to have some kind of inspiration from other practitioners. However, to create an altar with objects that have no meaning for you is somewhat pointless. If you find a wand silly or off-putting, it won't make sense to keep one on your altar just because a book told you to. Nevertheless, it doesn't hurt to know what these objects are for. Even if you don't include them on your altar, they might give you some ideas.

The purpose of an altar is to function as a personal place of power. This power is not necessarily some outside force or energy but something within you that you harness and give a physical form. Choose meaningful symbols and objects for your altar that elicit positive emotions. Every time you look at it, you will feel a sense of empowerment. The altar is a place for magic, for ritual, or just to sit and think, strengthening your resolve when facing life's challenges.

First, I'll give a brief overview of a "traditional" altar based on old-school Satanism, then some information about Luciferian altars, and then some ideas for creating your own. You may wish to integrate all, some, or none of the elements described here.

LaVey's Altar

LaVey based a lot of his rituals on ceremonial magic mixed with details from literature and history. While you may not approve of LaVey, it's worth contemplating his style of altar and noticing which bits of history inspired it. Instead of a table, his altar was sometimes a consenting naked woman lying on her back. Ceremonies were carried out on her abdomen, just like in the alleged Black Mass during the Affair of the Poisons.

There was a picture or sculpture of Baphomet present, and candles were lit to represent the light of Lucifer. Only black candles were to be used in ritual and for illuminating the room, except for a single white candle. A black candle was placed to the left of the altar to represent the left-hand path. The white candle was placed to the right to represent the "hypocrisy of white light 'magicians' and the followers of the right-hand path."[278]

On the altar were several things hearkening back to ceremonial magic. A chalice was required, but it must *not* be made of gold, as gold was associated with the heavenly realm. Any other material was acceptable.[279] There was a phallic symbol, which could be any object of the appropriate shape, to represent aggression and fertility. Also signifying aggression was a sword, which was used much like a wand to direct energy. Gongs and bells were on hand to be rung at the beginning and end of ceremonies. Last was parchment made from sheepskin for writing curses or requests on.

In addition to these things, LaVey emphasized the benefit of choosing your own altar ideas, such as pictures and scents, to intensify the emotions needed for the ritual.

---

278. LaVey, *The Satanic Bible*, 137.
279. LaVey, *The Satanic Bible*, 137.

Luciferian Altar

Luciferianism is much more complicated than Satanism, and the meanings attributed to altar tools are many-layered. Here is an extremely simplified explanation of what you might find on a Luciferian altar and why.

Here too is a chalice and parchment, but instead of a sword, there is an athame or dagger that represents the power within the magician as either air or fire, based on ceremonial magic and the magician's goal.[280] There is also a wand representing the will of the practitioner and a disk or picture of the inverted pentagram symbolizing carnality, the womb, the physical realm, and self-mastery.

Unlike LaVey's altar, different colors of candles can be used depending on the purpose of the ritual.

Personal Altar

The third kind of altar, and the most powerful in my opinion, is the one you create based on your own desires, will, and beliefs. Many of the above tools, like chalices and swords, are elements of ceremonial magic. If they have meaning to you, then, by all means, include them.

Your altar should be as visually appealing to you as possible. If it aligns with your personal sense of beauty, you will feel good when you spend time there, and that is at the top of the list of reasons for having an altar in this context.

If you're not versed in ceremonial magic and take a more individualistic approach, as I do, here are some suggestions for building your own altar to the devil in whatever form you understand him to be.

- A statue or picture of the devil. To some, this could be a representation of the folkloric devil, a goat, or a picture of Baphomet.
- Candles. For providing light, use the color of candle you personally prefer. While I understand the idea behind black candles, not everyone enjoys that look. If you like pink, use pink ones. In fact, make the whole altar pink if you want. This altar is

---

280. Ford, *Apotheosis*, 149.

all about you and your personal power. Include a single candle that is noticeably unique from the others to represent the light of Lucifer or the fire of Satan. This candle might be a different color, a special shape, scented, or whatever you like. I use a yellow or red seven-day candle in glass that is painted with symbols representing my ideals, which I light at each session and extinguish in between.

- An offering dish. Even if you don't believe in the actual existence of the devil, placing incense, coins, or wine in front of the statue or image can be affirming to your beliefs. In its most atheist form, it could be thought of as an offering to the self since the devil, in this case, represents individualism. Put something you love there, like a shot of your favorite whiskey or candy. Otherwise, you can think of it as an offering to the devil in whatever form you feel he takes.

- An inverted pentagram. The inverted pentagram reminds you that you are focused on the here and now, on real goals. You are embracing your human and animal self and are not putting spirituality on an unreachable pedestal. It's a reminder that you can materially change your own life and do as you will. Like the horns of an aggressive goat, which fit nicely into the two uppermost points of the star, you will push forward to fight for what you desire on the material plane, taking concrete action to achieve it.

- Things that make you happy. If you are proud of a diploma you've earned or a painting you created, why not put it on the altar? If you like bones and skulls, include them. The same applies to flowers, kittens, and sparkles if that's what you're into. Add whatever creates an aesthetic that you love.

- Objects or images aligned with your will. If your will is to achieve wealth, you could have a money symbol on the altar. If you are seeking a sexual partner, make like a witch and put an image of a phallus or vulva on it. Be creative, and don't worry about what anyone else thinks. It's not about them.

Now that you have an altar set up, you can try out some simple rituals at your altar, like those mentioned earlier. If it's your first time doing so, it may take a while to get comfortable. Allowing yourself to be fully emotionally immersed in a symbolic act during a ritual doesn't come easily to everyone and might take some practice.

◆ ◆ ◆ ◆ ◆

Lucifer is the light-bringer. As such, he can shine knowledge upon the darkest corners of the self, allowing you to see the full truth. This helps you identify your will and pursue it.

Discovering the shadow self is not unlike eating from the Tree of Knowledge. Everything is just hunky-dory so long as we don't bite into the real truth. What you discover in the shadow self may at first seem like pain and hardship, just as when Eve ate the apple and her eyes were opened to the human condition. What the story left out is just how many positive, amazing things come with knowledge.

CHAPTER 9

SATANIC SIGILS AND SYMBOLS

There are many seemingly random concepts in Western culture that are considered devilish. Certain words, objects, and symbols are seared into our subconscious as being satanic, but we don't necessarily know *why* the association is there.

Symbols are of great importance to people, religious or not. Consider how a shape or design can elicit a collective response, such as a national flag. A symbol triggers a strong emotion or, at the very least, makes us think of a certain thing. This chapter will explore the well-known symbols of the devil and Satan, explaining their origins and significance.

666

The number 666 was popularized by Aleister Crowley, who called himself "the Beast 666," although he did not create the infernal number's significance.

There is a widespread theory that the number is associated with Roman Emperor Nero because some versions of that name, when transliterated in Hebrew from letters into numbers, loosely made up the number 666. Nero happened to be the first Roman emperor to persecute Christians, which may have had something to do with him receiving the number of the Antichrist.

The book of Revelation says, "Let him that hath understanding count the number of the beast: for it is the number of a man; and his number *is* Six hundred threescore *and* six."[281] It also says that anyone who worships the beast, or image of the beast, will have the number permanently stamped on their head or hand and be tormented with fire and sulfur for eternity.[282]

666 Symbol

While Crowley labeled himself with the number 666 to identify as a beast, he also did so based on its meaning in the Kabbalah, in which the number denotes the creation of a perfect world and all life on earth. But due to its association with the Antichrist, 666 has a bad rap on par with the unlucky number thirteen.

BAPHOMET

Baphomet, who has come to symbolize Satanism, is a nonbinary figure designed by Éliphas Lévi.

In the 1300s, a military order called the Knights Templar was accused of heresy by King Philip IV of France. The knights were subjected to torture and forced to confess that they worshipped a horned, four-legged devilish idol, later called Baphomet. They were also coerced into admitting they had sex with demons, rubbed baby's lard on Baphomet's head, and trampled on the cross.[283]

What some people may not realize is that there is a lot more to Baphomet than meets the eye beyond their scary appearance.

Every part of Baphomet's form holds significance. They have a goat's head, horns, weirdly human eyes, an upright pentagram on their fore-

---

281. Revelation 13:18 (King James Version).
282. Revelation 13:15–17 (King James Version).
283. Faxneld, *Satanic Feminism*, 53.

head, and a flame between their horns. One arm points up, the other down, with two pointing fingers. They have feathered wings, breasts, cloven hooves, and a caduceus in their lap.

All these things come together to convey the union and balance of opposites, microcosm and macrocosm, and the universal life force.

Baphomet

In the original drawing of Baphomet, the background shows a white moon above the figure and a black moon below it, which represent mercy and justice. Baphomet has one male arm and one female arm, unifying genders. On one arm is the word *solve*; on the other, *coagula*. *Solve et coagula* is a principle in alchemy that means dissolve and coagulate. According to this principle, a substance must be broken down for something new to appear, encapsulating the symbiotic relationship between destruction and creation. One arm points to the sky and the other to the earth, meaning "as above, so below." The hands have two fingers outreached in what Lévi called the "sign of the occultist." The breasts represent humanity and the caduceus, eternal life. On Baphomet's forehead is an upright pentagram, which means soul over matter. The scales near the caduceus signify water, and the semicircle above the scales is the atmosphere. There are snakes entwined around the caduceus, which are the two currents of magnetism: one is a serpent of light and creation and the other is of fire and destruction. The wings stand for the volatile. Lévi said the goat's head was "the horror of sin," or earthly matters and flesh. Between the horns is a torch bearing the flame of intelligence.[284]

Today, Baphomet is perhaps most well-known to the public in connection to The Satanic Temple, which built a gigantic, solid bronze statue of the idol. This glorious monstrosity stands on display in the temple today, with people traveling to Salem to see it in person.

Baphomet has become almost mainstream. You can find plush toys and even socks bearing their image.

THE GOAT

The goat is known as Satan's best friend for a myriad of reasons. This partnership can be traced to the Bible and to folklore told by rural people, for many of whom the goat was an everyday part of farm life. Goats were considered a lowly, dirty kind of animal due to their voracious sexual appetites and mischievous personalities. They're also pretty famous for being stubborn and difficult to control. Then there are the horns and hooves, which perhaps connected them to some of the older gods too.

In the Old Testament, there is a story about two goats.[285] One goat was named Yahweh and dedicated to the Lord. This goat was blessed and sacrificed. The other goat, named Azazel, was symbolically loaded with

---

284. Éliphas Lévi, *Transcendental Magic: Its Doctrine and Ritual*, trans. Arthur Edward Waite (London: Rider and Co., 1896), 377–78.

285. Leviticus 16:5–26 (King James Version).

the sins of the community and cast out into the desert to die, taking all the problems of the people with him. This is where the term scapegoat comes from.[286]

In scripture, there's a notable difference between sheep and goats. Sheep are dependent on and trust their leader, the shepherd. They stay with the herd at all costs, never questioning what direction they're headed in. Goats, on the other hand, are nearly impossible to control. In the book of Matthew, there is a reference to the Son of Man separating the goats from the sheep on Judgment Day. He puts the sheep to his right and the goats to his left. The sheep inherit the kingdom and go forth into heaven as a reward for their good behavior. The goats do not.[287]

Another old story that brings the goat and the devil together is a Grimm fairy tale called "The Lord's Animals and the Devils." In it, God creates all the animals but forgets to make goats. The devil decides to make them himself, giving them great long tails. When he discovers that these long tails get caught in hedges all the time, he becomes frustrated with having to untangle them and bites them all off. Over time, God notices that the goats have destroyed many of his plants and trees. He summons some wolves, who tear the goats to smithereens. The devil confronts God, asking why he'd do such a thing. God answers that the goats only caused trouble and nothing more. The devil's defense is that he, himself, is made of trouble, so everything he creates will be too. He demands money for the damage done to his goats. God promises that when the oak trees lose all their leaves, he will pay the devil. In the autumn, the devil comes to collect, but God tells him there is still one single oak tree with its leaves, that can be found in a church in Constantinople. In a fit of rage, the devil stomps off to find this tree, which takes him six months. When he finally returns, all the trees have once again opened their leaves. He has been fooled. He gets so angry that he pokes out the eyes of all his

---

286. Hope Bolinger, "Why Is Satan Depicted as a Goat in Scripture?" Crosswalk, October 12, 2020, https://www.crosswalk.com/faith/bible-study/why-satan-shows-up-as-a -goat-in-scripture.html.

287. Matthew 25:32–46 (King James Version).

goats and puts his own eyes into their heads instead. This story, according to the Grimms, explains why the devil has such a fondness for goats and why they have devil's eyes and short tails.[288]

GOAT HANDS

You've probably seen the infamous hand gesture for the devil: thumb, middle, and ring finger tucked in, with the pointer finger and pinkie sticking up, creating what looks like a goat's head. While many of us equate this gesture with the devil because of its shape and association with heavy metal music, its origins are far removed from that.

In Italy, the gesture is made to invoke the strength of a bull while repelling the evil eye and bad luck. In this case, it's done with the hand facing down. Upright, the gesture is called "cuckold's horns" and mocks someone whose partner is cheating on them.[289] It's considered very insulting to aim it at someone.

So how did this hand gesture go from its original meaning to a sign of the devil? Some say it can be accredited to heavy metal musician Ronnie James Dio who, in 1979, walked on stage at a Black Sabbath concert making the hand gesture at the audience. When asked if the gesture was satanic, he said no, explaining that he'd learned it from his Italian grandmother.[290]

However, it seems heavy metal fans preferred the satanic version, and that's what took hold instead. I suppose one could say that context matters when it comes to throwing the horns.

INVERTED CROSS

The inverted crucifix is usually considered a form of blasphemy and a symbol of anti-Christian belief. It was popularized in the 1980s during

---

288. Jacob Grimm and Wilhelm Grimm, *Grimm's Household Tales*, trans. Margaret Hunt, vol. 2 (London: George Bell and Sons, 1884), 217–18.

289. Emma Garland, "Throwing the 'Metal Horns' Is the Same as Calling Someone a Cuck," Vice, February 2, 2018, https://www.vice.com/en/article/a34wk8/throwing-the-metal-horns-is-the-same-as-calling-someone-a-cuck.

290. EvilG, "Ronnie James Dio," Metal-Rules.com, September 14, 2006, https://www.metal-rules.com/2006/09/14/ronnie-james-dio-2/.

the satanic panic when cult "experts" listed the inverted crucifix as one of the signs that your teenager was a secret devil worshiper.

Éliphas Lévi credited prophet and spiritual leader Eugène Vintras (1807–75) with the inverted cross. Vintras included it in his ceremonies, wherein he allegedly manifested miracles, caused the host to sweat blood, and made wine appear.[291] This character is a story in and of himself, but for now, we'll leave it at that.

The inverted cross is not always considered anticlerical. It is also the cross of St. Peter, the apostle who requested to be crucified upside down because he didn't consider himself worthy of dying the same way Jesus did.

For many people, wearing the inverted cross is a statement rejecting the moral code of the church and a symbol of rebellion against oppressive teachings that stem from it.

THE LEVIATHAN CROSS

Leviathan is a biblical and mythological sea serpent that represents chaos and envy and is considered a demon in some cases.

The Leviathan cross, also called Satan's cross, is the old alchemical symbol for brimstone. Hell is said to be filled with burning brimstone, frying away the sins of its inhabitants and letting off the stench of sulfur, which is similar to rotten eggs. The term *fire and brimstone* is used to describe the kind of preaching that focuses on hell and damnation.

Leviathan Cross

291. Éliphas Lévi, *The Mysteries of Magic: A Digest of the Writings of Éliphas Lévi*, ed. Arthur Edward Waite, 2nd ed (London: Kegan Paul, Trench, Trübner & Co., 1897), 460–61.

The infinity symbol at the base of the cross, which looks like an eight on its side, represents the sea serpent and the never-ending cycle of death and rebirth, destruction and creation. The double-armed cross is sometimes viewed as an equal sign, representing equality.

THE PENTAGRAM

The upright pentagram, with one point at the top, is popularly known as a positive symbol in contemporary witchcraft. The points represent earth, air, fire, and water, with the uppermost point meaning spirit. In some ways, this conveys that spirituality is above earthly realms and, to some, considered more important.

Image 3: Upright Pentagram

When the pentagram is inverted with one point down, it places matter above spirit. That's why it is associated with Satan.

Image 4: Inverted Pentagram

Occultist Éliphas Lévi wrote that the upright pentagram represented Christ, while the two points of the inverted pentagram were the horns of a goat. He wrote, "The pentagram, when pointing two of its rays upwards, represents Satan or the goat of the sabbath, and it represents the Saviour when it points a single ray upward."[292] This meaning makes the inverted pentagram alluring for those who are against all forms of religion and spirituality, like some Satanists.

The inverted pentagram has changed a little since Lévi's explanation and isn't typically associated with Jesus anymore. It's been embraced by occultists, witches, and Satanists as representing materiality and reason over blind faith.

SIGIL OF BAPHOMET

The Sigil of Baphomet is the official logo for the Church of Satan. The sigil is based on a drawing in *Le Serpent de La Genese: La Clef de La Magie Noire* by Stanislas Guaita, which depicts a goat's head inside two circles with the words Samael and Lilith.[293] Hebrew letters on the points of the stars spell *Leviathan*. This drawing was based on the descriptions of the pentagram by Levi. This sigil encompasses all the meanings of the inverted pentagram, along with some of LaVey's own beliefs.

The horned goat within an inverted pentagram has become a symbol for Satanism in general and is also seen in the logo for The Satanic Temple.

Sigil of Baphomet by Stanislas de Guaita (1897)

292. Lévi, *The Doctrine and Ritual of High Magic: A New Translation*, 240.

293. Stanislas Guaita, *Le Serpent de La Genese: La Clef de La Magie Noir (Livre II)* (1897; repr. Paris: Henri Durville, 1920), 417.

THE SIGIL OF LUCIFER

The sigil of Lucifer was discovered in the eighteenth century in the *Grimorium Verum*, which means the "True Grimoire." This grimoire of ceremonial magic contained lists of demons and instructions for summoning them. One was Lucifer with his accompanying sigil.[294]

Sigil of Lucifer

There are various interpretations of this sigil and what each of the lines and shapes signify. It resembles a chalice, which means creation. It's said that the X represents the earth and material plane, the upside-down triangle means life-giving water, and the V at the bottom indicates the balance of opposites.

A more complex theory connects this sigil to the pineal gland, which many people know as the third eye. In *Treatise on the Human Mind* (1664) by Louis de La Forge, a very old book about the human body and nervous system, there is an illustration about the pineal gland and mind-body dualism that looks an awful lot like the sigil of Lucifer.[295] This connection is only theoretical, but the concept of a third eye and the pineal gland is widespread, holding spiritual significance in many cultures. For this reason, the sigil of Lucifer may be loosely based on it.

---

294. Joseph H. Peterson, trans., *Grimorium Verum: A Handbook of Black Magic* ([1517?]; repr., Scotts Valley, CA: self-pub., CreateSpace Publishing, 2007), 12.

295. Louis de La Forge, *Traitté de l'esprit de l'homme: De ses facultez et fonctions, et de son union avec le corps* (Paris: Michel Bobin & Nicholas le Gras, 1666), 327.

Louis de La Forge's Pineal Gland Diagram

The pineal gland contains cones and rods like our regular eyes and can therefore detect light, further linking it to Lucifer. Information about the pineal gland is mostly mystical, and it's believed to bring about spiritual enlightenment when fully functioning. In other words, bringing light, knowledge, and inspiration, just like our friend Lucifer.

CHAPTER 10

THE DEVIL'S APOTHECARY

For a long time, I've been fascinated by plants with *devil* in their name. Curious to know the story behind them, I started digging around and built a list. Some are associated with the archfiend because they're poisonous, prickly, or smelly. Other times, the link seems quite random and the folklore illogical. If you're like me, you'll enjoy this section of devilish plants for curiosity's sake, or if you're a practicing witch, you might discover some new herbs and roots to add to your collection. Most of the plants on the list have *devil* in their title, and those that don't come with relevant folklore attached to them.

I should mention that, like many people, I believe in making magical use of the plants that grow in my own area. You'll notice some on this list are expensive or hard to find. Don't feel obligated to seek out pricey plant materials from the other side of the globe unless that is what makes them feel powerful to you. Many of the herbs listed here can be swapped for something more accessible. For example, many of the devil's plants are named so because they're invasive, and there's no shortage of invasive species all around you to choose from.

Many plants on this list are poisonous, so be sure to use caution if you choose to handle them. Others, like apples and parsley, are perfectly harmless.

Apple (*Malus domestica*): Also known as fruit of the underworld, the apple is what started the whole debacle in the Garden of Eden. It's the fruit of carnal knowledge and is associated with sexuality. Apples are often included in love spells, and they pop up as symbols everywhere from old fairy tales to modern movies. In the Middle Ages in Europe, it was said that the devil would approach a girl in the dead of the night for sexual relations. As a token of his affection, he would give her an apple with a worm in it.[296] The apple revealed the law of gravity to Newton, linking it to enlightenment, which fits our understanding of Lucifer as a light-bringer. It was said that you should always wipe an apple clean before eating it because if you didn't, you were challenging the devil.[297]

Blackberry (*Rubus*): Also known as briar, bramble, and thimbleberry, the blackberry is a common thing to find in the grocery store, but according to English folklore, Lucifer became entangled in a blackberry bush upon his expulsion from heaven. In a fit of rage, he urinated on it, spat on it, and cursed it so its berries would not be edible. In some parts of England, the berries are never eaten after Michaelmas (September 29), which was when he was said to have fallen.[298] After the first frost, blackberries' flavor does change, and they're no longer good to eat, as they start to decay and grow mold, lending some credence to the story.

Creeping Devil Cactus (*Stenocereus eruca*): This creepy cactus is known for moving along the deserts of northwestern Mex-

---

296. Venetia Newell, *An Egg at Easter: A Folklore Study* (London: Routledge & Keagan Paul, 1971), 70.

297. D.C. Watts, *Dictionary of Plant Lore* (San Diego, CA: Elsevier, 2007), 11.

298. Mary Beth Albright, "Michaelmas: The Day the Devil Spit on Your Blackberries," *National Geographic*, September 28, 2015, https://www.nationalgeographic.com /culture/article/michaelmas-the-day-the-devil-spit-on-your-blackberries.

ico like a very slow animal. It resembles a tangle of snakes lying low to the ground. It pulls itself along by laying down new roots while simultaneously killing off old ones. In this way, it appears to be a sinister, serpentine creature slowly slithering along the sand.

Devil Chaser (*Dipsacus*): Also known as teasel, this thorny plant, native to Russia, has a blue flower. It was said that when a person was in mourning, they could keep the devil away from the soul of the departed by waving a sprig of this flower and chewing camphor seeds while combing the hair of the deceased.[299]

Devil's Backbone (*Polemonium*): Also known as Jacob's ladder, devil's ribcage, devil's spine, and slipper plant, the devil's backbone is a common garden plant named for its thick, zigzagging stems that resemble bones. It's interesting that it has so many devilish names, because the story of Jacob's ladder is about the connection between humans and the divine. I suppose, like everything, it's a matter of how you choose to look at it.

Devil's Bit (*Scabiosa*): Also known as scabious and pincushion flower, this pretty purple garden flower has dark-colored roots that appear short or cut off. English legend has it that these roots could cure skin conditions in humans, so the devil bit them off to prevent people from healing.

Devil's Butter (*Tremella mesenterica*): Also known as witches' butter, this yellow, jelly-like fungus was said to contain an evil spirit that would harm farm animals and was therefore burned when it appeared.[300] Devil's butter grows out of dry wood like door frames and gateposts. In Eastern European folklore, its appearance meant your house had been cursed, and to counter

---

299. Richard Folkard, *Plant Lore, Legends and Lyrics: Embracing the Myths, Traditions, Superstitions, and Folk-Lore of the Plant Kingdom* (London, 1884), 86.
300. Boyer, *Plants of the Devil*, 27.

the curse, you must drain the fungus with a pin or other sharp object.[301] The problem is this fungus lives inside the wood, and once it's taken hold, it will keep coming back.

Devil's Cactus (*Opuntia*): Also known as prickly pear cactus, devil's cactus is so invasive across America that it's illegal to possess in some areas. It's known for destroying agriculture, hurting wildlife, and injuring the mouths of grazing farm animals.

Devil's Cherries (*Atropa*): The devil's cherries are also called belladonna, deadly nightshade, devil's rhubarb, and Satan's cherries. Long ago, parents warned their children that if they touched the berries of the deadly belladonna plant, they would find themselves face-to-face with the devil. According to folklore from Bohemia, the devil watched over this plant, and the only way to dispose of it was to let a black hen loose on your property on Walpurgis Night (April 30). While the devil was distracted by the hen, the plant could be uprooted and thrown away.[302] Belladonna was a popular ingredient in flying ointment, and those who experienced its poison claimed they could feel themselves growing fur and transforming into animals.[303] The berries are supposed to be incredibly sweet but deadly, encapsulating temptation and its consequences.

Devil's Claw (*Harpagophytum procumbens*): Also known as grapple plant and wood spider, the devil's claw plant is native to southern Africa and bears fruit that is covered in little hooks that resemble claws. When dried, the fruit is used in medicine,

---

301. Thomas Roehl, "#059 *Tremella mesenterica*, Witch's Butter," Fungus Fact Friday, last modified October 20, 2017, https://www.fungusfactfriday.com/059-tremella -mesenterica/.

302. Charles M. Skinner, *Myths and Legends of Flowers, Trees, Fruits, and Plants in All Ages and in All Climes* (Philadelphia, PA: J. B. Lippincott Company, 1911), 30.

303. Watts, *Dictionary of Plant Lore*, 102.

but it has a particularly sinister look to it. Devil's claw root is used for protection magic.

Devil's Claw Root

Devil's Cotton (*Abroma augusta*): Also known as abroma, when fully opened, this unusual tropical flower contains a web of fibrous hairs that are extremely irritating to the skin. It's sort of like opening a beautiful flower to find a noxious spider and its web inside. The terrible fibers resemble cotton, which is where it got its name. One might be tempted to touch the soft-looking fibers, only to be in for a painful surprise.

Devil's Droppings: *Devil's droppings* refers to mushrooms and fungus in general, perhaps because they grow in animal waste and decaying, dark places.

Devil's Dung (*Ferula assa-foetida*): Devil's dung, or asafetida, is a gum that is extracted from a type of fennel. It naturally contains sulfur and smells terrible when broken open. Another name for sulfur is brimstone. The phrase *fire and brimstone* is often used when speaking of eternal damnation, hell, and the wrath of God. It's said that hell smells of burning sulfur, in reference to the burning rock beneath the earth.

Devil's Dye (*Indigofera*): This plant, also known as indigo, has purple flowers that, when processed correctly, produce a dark blue dye. During the reign of Elizabeth I, it was called "food for the devil."[304] King Henry IV of France threatened the death sentence for anyone found to be using indigo dye, claiming it was extremely harmful. In truth, it was because indigo was competition for local dye from a flower called woad. Simply calling it "devil's dye" would have been effective in keeping people away from it at that time.

Devil's Eyelash (*Tribulus terrestris*): Also known as goat's head, devil's thorn, and puncture vine, the devil's eyelash is an invasive weed that grows in dry, warm parts of the world. It produces burs with four sturdy, sharp spines. They're so strong that they've been known to puncture shoes and even wheels. The burs, which injure the mouths of livestock, look like goat heads. While there's not much folklore to be found about the devil's eyelash, its sharpness and goatlike appearance make it ideal for devilish or baneful magic.

Devil's Eyes (*Hyoscyamus*): Native to Europe and Siberia, devil's eyes, or henbane flowers, are yellow with black centers. Henbane was a common ingredient in flying ointments, a poison that when put on the genitals or armpits was said to create the feeling of flying. Perhaps it gets the name devil's eyes because it allows a person to see through the eyes of a witch as they fly to the Sabbath.

Devil's Fingers (*Phallaceae*): Also known as stinkhorn fungus, devil's horn, and octopus stinkhorn, this fungus grows around the world but mostly in tropical regions. It smells of rotten flesh and grows in appendages that resemble fingers. It is birthed out of a slimy sack of gel, giving it the appearance of something alien. Its terrible stench attracts flies and worms. The fungus is a devilish red color with black bits on it that resemble coal. There doesn't seem to be much folklore regarding this fungus, so one

---

304. Watts, *Dictionary of Plant Lore*, 207–8.

can surmise that it gets its name from its color, stink, and disturbing appearance.

Devil's Fingers, or Stinkhorn Fungus

Devil's Flight (*Hypericum perforatum*): More commonly known as St. John's wort, this plant is best known for its medicinal use as an antidepressant. This plant has yellow flowers and is said to fight off demons and evil spirits.[305]

Devil's Flower (*Centaurea cyanus*): Also known as bachelor's button, cornflower, and hurtsickle, this small blue flower was carried by men for love and divination. In Europe, it was worn to signify if they were single or interested in a partner. If the flower wilted too quickly, it meant that his love would go unrequited. Sometimes, the flowers also stood for bitter singleness or being thwarted in love. This flower is native to the United Kingdom and is a common garden plant.

Devil's Fuge (*Viscum album*): Devil's fuge is most well-known as mistletoe. "Fuge" means to drive something away—in this case, Satan. Pliny claimed it had been used in ancient druid rituals.[306] In the Middle Ages, mistletoe was forbidden in churches

305. Folkard, *Plant Lore, Legends and Lyrics*, 52.

306. Pliny, *Natural History, Volume IV, Books XII–XVI*, Loeb Classical Library 370, ed. H. Rackham (1945; repr., Cambridge, MA: Harvard University Press, 1960), 549.

because of its Pagan associations. It is a berry-producing parasitic vine that latches onto trees, feeding on them until they die.

Devil's Guts (*Cuscuta americana*): Also known as dodder, devil's threads, devil's nets, devil's hair, and devil's ringlets, this plant belongs to the morning glory family and is an invasive plant that will take over entire gardens across North America and Europe. It survives by sending out a tiny vine that attaches itself to a plant, on which it feeds. Once established, it will detach from the earth and survive by sucking the life out of the host plant. Its stringy vines look like guts or hair.

Devil's Helmet (*Aconitum*): Also known as aconite, wolfsbane, and monkshood, this deadly, poisonous plant grows in Europe, Asia, and North America. The flowers look like a cluster of hooded heads in prayer or like helmets. The devil's helmet is said to ward off werewolves, probably because it was also used to poison real wolves in North America and Europe. It was put into raw meat and left out as bait.[307]

Devil's Horn (*Proboscidea louisianica*): This flowering bush, also known as ram's horn, is native to Mexico and Texas. It produces fruit that, when dried, splits into two to release its seeds. Afterward, the dried seed pod looks like curved horns. The leaves and stems are covered with foul-smelling slime, and the dried pods become sharp, protruding hooks. They can be painful when they latch onto a person or animal. All these unpleasant qualities combined are probably how it earned its name.

---

307. Raychelle Burks, "The Dead of Aconite," Chemistry World, October 22, 2021, https://www.chemistryworld.com/opinion/the-dead-of-aconite/4014423.article.

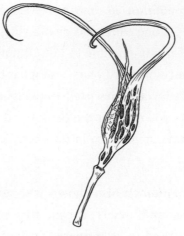

Devil's Horn

Devil in the Bush (*Nigella damascena*): Native to the Mediterranean and North Africa, the flowers on this bush are surrounded by leaves with soft, thread-like spikes, which appear to either imprison the flowers or embrace them, depending on your intentions. In this way, the plant can be a trickster, like the devil. It's also known as love-in-a-mist and Jack-in-a-tangle. From the names and appearance of this flower, we can see that, just like love, it can be either wonderful or terrible. Used in love spells, it would be extremely binding and harsh. To me, devil in the bush signifies rejection in love or manipulation in relationships.

Devil in the Bush

Devil's Ivy (*Epipremnum pinnatum*): Also known as golden pothos, centipede tongavine, and devil's vine, this long, trailing houseplant is nearly impossible to kill. I know because I've had the same one for twenty-five years, and it has been through a lot. In nature, devil's ivy attaches itself to plants above ground and then sends fibers down under the earth to take root and spread. It thrives and stays green even in darkness, lending it a sinister aura.

Devil's Leaf (*Urtica dioica*): Also known as stinging nettle, naughty man's plaything, and devil's apron, this plant has invasive weedy leaves covered in little fibers that irritate the skin when touched. It is said that when Satan and the other fallen angels landed on earth, stinging nettle sprang up wherever they stepped. There's also a morbid rumor that it grew out of the bones of dead bodies.[308] In another story, an angel happened upon the devil, who was singing about the fields of oats and buckwheat. The angel was afraid that the devil would steal the crops from humans, leaving them to go hungry. So the angel started singing about thistles and nettles to confuse Satan, causing him to accidentally do the same. The fields turned into nettles, and the devil was so angry that he bestowed them with stinging, itching properties. Stinging nettle grows all over North America.

Devil's Milk (*Ranunculus ficaria*): Also known as celandine, pilewort, fig buttercup, and crow's feet, this invasive yellow flower, which grows mostly in the north temperate zone, has poisonous milky juices in its stems and leaves that can kill animals when eaten, and it causes an itchy rash when touched. It's said that

---

308. Watts, *Dictionary of Plant Lore*, 264.

beggars stomped on the leaves to create blisters on their feet and arms, eliciting pity so people would give them more money.[309]

Devil's Nettle (*Achillea millefolium*): Also called yarrow and devil's plaything, this plant is a common perennial with various colors of flowers. Yarrow was believed to be the devil's favorite plant, although it is unclear where this belief originated or why. In Irish folklore, no illness could withstand its virtuous healing powers.[310] Strangely, it's also believed to disperse evil spirits. Yarrow is often used in love divination and love spells.

Devil's Nightcap (*Stellaria holostea*): Also known as stitchwort, devil's ears, devil's eyes, and addersmeat, this common wildflower is believed to be protected by fairies who will snatch you away if you dare to pick it.[311] In Cornish folklore, it is said that if you pick the devil's nightcap, you'll be bitten by a snake.

Devil's Oatmeal (*Petroselinum crispum*): It's surprising how much superstition there is regarding parsley, an ordinary leafy green herb that can be found in any grocery store or garden. According to German folklore, it was incredibly bad luck to transplant the devil's oatmeal, or parsley, because you or someone you knew would die. There was a medieval belief that you could kill someone by saying their name while simultaneously pulling parsley out of the ground. Planting the seeds was dangerous and had to be done by placing them on a page of the Bible and then blowing them onto the earth.[312] For extra precaution, it was advised that you plant the seeds on Good Friday and then douse them with boiling water. Parsley seed takes a long time to sprout and grow because, it's said, it has to go to the devil and back

---

309. Watts, *Dictionary of Plant Lore*, 52.
310. Jane Wilde, *Ancient Legends, Mystic Charms, and Superstitions of Ireland*, vol. 1 (Boston, MA: Ticknore and Co., 1887), 198.
311. Skinner, *Myths and Legends of Flowers, Trees, Fruits, and Plants*, 23.
312. Watts, *Dictionary of Plant Lore*, 285.

nine times before flourishing above ground.[313] Another belief was that only witches could successfully grow parsley, and if a virgin planted the seeds, she would be impregnated with Satan's offspring.

Devil's Paintbrush (*Hieracium aurantiacum*): Also known as fox and cubs and orange hawkweed, this flower is bright orange like fire and tends to aggressively overtake meadows and fields, somewhat like flames spreading. One can imagine the devil sweeping a brush across the canvas of a field, spreading fire-colored pests. It is native to central and southern Europe.

Devil's Pumpkin (*Passiflora suberosa*): Another parasite, the devil's pumpkin, also known as corky stem passionflower, is native to the southeastern States. It winds itself around a host plant to survive. The stems and leaves are poisonous, as are the berries, which turn black as they ripen. Its folk name comes from its parasitic, poisonous nature and black berries.

Devil's Snare (*Datura stramonium*): This plant is also known as jimsonweed, devil's weed, devil's trumpet, devil's cucumber, devil's breath, devil's apple, and thornapple. Extremely poisonous and invasive, it grows across North America and has white or purple flowers. The seed pod is round and covered in spikes with black seeds inside. The seeds of the devil's snare were allegedly used in baneful magic, and it was said that witches burned them at their sabbaths as an aphrodisiac. Other lore from around the world claims that the devil's snare could make someone invisible and be used in love potions. In folklore from Maryland, it could even unlock doors and recover lost objects.[314]

---

313. Watts, *Dictionary of Plant Lore*, 104.
314. Watts, *Dictionary of Plant Lore*, 380–81.

Devil's Snuff Box (*Lycoperdon perlatum*): This fungus is also called puffball mushroom, devil's soot bags, and puck's stool. A funny fact: the name *Lycoperdon* means "wolf fart." When fresh, this mushroom is edible. However, if you happen to disturb a dried one, spores will come flying out of it like a puff of soot. These spores are rumored to cause blindness. The devil's snuff box can be found in damp regions almost everywhere, especially after rain.

Devil's Tears (*Phygelius*): The long, cylindrical blooms of the devil's tears, also known as cape fuchsia, are native to South Africa and grow in a clump with the flowers pointing down toward the earth. The flowers are shaped like long teardrops. They may be called devil's tears because of their downward-pointing faces and crimson color.

Devil's Tongue (*Amorphophallus konjac*): Also known as konjac, this bright red flower, which grows in east and southeast Asia, has a protrusion in its middle like a tongue. It is related to the corpse flower and smells like decaying flesh. Devil's tongue is also another name for some types of hot peppers because of their shape and spiciness.

Devil's Tongue Cactus (*Ferocactus*): This cactus's appearance and sharp spines are responsible for its name. It has reddish-colored spikes that resemble tongues sticking out and is native to North and South America. It's also known as barrel cactus.

Devil's Walking Stick (*Aralia spinosa*): Also known as Alaskan ginseng and devil's club, devil's walking stick is a shrub covered in spines that can become embedded in your skin and cause infections. It grows across North America. Its berries attract pollinators but are poisonous to humans. It gets its name because its branches are the right size to use as a walking stick, but anyone who grabs onto it will be sorry.

Elder Tree (*Sambucus*): The elder is also known as old gal and pipe tree. In England, it was believed that elder wood was used to craft the cross on which Jesus was crucified and was also the tree from which Judas hanged himself. It was said that babies whose cradles were made of elder wood would become sickly or be teased by fairies. Burning elder wood could bring the devil down your chimney into your home.[315] The dwarf elder was said to only grow where blood had been shed, and if someone built a house out of elder wood, they would forever feel like their legs were being pulled on by unseen beings.[316]

Garlic (*Allium sativum*): This everyday culinary bulb, also known as camphor of the poor, has been used for everything from warding off vampires to divination. A Turkish legend says that when the devil stepped into the Garden of Eden, garlic sprung up around his left foot and onions around his right.[317] Despite this, it's been used in all kinds of protection magic around the world. There's a Palestinian belief that garlic would protect a baby from Lilith and prevent the mother from going insane.[318]

Purple Devil (*Solanum atropurpureum*): Also called malevolence and five-minute plant, purple devil is a thorned woody shrub native to Brazil that can be used to build a hedge that no one would dare cross. It can grow up to ten feet tall, and its poisonous thorns cause skin irritation and therefore keep people and animals off property. It's related to the potato and bears poisonous berries.

---

315. Robert Graves, *The White Goddess: A Historical Grammar of Poetic Myth* (New York: Farrar, Straus & Cudahy, 1948; repr., New York: Vintage Books, 1958), 191–92.

316. Skinner, *Myths and Legends of Flowers, Trees, Fruits, and Plants*, 105.

317. S. E. Schlosser, "Garlic: Superstitions, Folklore and Fact," last modified August 28, 2022, https://americanfolklore.net/folklore/2010/10/garlic_superstitions_folklore.html.

318. Watts, *Dictionary of Plant Lore*, 161.

Satan's Apple (*Mandragora*): Satan's apple is another name for mandrake. In Arabic, the mandrake is called the devil's testicles. You're probably familiar with mandrake and its root, which is supposedly shaped like a human being and makes a screaming noise when pulled from the earth. In medieval Europe, it was believed that anyone who heard this scream would die or lose their mind.[319] But if certain protocol was followed while harvesting the plant, the devil could be summoned to fulfill your desires. This required efforts to avoid hearing the scream of the plant. The strategy was as follows: On a Friday, a pure black dog without a single white hair on its body would be tied to the mandrake plant. The person who wished to summon the devil would stay a reasonable distance away with their ears covered and throw a chunk of raw meat nearby. The meat would make the dog come running, pulling up the plant as it did so. Unfortunately, the dog would hear the scream and die, but the person summoning the devil would have cheated death and madness.[320] In English folklore, if someone was unjustly hanged, the fluids that dripped from their body to the ground sprouted mandrake. A female victim would produce female mandrake plants, and a male victim would produce male plants (mandrake is a dioecious plant). This particular mandrake was considered especially magical.[321] When someone had mandrake in their possession, the devil kept his eye on it to ensure they would never be rid of it. They could burn it, throw it away, and take any measure possible, but it would always come back to them until their dying day. The only way to pass it on was to sell it for less than what was paid for it.[322]

---

319. Skinner, *Myths and Legends of Flowers, Trees, Fruits, and Plants*, 168.
320. Skinner, *Myths and Legends of Flowers, Trees, Fruits, and Plants*, 168.
321. Watts, *Dictionary of Plant Lore*, 239.
322. Skinner, *Myths and Legends of Flowers, Trees, Fruits, and Plants*, 169.

Sweet Briar Rose (*Rosa rubiginosa*): The sweet briar rose, native to eastern Asia and Europe, smells beautiful but has tough thorns that point down toward hell. The legend behind these unique thorns is that the devil planned to use them to build a ladder to heaven, but when he discovered they grew from only a small shrub, he became angry and made the thorns point downward. Lore in France says the devil himself planted sweet briar, and the rosehips that form on it are the devil's bread.[323]

PLANTS IN RITUAL USE

Many of these plants have earned their devilish connotations for one of these reasons: foul smell, sharp thorns, invasiveness, poisonousness, parasitic qualities, and random folklore. If you choose to use these plants (or similar ones) in your workings, there are a few ways to decide what role they will play. Again, I don't recommend tinkering with poisonous plants unless you are an experienced botanist, and definitely do not consume them.

Invasiveness

Invasive plants can be used for spells to spread something far and wide. If you practice baneful magic, this is a way to curse many people at once or to help spread information. You could also get revenge by causing negativity to propagate throughout a person's life.

Sharpness

Thorns can be included in defensive workings because their purpose is to protect the plant. They can also be used to inflict pain or misfortune. A large thorn can replace pins in poppets or be added to witch bottles for protection.

---

323. Watts, *Dictionary of Plant Lore*, 368.

Burrs

Burrs are seed pods with hooks on them. As animals brush against them, the burrs get caught in their fur, and the animals unknowingly spread the seeds. Burrs range from being slightly annoying to utterly painful. If you've ever had a curious pet wander into a patch of burrs, you know how awful they can be to remove from fur. You can use burrs in workings to get "hooks" into someone or to attach energy to a person or thing. The sharp ones can be used in curses.

Foul Smell

Plants with a noxious odor can be included in spells to repel or ward off a person or situation. They might also be used to make a person seem unappealing to others.

Parasites

Parasitic plants are basically vampires. They live off the life energy of a host until it is drained. You can use a parasitic plant to drain energy out of a person or a situation that needs de-escalation. Parasitic vines that overtake other plants can be used in magic for making yourself outshine another person when in competition.

BLOOD IN RITUAL AND MAGIC

Not all magical ingredients are plant-based; some workings call for a drop of blood.

Blood is life. It is carnality in liquid form. Blood is of your flesh; it is everything you have been or will be; it's the DNA of your ancestors and all you have lived, breathed, or consumed. Your blood is 100 percent unique to you. Perhaps that's why the devil demands it in so many stories.

When meditating or working magic, consider focusing not on light or vibrations but on your blood. Your blood is the material world. It contains iron like the earth. It's your strength and virility. You can feel blood moving through your body and heart, making it an accessible focal point in ritual for those who find visualization difficult. Feeling your blood moving through your veins instead of imagining energy or light is an alternative.

Blood brings out peoples' most primal instincts. This is why phrases like "bathing in the blood of one's enemies" elicit strong emotions even when not meant literally. It implies a satisfying mixture of violence, survival, victory, and hedonism.

Using blood in witchcraft and ritual creates a physical and very personal link between yourself and whatever energies you believe you're working with. It can also be powerfully affirming and feel like a pact is being made because you have signed your name in blood, so to speak.

Whole grimoires have supposedly been written in blood, and in folklore the devil almost always demands it. Due to its symbolism and history, there is the option to include blood in the rituals in this book.

Before going any further, I must stress that the following information is not intended to encourage self-harm. If you have a history of self-harm, including blood in rituals may be best avoided. Feel free to skip this section if you find it triggering. Some of the following recipes and rituals include blood as an optional ingredient. If this makes you uncomfortable, simply omit it from your work. It is by no means mandatory.

Should you choose to include blood in your rituals, please consider the following safety tips:

- Use a single-use sterile lancet and dispose of it properly in a biohazardous waste container. Do not use knives, razors, or any other tool, as they are difficult to control and you could accidentally injure yourself badly. Also, they're not usually sterile, which can lead to infection.

- Prick only your finger. Just a tiny amount of blood is necessary. Any other part of your body might bleed unpredictably, and it's better safe than sorry.

- Don't touch the blood of another person unless you are in a fluid-sharing relationship. Many diseases are spread through blood, and sometimes people are unaware that they have them. Use gloves and common sense.

- It's illegal to feed your blood, or any bodily fluids, to another person without their consent. Besides that, doing so goes against satanic belief. If you cause someone to ingest your blood without consent, you are violating their free will.

THE RECIPES

As mentioned, ritual can be enhanced by including visuals, scents, tools, and actions that create necessary emotions. To some, these tools are purely aesthetic, while for others, they are considered magical. The following are some suggested recipes for ritual ingredients, whether you believe they have power in and of themselves or that they are mere tools. Whatever gives them power to you is what matters. Some of these items are suggested in the rituals in chapter 12.

Incense of the Damned

Decadent-era writer Joris-Karl Huysmans wrote a hugely popular novel called *Là-Bas* (*Down There*) in 1891. This shocking, sexual, and scandalous (for its time) story follows a fellow who finds himself lured into the shocking world of Satanism and attending a Black Mass. The description of the Black Mass in *Là-Bas* influenced future ideas about devil worship. The following incense is based on that described in the story: "'Asphalt from the street, leaves of henbane, datura, dried nightshade, and myrrh. These are perfumes delightful to Satan, our master.'"[324] If you don't have all those ingredients, as three of them are poisonous and possibly difficult to obtain, I've swapped them for accessible substitutes with appropriate folkloric associations.

MATERIALS

Pinch of asphalt or dirt from the street

1 tablespoon shavings of elder wood

1 tablespoon blackberry brambles, cut small.

---

324. J. K. Huysmans and Robert Irwin, *Là-Bas (Lower Depths)* (1891; repr., London, England, United States of America: Dedalus Ltd., 1986), 244.

1 tablespoon dried tobacco (it's in the nightshade family)
1 tablespoon myrrh

This loose incense is to be burned on a charcoal disk during ritual or whenever you feel like bringing some devilish energy into your space.

Devil's Water

Water is used in religious rituals of all kinds, for cleansing, banishing, and more. This devil's water can be used to replace regular water in any ritual you do. You can sprinkle it around the home as part of a cleansing ceremony, add it to the bath, or use it for the rituals in this book. Drinking it is not recommended.

MATERIALS

1 cup water from the ground. The source should be as close to hell as possible. This might be found in a deep canyon or simply a puddle—whatever is available. A sulfur spring would be the absolute best, but those are not usually easy to come by.

Ashes from burned incense, particularly if left over from a previous ritual

6 thorns of any kind

6 apple seeds

6 hairs from a black dog or a goat

Scent of your choice

1 drop of your blood (optional; revisit the safety information on page 214)

Inverted pentagram picture or disk

Put these ingredients in a jar with a tight lid. Place the jar on the inverted pentagram disk or picture overnight. If you like, you can strain the liquid when it's complete. This allows you to put it in a spray bottle if you want.

Devil's Ink

Some of the rituals in this book include writing pacts or other things. To ritualize the task, you might choose to use a dip pen or a brush with ink.

The following recipe is a blackberry-based ink, which is fitting as it's said that when Lucifer was expelled from heaven, he fell into a blackberry bramble. This ink is made of natural materials and will dry to a light, transparent color, but the plus side is that all the materials are linked to the devil in some way. After your ink is made from the berries, you'll be adding more ingredients to it.

MATERIALS

1 cup of fresh blackberries, preferably gathered after the first frost

2 teaspoons white vinegar

1 teaspoon salt

Piece of charcoal about the size of your thumb

6 drops of devil's water

1 drop of your blood (optional; revisit the safety information
   on page 214)

To make the blackberry ink, heat the berries in a saucepan. While they warm for about 5 minutes, squash them with a masher. Allow them to cool, and then strain the liquid from the pulp using a sieve or cheesecloth, pushing as much juice out as possible into a jar. Discard the pulp. Add the white vinegar and salt to the liquid and stir. This is your blackberry ink. The vinegar preserves the color, and the salt prevents mold.

Using a mortar and pestle, grind the charcoal to a powder. Mix it with the ink, devil's water, and blood and stir. Keep the ink in a sealed container. Shake before using.

This ink should keep for about 1 month at room temperature and 2 months in the refrigerator.

If you'd prefer to write in a darker hue, you can replace the blackberry ink with any ink of your choosing, adding the other ingredients to it.

Devil's Cursing Powder

For those who practice magic, this foul powder can be used to ward off enemies or unwanted influences. Go outside with some powder in your hand, and then blow it away from you. Make sure to note which way the wind is blowing.

MATERIAL
½ tsp. ground garlic
½ tsp. ground onion
1 tsp. ground charcoal
½ tsp. dried ground parsley
½ tsp. cayenne pepper
Tip of a match
1 drop of blood (optional; revisit the safety information on page 214)

Grind everything together with a mortar and pestle.

The garlic and onion are chosen for their foul smell and because they grew at the devil's feet when he stepped into the Garden of Eden. Parsley, also known as the devil's oatmeal, was considered a cursed, evil plant in folklore. The charcoal and sulfurous matchhead represent the devil's domain.

CHAPTER 11

DEMONS AND OTHER SPIRITS

It's difficult to discuss the history of the devil without mentioning demons, as the two seem to come hand in hand in the Bible and beyond. Demons have been popping up since before the Old Testament, with many explanations of what they are. Most of us know something about demonic possession (even if only from movies), have heard vague stories about fallen angels, or are even familiar with names like Beelzebub and Astaroth. But what exactly are demons, and where did they come from?

THE ORIGIN OF DEMONS

Demonology is extremely complicated with many different approaches and theories. In many cases, the names of demons were based on gods belonging to older religions of Babylonia (formerly Sumer), Assyria, Canaan, and Phoenicia, which fall into the overall area of Mesopotamia. Mesopotamia was one of the world's oldest civilizations, located where Iraq, Syria, Turkey, and Iran are today. When you examine beings such as Canaanite Tiamat, the serpent-goddess of the sea, and Nergal, the disease-spreading Mesopotamian god of the underworld, you might recognize bits and pieces of them in modern-day demons.

These, and other old deities, were first altered by the Hebrew faith and then changed even further by the Christian faith. Many demons do not resemble their original form. For example, the Canaanite fertility goddess

Astarte became the male demon Astaroth and Tiamat may have become the evil serpent Leviathan.

Greek Daimones

In ancient Greece, demons were referred to as *daimones*. Daimones were neither human nor divine. They were not always evil and can almost be compared to what we might now call spirit guides.

The famous Greek philosopher Socrates claimed to have a daimon within him that functioned as a guiding force. The public thought this was the same thing as consorting with evil spirits. They accused him of corrupting his students and claimed he was an occultist who conversed with new gods. He was executed by poisoning.

Socrates' daimones were later described in detail by different philosophers, such as Plato and Xenophon. Sometimes they were called the voice of God and other times an oracle.[325]

The Greek daimon wasn't necessarily a being in itself, but an abstract feeling within. A daimon could manifest as a supernatural will or desire that drove a person to action.[326] Daimones were considered a form of intelligence living between humans and the gods. A good daimon was called an *agathodaemon* and a bad one was called a *kakodaimon*.[327] Daimones weren't intentionally summoned but were attached to a person from birth, somewhat like fate. It was said that a happy person was born with a good daimon and an unhappy person with a negative one.

Our understanding of demons today is that they exist in the middle ground between humanity and the devil, similar to the way that Greek daimones lived between humans and the divine.

---

325. Georg Luck, *Arcana Mundi: Magic and Occult in the Greek and Roman Worlds* (Baltimore, MD: Johns Hopkins University Press, 1985), 185.

326. Walter Burkert, *Greek Religion: Archaic and Classical*, trans. John Raffan (Malden, MA: Blackwell Publishing, 1985), 180.

327. Luck, *Arcana Mundi*, 172.

Demons in Judaism

Scholars studying the origins of Israelite religion researched Mesopotamian deities to figure out where their own evil spirits, like Azazel and Lilith, may have come from.[328] Many Jewish demons can be traced back to Babylonian spirits.

In general, demons in Judaism are not ruled by the devil but are agents of God who carry out punishment under his instruction. Demons in Jewish and Talmudic traditions are omnipotent evil beings who bring misfortune and calamity upon humans. Some stories say that demons are the children of Lilith, who disobeyed Adam, mated with monsters, and birthed all kinds of evil creatures. They are also born of female demons who had sex with Adam after his expulsion from the Garden of Eden. Sometimes they are the souls of deceased people who had poor morals in life, and other times are created by nightmares.[329]

There are evil spirits called *mazziqin* or *mazzikin*, which means "harmful spirits," and under that umbrella are three kinds of demons. The *Lilin*, night spirits who harass men and murder babies and mothers, the *Shedim*, which means "the violent ones," and the *Ruchin*, demons of storms and wind.[330] The Shedim are born of a man and a succubus. They weep by the gravesides of recently deceased men, so living children are warned to stay away during the burial. In other lore, the Shedim live in the woods, where they dance wildly and play tricks on humans.[331]

Jewish demons create emotional pain and physical sickness for humans, but unlike Christian demons, they were always acting as agents of God, not Satan.

---

328. Judit M. Blair, *De-Demonising the Old Testament: An Investigation of Azazel, Lilith, Deber, Qeteb and Reshef in the Hebrew Bible* (Tubinger, Germany: Mohr Siebeck, 2009), 1.

329. Guiley, *The Encyclopedia of Demons and Demonology*, 56.

330. M. Belanger, *The Dictionary of Demons: Names of the Damned*, rev. ed. (Woodbury, MN: Llewellyn Publications, 2021), 221.

331. Guiley, *The Encyclopedia of Demons and Demonology*, 233.

Djinn

The *jinn* or *djinn* of Arabic lore are sometimes compared to demons because of a text called *The Testament of Solomon*, which is referenced across several religions and which you'll learn about in this chapter. However, djinn are very different from Western demons. They are sometimes known as genies who can grant wishes and are kept in bottles, an idea from Arabic folktales.

In Muslim lore, djinn can be both good and evil. They are said to have existed before Adam and Eve. Their ruler, Iblis (Shaytan), was cast out of heaven along with his followers when he refused to prostrate before Adam. The followers turned into djinn.[332]

Djinn have free will and their purpose is to worship God, who is their creator. Just like humans, they'll be judged at the end of their time on earth, and possibly sent to hell, depending on their behavior. They are said to be found in unclean places like bathrooms, animal stalls, and cemeteries. They cannot stand listening to prayer and will flee at the sound.[333] They possess speed and movement that humans do not.[334]

The djinn are invisible but can take on human or animal form. There is a story that if you find a snake in your house, you must not kill it, because it might be a good djinn in disguise. Call out to the snake three times. If it leaves, it is a djinn. If not, it is just a snake.[335]

Each person is said to have two djinn that stay with them throughout life. One urges them to do good, the other evil. They can impact a person's mind and body, but they cannot impact their heart or soul.[336]

---

332. Umar Sulaiman al-Ashqar and Jamaal al-Din M. Zarabozo, *The World of the Jinn and Devils* (Denver, CO, United States of America: Al-Basheer Publications and Translations, 1998), 13.

333. Sulaiman al-Ashqar and Zarabozo, *The World of the Jinn and Devils*, 24–25.

334. Sulaiman al-Ashqar and Zarabozo, *The World of the Jinn and Devils*, 29.

335. Sulaiman al-Ashqar and Zarabozo, *The World of the Jinn and Devils*, 34–35.

336. Guiley, *The Encyclopedia of Demons and Demonology*, 68.

The djinn have no power over the truly pious, but they have been known to possess people who have harmed them or who spend too much time alone.

Some djinn are righteous and others are evil, but the evil ones can be converted to righteousness just like a person can.

The djinn are ruled by God and are acting upon his instruction, unlike Christian demons, who belong to the devil.

DEMONIC TEXTS

Three major sources have shaped our understanding of demons. Here I'll briefly explain the book of Revelation, the book of Enoch, and the Testament of Solomon. These stories are each vaguely connected.

The most well-known Western origin story of demons centers around Adam and Eve and the Garden of Eden. Demons in this case were once angels who joined Lucifer's army in heaven and were cast down to earth alongside him.

The Book of Revelation

In the book of Revelation a great red dragon with seven crowned heads, each with seven horns, attacks the earth. The dragon scoops a third of the stars from the sky, throws them to the ground, and starts a battle. A war ensues in heaven between the dragon's army and that of the angel Michael: "And the great dragon was cast out, that old serpent, called the Devil and Satan who deceiveth the whole world: he was cast out into the earth, and his angels were cast out with him." The dragon represents Satan and the fallen stars are his army of demons.[337]

The Book of Enoch

If you're familiar with ceremonial magic, you've likely heard of the book of Enoch. The book of Enoch is one of the Dead Sea Scrolls, which are ancient Hebrew texts from before the first century. This book explains

---

337. Revelation 12:1–17 (King James Version).

why the great flood in the Bible occurred, including information about the origin of demons and the fate of fallen angels. While the character named Enoch is mentioned in the books of Genesis, Luke, and Hebrews, it is only a brief reference to his lineage in relation to other prominent figures.[338] The book was once included in scripture but was removed from the canon because biblical scholars doubted its authenticity. They concluded it had not actually been written by Enoch of the scriptures and therefore was not the word of God.[339]

The book of Enoch tells the story of the watchers. The watchers are angels sent to earth by God. They lust after human women and eventually have sex with them. These women give birth to giants and *Nephilim*, creatures who mercilessly murder and drink the blood of people and animals. The watchers themselves are devious angels, adept at evil magic. They teach humans sorcery, astrology, and how to make weapons of war. This forbidden knowledge in the hands of humans wreaks havoc and leads to the destruction of the earth. Eventually, the humans can't handle the monstrous Nephilim anymore and cry out to God to help them.

God sends Enoch to warn the watchers that they are soon to be destroyed. Enoch has a vision of hell in which he sees a prison for the fallen angels. God sends four more angels, who trap the leader of the watchers and send others to hell.

In the end, the watchers and their offspring become demons.[340] Stripped of their earthly forms, they would try to possess human bodies as a means of returning to the earthly realm.[341]

Enochian magic was created by John Dee and Edward Kelley in the 1500s. Divine beings supposedly used Dee as a conduit to share magical information, including the Enochian language and the Enochian keys,

---

338. Genesis 4:17–18, 5:18–24; Luke 3:37; Hebrews 11:5 (King James Version).

339. Brooks Manley, "Why Was the Book of Enoch Removed from the Bible?" Understanding the Bible, accessed July 10, 2023, https://understandingthebible.org/why-was-book-of-enoch-removed-from-bible/.

340. Richard Lawrence, trans., *The Book of Enoch* (Oxford, UK: John Henry Parker, 1838), 7:1–10:29.

341. Belanger, *The Dictionary of Demons*, 440.

which are a series of incantations. Reciting the Enochian keys is believed to open the gates to other planes of existence and invoke angels. LaVey mentions the Enochian Keys in *The Satanic Bible*, which make them relevant to Satanism, even if only tenuously, as the original Enochian language was considered angelic and godly.

The book of Enoch is apocalyptic and describes the end of the world. It follows the same storyline as Revelation, with a messiah, salvation, resurrection, and heaven, but with variations of names and some details.

The Testament of Solomon

One of the largest influences on demonology today is the Testament of Solomon, written sometime around the first century. This text is attributed to King Solomon, the monarch of ancient Israel, although he didn't actually write it. His name was assigned to the text to lend it legitimacy because he was believed to have great mystical powers. The testament was shaped by a range of religions, including Greek, Jewish, and Christian, and is said to have influenced Islam. The book has been compared to *Arabian Nights*, a collection of Middle Eastern folktales compiled between the eighth and thirteenth centuries. It was one of the first writings to claim that demons, called the watchers in the book of Enoch, could be overpowered and controlled.[342]

Although not considered a holy scripture, the book was taken as truth by many. Solomon's power was revered by Talmudic Jewish tradition, then Christianity, then Islam. Solomon's summoning, binding, and controlling of demons laid the groundwork for Western ceremonial magic, contributing to many magical grimoires.[343]

There are several references to the book of Enoch and the story of the watchers within the Testament. The red sea is mentioned in both, and the demon Asmodeus claims to be born of a woman and an angel, like the Nephilim.

---

342. Belanger, *The Dictionary of Demons*, 3.
343. Belanger, *The Dictionary of Demons*, 443.

In the story, King Solomon is given a magic ring that bears the seal of Solomon, a symbol that appears repeatedly in later grimoires such as *The Lesser Key of Solomon* (c. 1600s CE), also known as the *Lemegeton*.

Seal of Solomon

In the story, King Solomon sets out to interrogate every demon of hell to learn their supernatural abilities, their station, who controls them, and how they can be bested. He writes the testament to teach the children of Israel how to identify and fight demons. He also forces the evil beings to do the hard labor of building the Temple of Jerusalem.

The tale begins when one of King Solomon's favorite workers complains that they're being harassed by a demon called Ornias. Ornias steals his food and money and sucks the life out of him through the worker's right thumb. Solomon prays over the problem and is given a magic ring that can control demons. He then overpowers Ornias and condemns him to work cutting stones for the temple. With Ornias under his power, Solomon commands that he bring all the princes of hell before him. Ornias summons Beelzeboul, the exarch of demons, who promises to bring all the "unclean spirits" to Solomon. Solomon is particularly curious about female demons, so Beelzeboul brings him Onoskelis, an evil beauty who pretends to be human to seduce men and strangle people. Solomon puts the murdering seductress to work spinning hemp for the temple. Next comes Asmodeus, who tells Solomon that his job is to interfere with newlywed couples and prevent them from consummating their marriage. He also incites madness in men that makes them stray from their wives. Solomon gives him the job of making clay for the temple by treading it with his feet.

More demons continue to be summoned, interrogated, and put to work. Among them are seven female demons who rule over deception, strife, battle, jealousy, power, and error, with the seventh representing several goddesses altogether. Solomon makes them dig the foundation for the temple.

This continues for some time, with Solomon speaking to many lesser demons about why they exist, their celestial association, and whose command they are under. The demons all have specific evil jobs. One is responsible for giving children hearing and vision problems. Another strangles babies, and one impregnates women while disguised as a man. Interestingly, one demon says they can be invoked by the name *Kronos*, which is actually the Greek god of abundance and harvest.

Next come thirty-six spirits, each of whom inflicts a specific kind of pain and calamity upon humanity. They have the heads of dogs, donkeys, oxen, rams, and birds. Among them are the animals representing the twelve signs of the zodiac.

Some of the demons described sound a lot like older deities. One has the front end of a horse and the tail of a fish, and his job is to destroy ships and cause sea sickness. He could be likened to the Greek god Poseidon.

The antidotes that send these spirits running are as strangely specific as their evil jobs. One technique is to etch magic words onto a piece of copper that has been taken from a ship and then tie it to one's loin. Another is to smear one's lips with chopped coriander while uttering magical words.

Eventually, Solomon receives a letter from an Arabian king, who tells him of a terrible wind spirit tormenting his people. Solomon instructs a youth to take the magic ring to Arabia to retrieve the wind demon by trapping it in a leather flask. When King Solomon asks this demon who rules him and how he can be bested, the demon says that there is only one who can: a god who was born to a virgin and crucified by Jewish people. This story of the Arabian demon trapped in a drinking flash is possibly associated with the djinn and the well-known legends of genies in bottles.

For some time, Solomon lives out his life peacefully and acquires many wives. He eventually meets a Shunamite woman and falls in love. He wishes to marry her as well, but she is from a place where different gods are worshipped. Her people tell Solomon that if he wishes to marry her, he must make a sacrifice to their gods, called Raphan and Moloch. He has no intention of doing so, but a demon named Eros (which also happens to be the name of the Greek god of love and sexuality) brings the woman five grasshoppers. Eros convinces her to tell Solomon that if he would just sacrifice the measly insects to Moloch then they can be wed. Solomon crushes them up as instructed. He immediately loses all the powers that God had bestowed upon him, becoming weak and wretched. He is then forced to do hard labor building a temple for the "idols" Baal, Raphan, and Moloch. The book abruptly ends with an amen.[344]

From this book, we can see that some of the demons were named after Greek deities and stripped of their original traits. We also see, once again, a woman being the cause of man's downfall. This book names many well-known demons but also many obscure ones about whom very little information can be found.

DEMONIC HIERARCHY

According to occultists like Agrippa, there is a hierarchy of demons in hell similar to the feudal system of the Middles Ages. In *The Lesser Key of Solomon* (1901) by Mathers and Crowley, there are seventy-two demons positioned as kings, dukes, princes, marquises, presidents, and knights.[345]

---

344. F. C. Conybeare, "The Testament of Solomon," *The Jewish Quarterly Review* 11, no. 1 (October 1, 1898): 1, https://doi.org/10.2307/1450398.

345. S. L. MacGregor Mathers and Aleister Crowley, *The Lesser Key of Solomon: Goetia: The Book of Evil Spirits, Lemegeton-Clavicula Salimonis Regis* (1904; repr., Fairhope, AL: Mockingbird Press, 2016), 49.

Other magicians tried to classify demons based on their behavior or what particular brand of misfortune they wrought on earth. There has been a multitude of categorizations and ranking systems, some making more sense than others. Here I'll explain three of them. There is some confusion about whether Lucifer and Satan are the devil or demons in some of these texts. Twice the names are denigrated as belonging to demons.

King James I and Evil Spirits

King James I, who later commissioned the King James Bible, penned a dissertation called *Daemonologie* in 1597. He doesn't specifically name demons in his book, instead calling them spirits, but the title indicates they may have been one and the same to him. King James's evil spirits were categorized based on what kind of ills they inflicted on humanity.

Lemures or *spectra* were the unhappy, tormented dead. These evil spirits would haunt the houses of those who had offended God in some way. If the spectra were in spirit form, they could fit through any crack or cranny and gain entry to a dwelling. But sometimes they took the form of a reanimated dead human body, in which case they used a window or door. Spectra also tended to approach people while they were alone and vulnerable.[346]

Next came *incubi* and *succubi*. You may have heard of these demons who sexually assault sleeping people or plague their dreams. Incubi were male and succubi were female. According to King James, these were "more monstrous nor al the rest." Sometimes the spirit would steal sperm from a dead body. Other times it would inhabit a corpse, reanimate it, and have relations with a victim, in which case their semen was described as extremely cold.[347]

Inner and outer torment were inflicted on people by demons in the form of physical and mental illness, which could be called *possession* and *obsession*. Both afflicted those who were guilty of grievous offenses or

---

346. James I, *Daemonologie: In Forme of a Dialogie*, 46.
347. James I, *Daemonologie: In Forme of a Dialogie*, 52.

who needed to have their faith tested. These demons physically weakened people until they died and then snatched up their human souls. They also led people into sin by afflicting their minds with disbelief or blasphemous thoughts against God.[348]

King James claimed that "gentiles," a word for outsiders, were affected by *phairies*, who were evil spirits led by the goddess Diana. Phairies were known to transport people from place to place, sometimes physically and other times through hallucination. In the case of hallucinations, the devil deluded the victims into believing they had cavorted with the phairies, gone to the hills, and been given a magical stone. These phairies could visit both witches and regular people.[349]

The Numeric Scales

In the book *The Magus* (1801) by occultist Francis Barret, there is a detailed explanation of demonic hierarchy based on seven numeric scales, inspired by the work of Agrippa. According to Barret, demons existed to counterbalance God's benevolence by tempting humans into sin with earthly desires.[350]

The scales themselves are assigned numbers of one through twelve, with corresponding characteristics based on numerology. Numbers one through seven include charts that list six hierarchical worlds inhabited by corresponding beings. The six worlds are listed in descending order from the highest, or most godly, to the lowest, or most infernal. From top to bottom, the worlds are the Exemplary, the Intellectual, the Celestial, the Elemental, the Lesser, and the Infernal.[351] In each chart, the highest world, or Exemplary, is always God. The Infernal world way down at the bottom is where we find our demons and corresponding evils. I've listed the number of each scale and the corresponding demons, along with a couple of words regarding the significance of each number according to

---

348. James I, *Daemonologie: In Forme of a Dialogie*, 49.
349. James I, *Daemonologie: In Forme of a Dialogie*, 57–58.
350. Francis Barret, *The Magus: A Complete System of Occult Philosophy* (New York: Carol Publishing Group, 1989), 132.
351. Barret, *The Magus*, 101.

The Magus. Some scales include things besides demons, such as places, sensations, and even types of people.

Scale 1: One is the number of unity and God, the center from which all else radiates. The demon for this scale is Lucifer, the Prince of Rebellion, angels, and darkness.

Scale 2: Two is the number of procreation and science but can also be negative, as it represents confusion and uncleanliness. The two chiefs of the devil are the demons Behemoth and Leviathan.

Scale 3: Three is the number of perfection. In the third scale, there are nine demons split into three groups:

Three Infernal Furies: Alecto, Minos, and Wicked

Three Infernal Judges: Megara, Acacus, and Apostates

Three Degrees of the Damned: Ctesiphone, Rhadamantus, and Infidels

Scale 4: Four is a number of solidity, and there are Four Princes of Devils: Samael, Azazel, Azael, and Mahazael

Scale 5: Five is the number of justice, and on this scale are Five Corporeal Torments: deadly bitterness, horrible howling, terrible darkness, unquenchable heat, and piercing stink.

Scale 6: The number six is the world. There are six devils on this scale who are called Authors of All Calamity: Acteus, Megalesius, Ormenus, Lycus, Nicon, and Mimon.

Scale 7: Seven is a magical number of power. This scale tells of the Seven Habitations of Infernals: hell, the gates of death, the shadow of death, the pit of destruction, the clay of death, perdition, and the depth of the earth.

In this system, human souls are included as the wicked, apostates, and infidels, confined to the third scale.

Using these scales is dependent on understanding numerology: "He who knows how to join together the vocal numbers and natural with divine, and order them into the same harmony, shall be able to work and know wonderful things."[352] This quote somewhat explains that underlying all the universe, the earthly, and the divine are numbers, and within numbers are many worlds, ranging from holy to hellish.

The Seven Deadly Sins

The seven deadly sins were the creation of German witch hunter Peter Binsfeld, who wrote the *Treatise on Confessions of Evildoers and Witchcraft* (1589). The seven deadly sins were things that God supposedly disapproved of, including pride, envy, wrath (anger), lust, sloth (laziness), avarice (greed), and gluttony. In some demonological systems, each deadly sin is paired with a corresponding demon. Binsfeld equated Lucifer with pride, Mannon with avarice, Asmodeus with lust, Satan with wrath, Beelzebub with gluttony, Leviathan with envy, and Belphegor with sloth.[353] These demons were sometimes called the "Seven Princes of Hell." Again, we see the names Satan and Lucifer downgraded to the status of demons.

NAMES OF DEMONS

To explain the whole of demonology would fill many tomes. Here, I'll give a brief overview of the most well-known demons. The short list barely scratches the surface but will give you a general idea of what each of these beings are. If the topic interests you, there are some books in the recommended reading list that you might like.

In the Testament of Solomon and later occult teachings, knowing and saying a demon's name was a means of controlling it. Even today, speaking the name of an evil being is looked upon with great fear by some who believe that doing so can attract the demon and cause it to possess the speaker or otherwise bring misfortune. This fear is the reason the

---

352. Barret, *The Magus*, 102.
353. Guiley, *The Encyclopedia of Demons and Demonology*, 29.

devil was nicknamed Old Scratch and Old Nick in the Middle Ages in Europe.[354]

Abaddon: In the Bible, Abaddon was the angel who ruled over the "bottomless pit," a place of misery from which smoke and locusts spring forth.[355] He was the angel of death and destruction and could be summoned for help with baneful magic. Often "Abaddon" was used in reference to a place rather than a demon and is equated to Greek Apollyon.

Asmodeus: The demon of lust, Asmodeus was a fire-breathing monster with three heads, wings, the tail of a serpent, and the feet of a rooster. He existed to ruin marriages, tempt people into adultery, and prevent sex between married couples. In several stories, he was thwarted by the smoke of burning liver and gall of a fish. In the book of Tobit, Asmodeus falls in love with a young girl named Sarah. Seven times Sarah gets married, and seven times Asmodeus kills her husbands before they can consummate the marriage, in hopes of having Sarah for himself. Tobias (who wrote the book of Tobit) eventually marries Sarah and drives Asmodeus away.[356] In 1647, Asmodeus was deemed responsible for the demonic possession of eighteen nuns in Louviers, France, luring them into sexual acts and heretical beliefs. You might also recall Asmodeus was named as the future husband of Diane Vaughan during the Taxil hoax.

Astaroth: Astaroth rode on an evil dragon, wielding a viper in his right hand. His breath was so bad that magicians had to protect themselves from it with a silver ring. He was said to know occult secrets and to be skilled in science. He could see into the past,

---

354. Belanger, *The Dictionary of Demons: Names of the Damned*, 2–3.

355. Revelation 9:11 (King James Version).

356. Frank Zimmerman, trans., *The Book of Tobit* (New York: Harper & Brothers, 1958), 63, 67.

present, and future and would truthfully answer the questions of those who summoned him.[357]

Azazel: Azazel appeared as the scapegoat in the Torah.[358] In this story, two goats were chosen; one represented the Lord and the other Azazel. The goat representing the Lord was sacrificed. The goat representing Azazel, however, was loaded with the sins of the people and then sent out into the desert to perish, symbolically removing evil from the community. Azazel also appeared in the book of Enoch, where he gave humans sinful gifts like carnal knowledge and weaponry.[359]

Baal: *Baal* was the Canaanite and Syrian word for "lord." Male gods were called Baals and female goddesses were called Astaroths (just one example of how demonic names are used repeatedly in different contexts). Ancient people of the areas worshipped different Baals depending on location. The religion of Baal was in competition with the religion of Yahweh, which eventually caused several different Baals to be turned into demons.

> *Baal-Zebul:* Canaanite and Phoenician lord of the heavens and the divine abode who became *Beelzebub*, which means "lord of the flies."

> *Baal-Hadad:* A storm god of the Canaanites and Syrians who also became Beelzebub.

> *Baal-Peor:* A Canaanite god associated with sensuality, Baal-Peor was demonized into Belphagor. Part of worshipping Belphagor allegedly involved vulgar acts of showing one's private parts.[360]

---

357. Mathers and Crowley, *The Lesser Key of Solomon*, 25.

358. *The Torah: The Five Books of Moses* (Philadelphia, PA: The Jewish Publication Society of America, 1962), Leviticus 16:8–10.

359. Lawrence, *The Book of Enoch*, 68:2.

360. Belanger, *The Dictionary of Demons: Names of the Damned*, 84.

Bael: Bael ruled the East and could make people invisible. He presided over sixty-six legions of spirits. He took the form of a toad, a cat, a human, or a combination of all three.[361]

Beelzebub: Beelzebub was thought to manifest as a giant disgusting fly with skulls on his wings or a large ugly beast made of various animal parts. In Hebrew belief, he was one of the most powerful demons. Beelzebub has been used as a name for Satan and vice versa, but technically, they were two different beings, sometimes in competition with each other. In medieval times, he was said to preside over witches' sabbaths, where participants would chant, "Beelzebub goity, Beelzebub beyty," which means "Beelzebub above, Beelzebub below."[362] Supposedly, the witches lay down on the ground and drank a potion that rendered them unable to move, and Beelzebub had sex with them all. Beelzebub is associated with both envy and gluttony.

Behemoth: The word *Behemoth* means a dirty animal or unclean spirit in the Bible. He's described in the book of Job as a deadly beast with bones of bronze and limbs like iron, his tail as strong as a tree.[363] He represented insurmountable, primordial forces and could only be slain by God himself. He was believed to be a giant angry-looking beast with the head of an elephant, a huge belly, and big stomping feet. In some stories, he kills the serpent Leviathan.

Belial: The word *Belial* in Hebrew loosely translates to "worthless." Belial was beautiful, with a soft voice, but inside was filled with lies and wickedness. He would appear in a chariot pulled by dragons when offered a sacrifice. He was described as responsible for guilt and sexual deviancy in humans. Belial's name

---

361. Mathers and Crowley, *The Lesser Key of Solomon*, 13.

362. Guiley, *The Encyclopedia of Demons and Demonology*, 24–25.

363. Job 40:15–24 (King James Version).

was sometimes swapped with antichrist and Satan. Those who gained his favor would be given the best of familiars and positions of power. In The Lesser Key of Solomon, he was considered a mighty king who was ranked alongside Lucifer.[364]

Belphagor: Belphagor began as a Moabite god of fertility and sexuality and was worshipped in the form of a phallus. Morphed into first Hebrew and then Christian form, he became associated with the deadly sin of sloth, along with invention and treasure. He was said to rule over sexist, poorly behaving men. He took the form of a human for a while so that he could experience sexual pleasures on earth. He was associated with sloth because he invented things that made life easier, causing laziness in humanity.

Leviathan: Leviathan, who you might remember from the section about symbols, was a sea serpent that was nearly impossible to kill. Leviathan is described as huge, covered in scales, and breathing fire. Originally there were two leviathans, one male and one female, but God had to kill the female to prevent them from multiplying, for if they did, they would destroy humankind.[365] He was sometimes associated with the deadly sin of envy. The name *Leviathan* means "coiled" or "twisted" in Hebrew. Leviathan is possibly the Babylonian Tiamat.[366] Tiamat is the goddess of the ocean but is also known to personify chaos. Her lower half includes a scaly, shiny tail similar to a serpent or dragon, and her top half is a woman.

Lucifer: *Lucifer* is the Hebrew word for "morning star." His sin was pride. Most of Lucifer's mythology is not based on the Bible at all but has been created by stories and art over the centuries. In

---

364. Mathers and Crowley, *The Lesser Key of Solomon*, 44.
365. Job 41:1–34 (King James Version).
366. Belanger, *The Dictionary of Demons*, 245.

these stories, Lucifer was the brightest, most beautiful angel in heaven and was almost as powerful as God. He dared to question the hierarchy of heaven and God's position. He rebelled, caused a war, and was cast out of heaven along with his army of angels.

Mammon: Mammon is connected to avarice or greed. *Mammon* was an Aramaic word for "riches." He came to be known as a demon of greed during the Middle Ages, infamous for tempting and tricking humans. The name Mammon appears twice in the Bible. In Matthew 6:24 Jesus says, "Ye cannot serve God and Mammon."[367] In Luke 16:9–13, a similar message is declared.[368] Both passages are speaking of treasures in heaven, and Mammon is called unrighteous and associated with materialism.

Moloch: Moloch, who has the head of a bull, was a demon from Hebrew lore who was originally an Ammonite or Canaanite god of the negative aspects of the sun, like drought and burning. He also caused plagues. Sacrifices were made to Moloch to avert misfortune. There were huge bronze statues in his likeness, with large bellies containing blazing fires into which child sacrifices would be thrown.[369] In Leviticus 20:2–5, Moloch is mentioned by name when the Lord says that anyone who gives their children to him will be killed and stoned, and anyone who looks at such a person will also be punished.[370]

---

367. Matthew 6:24 (King James Version).
368. Luke 16:9–13 (King James Version).
369. Guiley, *The Encyclopedia of Demons and Demonology*, 178–79.
370. Leviticus 10:2–5 (King James Version).

CHAPTER 12

RITUALS

The rituals in this book are meant to inspire you and are all geared toward self-empowerment. You can follow the instructions to the letter or make them your own. For those who believe in magic and have an established practice, the rituals can be tweaked according to your preference. For those who do not believe in magic, they can be considered symbolic acts that benefit you psychologically and help you focus on attaining your goals.

Some of them have been written in such a way that you must make your own decisions about certain elements. One of the issues with many ritual books is that the words or materials don't align with the practitioner, rendering them empty of meaning. This would be especially so for satanic rituals due to their individualistic nature. While in witchcraft there are certain herbs, stones, and other tools believed to have magical properties based on centuries of folklore and tradition, satanic ritual doesn't have the same background.

If you're a practicing witch, feel free to augment these rituals with all the elements you would normally include in your rites. In instances where I have suggested materials, you can alter them according to your personal beliefs. What's important is that the ritual resonates with you personally.

Because imagery and symbols are so powerful, you might want to have devil-related aesthetics around you during rituals. This could be an entire altar decorated with black candles and a Baphomet statue, or something as simple as wearing an inverted cross necklace. Whether you include mystical elements in your practice or not, these visuals will invoke the appropriate mood.

THE SCIENCE OF RITUAL

Not everyone believes in spells and magic, and therefore, some might find participating in them uncomfortable or even pointless. However, there is much more than meets the eye in terms of the psychological and emotional benefits of ritual. You don't have to be a theist or have any spiritual beliefs at all to benefit from it.

A ritual is a symbolic action that results in a desired outcome, which can be anything from solace to inspiration, or even releasing anger.

Ancient civilizations and our collective ancestors all partook in ritual instinctively. In a time before established religion, people knew to come together and perform symbolic gestures in attempt to impact the world around them. This created a sense of agency, community, and in some cases alleviated the fear of natural disaster and death.

Rituals are often done when we face situations that are beyond our personal control, which explains why many people have good-luck superstitions for sports or gambling. Even those who deep down inside think rituals are silly take comfort from them.

Studies have shown that rituals performed after a loss alleviate feelings of grief and provide comfort, even in those who are not religious or spiritual.[371] Something in us is soothed by, is empowered by, or otherwise benefits from acts of ritual in a deep way that we may not consciously realize. Whether you call it magic, science, or brain chemistry, it works.

---

371. Carmen Nobel, "The Power of Rituals in Life, Death, and Business," Harvard Business School, June 3, 2013, https://hbswk.hbs.edu/item/the-power-of-rituals-in-life-death -and-business.

When it seems that your life is full of negative things that you cannot change, ritual can provide the first step to reharnessing your own agency. It can reset your mind, planting a seed of confidence that can grow into change.

When you conduct the spells and rituals in this book, you are invited to add your own flavors to them. If you want to call upon spirit, go for it. If you like to envision moving energy around, as I do, do that as well. If the ritual is a mere series of actions for you, you will still most likely discover that you feel powerful, or at least better, afterward.

ORGASM AND MAGIC

In some kinds of ceremonial magic, orgasm is considered an important part of ritual.

All sexual things have largely been labeled dirty and evil in monotheistic religion. Truthfully, there are still plenty of people who believe masturbation is sinful and that some kind of punishment will come crashing down on those who partake without repenting afterward. These two things combined make sex magic appealing to some on the left-hand path, as physical pleasure is in the devil's hands.

Orgasm in ritual is a form of energy work. To cast a spell, as some of us might call it, is to harness, build, and then release energy to create change. Animal sacrifice is performed in some practices for the same reason. The death throes of the sacrifice emit powerful energy, which the magician directs into manifesting their desire. Orgasm is sometimes considered a replacement for sacrifice because it is primal and biological like death and provides a similar expulsion of energy. I personally do not perform animal sacrifice and will not be providing further information on it here.

Orgasm with intention raises energy in the body, creating a physical sense of mounting power, which is then released. It's much like any energy-building exercise in which vibrations are raised via chanting, dance, or music.

To incorporate orgasm into a working, you would follow the required steps of the spell, like ingredients and actions. The spell would culminate in visualizing your goal while bringing on orgasm and mentally directing the energy to the universe, to a god or goddess, or whatever you believe in.

I mention this type of energy release here because it factors into certain left-hand path and satanic practices, but as with all things, it is optional.

RITUAL TRADITIONS

Just as there are traditional altar setups for various satanic groups, there are guidelines for satanic rituals as well. Some people use the same ritual routine regardless of its purpose, while others are more flexible. You don't have to follow any guidelines that don't resonate with you, but you can take inspiration from some existing traditions.

LaVey's Rituals

In *The Satanic Bible*, LaVey gives a general breakdown of how a group ritual should be performed within his organization. The book offers three kinds of rituals: sexual ritual, compassionate ritual, and destruction ritual. All spells would fall within these three categories. For example, a love spell is considered a sexual ritual, prosperity and health are in the compassionate category, and protection and curses are classified as destructive.

The book emphasizes that desire is the motivating factor behind all workings. To create the necessary emotional energy needed, the participant(s) must be genuinely invested in the results. If you are targeting a specific person, the ritual should be performed at the time of day that they are most vulnerable to incoming energy, such as during sleep or while bored. It's encouraged that participants include any imagery or objects that make them feel mentally attuned to the task at hand, like a picture of the person in question or a piece of their clothing.

According to LaVey, the altar should be facing the west. Male participants are to wear black hooded robes, and female members dress in provocative outfits to increase the sexual vibes in the room (remember, this was written by a straight man in the 1960s, and it shows). People may wish to cover their faces, allowing them to fully immerse themselves in the experience without insecurity or self-consciousness. Everyone is to wear a sigil of Baphomet or a pentagram amulet.

At the beginning and end of the ritual, participants walk widdershins, or counterclockwise, in a circle while bells are rung.

First, the leader, or priest, reads passages from *The Satanic Bible*, including a list of infernal names. The infernal names belong to ancient gods, goddesses, and demons. It's unclear what specific meaning these names held for LaVey, beyond being rejected by the Christian faith.

The priest drinks wine from the chalice, then uses a sword to call upon the four directions, in this case called the four Princes of Hell: Satan (south), Lucifer (east), Belial (north), and Leviathan (west). There is benediction of the phallus and then the priest reads the appropriate words as written in the book.

Requests written on parchment are read aloud and burned. The white candle is only used for cursing, while all other rituals use the black candle. After each burning, the congregation yells "Hail Satan" or "Shemhamforash," which means "the explicit name" and comes from the Tannaitic word describing the Tetragrammaton.

Before ringing the bell to close the ceremony, one of *The Satanic Bible*'s Enochian Keys is recited.

LaVey's ritual is very ceremonial and dramatic and follows the same course no matter the goal, changing only which words are recited.

Luciferian Ritual

Luciferian rituals are self-led and creativity is encouraged. Will, desire, and belief are the key ingredients to success.

According to Luciferian author Michael W. Ford's book *Apotheosis: The Ultimate Beginner's Guide to Luciferianism and the Left-Hand Path*, robes are worn based on color association: black for hidden knowledge, red for creativity, white for solar and lunar rituals, and green for earth-related workings.[372] Like LaVey's ritual, Luciferian rites begin and end with the ringing of bells. Unlike LaVey's workings, different colors of candles can be used. Black is for power, success, and invoking deities and demons. White candles are for well-being and health, blue for imagination, and red for seduction and lust.

Luciferian rituals often include evoking a spirit or demon into a sigil or object chosen specifically to house it. The spirit is magically bound to the object, and then each day the practitioner meditates upon it while visualizing their goals. Sometimes they make offerings of incense or libations. A similar ritual is invocation, in which the spirit or being is welcomed inside the practitioner's body.

Luciferian ritual makes use of circle casting to mark the magical space and to represent the serpent ouroboros, which is an image of a snake eating its own tail. This symbol stands for the cycle of life and death. There are multiple designs for Luciferian circles that all look different, such as the circle of the adversary and the grand Luciferian circle.

Luciferianism uses many elements of ceremonial magic, such as the athame and wand for directing energy. Rituals are mostly self-created and can involve recitations of words you make up yourself in alignment with your intent, sometimes in the form of hymns or poems. Because Luciferianism is so individualistic, there are no set ceremonies that one must follow. Like in many forms of witchcraft, the practitioner takes bits and pieces of various spiritual systems and puts them together how they see fit.

The Personal Ritual

Just as with the construction of an altar, I believe that the rituals you make up yourself are the most conducive to success. While prewritten rituals are useful to beginners to give them a starting point, you don't have to use them if you don't want to. Here are a few bits of advice for creating rituals.

---

372. Ford, *Apotheosis*, 154.

- Don't hold back. During ritual, feel free to laugh or cry or any-thing in between, as this emotion is key to success. It must be harnessed and directed.

- Not everyone can sit still in silence and visualize or meditate. If you force yourself to, you will lose the emotion of your working. Do whatever raises your focus and energy. This could be listen-ing to music, moving around, talking, pacing, or anything that works.

- Don't be self-conscious. Sometimes ritual can feel very strange and even silly if you're not used to it. Try not to let these kinds of insecurities get to you. Trust that it doesn't matter what any-one would think and focus solely on your purpose.

- As mentioned in the altar section of this book, incorporate items and actions that have meaning for you specifically. If casting a circle is something you already do and find helpful, include it. If not, omit it. You might light incense and candles for mood.

- You don't need a script, but you do need a clear intention. Sum up what you want in one sentence before deciding on a ritual.

- Go with the flow. Personally, I find the best workings are often spontaneous and require little preparation. Don't worry too much about theatrics and ceremony unless they're useful to you. If that's the case, decide on all the words and actions ahead of time.

The following instructions in this book will help you understand the form and function of a ritual. They are not traditionally structured and are simpler than the others described here. If you're new to ritual, try some of them out and soon you might find yourself creating your own.

DAILY DEVOTION

Daily devotion is not the same as worshipping something. This simple cer-emony is more like a statement of your own will paired with reflection. It doesn't include any kind of worship unless you choose to do so according to your beliefs. It can help connect you to the archetype of the devil in ways that apply to your situation.

From a purely nonspiritual perspective, taking a few moments each day to sit at your altar and contemplate your goals can only empower you to make moves toward them. It will rewire your brain to align with your desires and allow you to feel more confident about achieving them. All of this may sound very fluffy, but paired with the devil and all he symbolizes, it can be a mentally invigorating exercise. Besides, to focus on Satan and the unrelenting, rebellious energy of the devil is a call to action for yourself. If nothing else, the devil reminds you that this devotion is not an empty wish or prayer but a genuine intention to follow your will.

Daily Devotion Exercise

Here is an example of a simple daily devotion you can do. Feel free to alter it and make it your own.

MATERIALS

Stick or cone incense

Statue or picture of the devil

Devil's water (see page 216)

Candle in a jar. Novena candles are perfect for this. You can paint the glass with satanic imagery ahead of time.

Sit before your altar and light the incense. As the smoke begins to billow, pass it around your head in a circle, envisioning the light of Lucifer radiating from the crown of your skull. This light contains the will, strength, and power that you're taking with you into your day.

Pass the incense smoke around or over the devil image in the same manner, and then place the incense in a holder. The smoke creates an energetic connection between yourself and the devil. Even if you don't believe in energy, this act mentally connects you to the devil archetype.

Dab a small amount of devil's water on the center of your forehead. Say your intention out loud or in your mind. This might be as simple as "Hail Satan, hail myself," or it could be more specific, like "I am as vengeful as the fires of hell." Consider your situation and make a statement accordingly.

Light the candle in the jar and place your hands on the glass where you can feel the heat from the flame. If the glass is too hot, just hold your hands a few inches away from it. As you feel your hands getting warmer, close your eyes and consider this flame. It is so small but can burn an entire house down. It can illuminate the unseen, or it can destroy everything in its path. Like the light of Lucifer, this fire contains both destruction and creation. It's as old as nature, and it burns within you as well. You destroy and create your own path every single day in the choices you make.

When you are finished, extinguish the candle, and use it again the next day.

THE RITUALS

The following rituals address various parts of the self that are often not embraced. In keeping with the devil or Satan, these rites focus on the carnal: self-empowerment, materialism, banishing shame, and the flesh. Each one includes an introduction that hopefully helps explain the significance of the ritual as it pertains to your daily life, as well as to the folklore and philosophies you've learned throughout this book.

The Devil's Book

In folklore, consorting with the devil often involved the signing of a book. Sometimes the book is described as plain black. Other times, it is bound in human skin. A witch or devotee would sign their name in blood to express their dedication.

In addition to signatures, in some lore the black book was supposed to contain instructions for summoning demons and performing spells. In German folklore, a cursed black book containing instructions for demon summoning was allegedly passed down through inheritance among a line of magicians. When it was read forward and then backward, its magical powers were awakened. The reader was endowed with great wealth and the power to perform baneful witchcraft. However, if they neglected to read the book backward, the devil would possess them. In the story, it seems the consequences of possessing this book were worse than any benefits. The only way to free oneself from its possession was if a minister nailed it to the inside of a drawer.[373]

All of that seems quite random, but it shows how mysterious books are often part of Satan's lore and is an example of his association with inversions and backwardness.

In this ritual, you're creating your own devil's book, devoted to the self. This book will help you pursue your desire while documenting your progress and include inspirational things to keep you focused. Writing something down has a finality to it and is a way to solidify a goal. It affirms that you can and will create the life you want. When in doubt, you can go back and read your previous entries for inspiration. When the book is full, it will be a record of your journey.

The devil's book is also a place where you can write out your absolute most honest feelings, desires, and opinions, no matter how foul and terrible. Rather than suppress these feelings or make them worse by doom scrolling, write them out. These feelings, which we're so often trained to be ashamed of, serve a very important purpose by acting as a guide to what you need to change.

You can use any notebook you like. You can make your own, purchase one with devil imagery on it, or just use a simple, plain, black, mysterious book. I suggest keeping the book hidden for the simple reason that it contains personal information that is no one else's business but also in case you might face disapproval if it's discovered.

On the first page, I recommend writing a dedication. You can make this process ceremonial by adding a drop of blood to ink and using fancy cal-

---

373. Guiley, *The Encyclopedia of Demons and Demonology,* 29.

ligraphy or by using colorful paint or markers. If you choose to include blood, please revisit the safety information on page 214.

Some forethought is required when writing your dedication. Do some brainstorming and consider what you wish to accomplish in line with the philosophy of Satanism and the devil. Here are some ideas:

- What is your will? Sum it up in one sentence.
- What specific knowledge do you seek?
- What logical, practical steps will you take to achieve your will?
- What do you refuse to tolerate? Consider this a pact with yourself.
- What or who are you fighting? Declare war on it here.

Sign your preferred name underneath. Your dedication is done.

Below is an example of a dedication. It's quite general but gives you the basics. You might prefer yours to be longer or more poetic. It's up to you.

My will is to succeed above and beyond those who underestimate me.

I seek the ability to see the truth in the intentions of others and the world around me.

I am pursuing education, gaining experience, and researching to get where I wish to be.

I refuse to allow disrespect or abuse from others. They cannot impact my dreams.

I declare war on those who wish to see me fail and who have harmed me with words and deeds. My success makes them irrelevant.

I am strong, intelligent, and unstoppable.

Hail Satan.

(Your name)

Any time you take steps toward your will, write it down and allow yourself to feel pride. When you succeed at keeping that pact with yourself, take note of it. Same with if you fail, as writing it out will help you let it go. If you're struggling to figure out what to write, you can try just stating your will in one sentence again. Repeated each day, this can be very powerful in shaping your attitude.

If someone gets in your way, write out what you'd really like to say to them. If someone in your past has a hold over you, write a page declaring that it is over. Some other things you might include are pictures or quotes from people you admire, images of the devil that appeal to you, and other ephemera that support your beliefs.

The important thing is that this is a book of power. This is not where you write down complaints or expressions of helplessness. Force yourself to reframe that thinking, funneling it into a strategy fueled by healthy rage, not victimhood. This is not to dismiss the experiences of victims but to invoke a sense of agency. Everything you write in this book should come from the perspective of self-empowerment. If you must, fake it till you make it.

Your own feelings might surprise you.

In time, when you go back and read the statements and thoughts from your past, you will see a clear pattern of growth.

The Devil's Mark

The notion of a devil's mark is rooted in the witch hunts. A devil's mark was a bump, brand, or scar said to have been placed upon the witch by the devil himself in exchange for their soul and to seal the bond between them. Witch hunters claimed that this mark was impervious to pain and would poke and stab it to determine whether the person was a witch. It was sometimes said that the witch's familiar would feed on blood from this mark like a baby at the breast. In reality, the mark in question was usually a very ordinary mole, scar, or birthmark.

During the witch hunts, having an unusual physical feature would have caused a person to be ousted from society and in some cases, tortured and killed. Nowadays the wounds inflicted on someone for their physical attributes are usually psychological, but still terribly damaging.

Almost everyone has at least one bodily feature that they feel ashamed of because society has taught them it deviates from the beauty standards or labels it a flaw. It may be something you were born with or something you acquired along the way, like a scar. It might even be something you chose, like a tattoo. Regardless, the end result of the ritual is the same: to affirm your sense of bodily autonomy and declare your right to comfortably exist, exactly as you are, without apology.

Loving your body is considered a satanic act in itself. Even more so when you love the parts of yourself that you've been forced to feel shame or embarrassment for. This ritual focuses on taking your "devil's mark" and reclaiming it, rejecting the judgment that's been cast upon you by others.

MATERIALS
2 pieces of paper
Pen
Devil's water (see page 216)
Candle in your choice of color
Fire-proof dish

Light the candle. On one piece of paper, write down at least three negative words that others have attributed to your devil's mark. For example, you may have been made to feel that a scar is *gross*, *ugly*, and *shameful*. On the other piece of paper, write at least three words that are the opposite, with positive connotations. In this case, *unique*, *survivor*, and *powerful* could work. This might seem difficult, but consider that stretch marks are often a result of growth or giving life, and many scars are a result of surviving difficulty or injury. If your mark is something you were born with, consider the unique perspective you have developed because of it. It has molded your worldview and given you wisdom from experience that others do not possess.

Look at your devil's mark and consider those painful words written down. Now take some devil's water and pour or wipe it over the mark, symbolically cleansing away the attributes others have cast upon it. Burn the paper with negative attributes in the fire-proof dish, and as it burns, say aloud the three positive words to replace the old ones. You might throw in a "Hail Satan" here if you wish.

From then on, when you catch a glimpse of your devil's mark, remember this empowering ritual and the three new names you have given it. Remembering this will reinforce the positive perspective you've chosen, affirming it in your brain. To take it a step further, you can periodically put devil's water on it and repeat the words you've written. Eventually, your feelings about this mark will change into pride and empowerment. You might also experience a healthy sense of disgust for the unsolicited opinions of others who are not worthy of dictating how you feel about yourself.

Devil's Oatmeal

This is a curse based on the folklore in which parsley, known as the devil's oatmeal, is an extremely evil plant. It was believed that if you said your enemy's name while pulling parsley from the ground, they would die. This can be broadened into a working to remove any situation from your life that's bringing unhappiness. You can perform this ritual with an individual in mind if you like, but the odds of it killing them are extremely slim. It should be seen as a symbolic gesture, in which you are mentally and physically rejecting their power over you.

I believe that the more time and effort put into something, the more meaningful it becomes. If you share this view, consider growing parsley just for this working. It may take a while, but legend says that's because it must go into the earth and meet with the devil nine times before growing fully. You may not have anyone in mind to curse at the moment, but it never hurts to be prepared. Parsley can be grown indoors in a pot or outdoors in warm weather.

If you really want to get into the superstitious part of things, you can plant the parsley seed according to the recommendations of folklore: place them on the pages of a Bible and then blow them into the soil.

While the parsley grows, remember the story of its diabolical evil every time you water it. If you do practice magic, consider this a way of empowering it with a purpose. If you do not believe in magic, this will still give the plant psychological power through association.

For this ritual, you are going to yank the plant from the ground while saying the name of your enemy or naming the problem you are banishing. Think of it like pulling a diseased parasite from your life and getting rid of it.

MATERIALS

Pot with parsley plant and soil

Black candle

6 garlic cloves

After planting and growing your parsley to a satisfactory size, it's ready to be used. Go to your plant after dark and light a black candle to see by. Place the garlic cloves around the plant in a circle to protect yourself from the vile energy of what it represents. Hold your hands above the plant and envision the person or undesirable situation. Allow yourself to feel all the annoyance and negativity this invokes. When it feels right, grab the plant close to the roots. State the name or the problem out loud and yank the parsley from the dirt. The roots will probably come up too, much like pulling a painful splinter from the skin. Imagine you're ripping the problem out of your life.

You can throw the garlic, soil, and parsley in the compost or garbage, and then wash your hands. Alternatively, you can lay the plant somewhere you can watch it decompose, content in the knowledge that your issue is withering away to nothing.

Banishing Shame

Shame is perhaps one of the most powerful tools of oppression and manipulation there is. Shame works on large and small scales, often irreligiously. On a large scale, the beauty industry shames us into hating our bodies and appearance so we'll buy their products. The patriarchy shames men for having emotions or empathy, thus upholding a system based on violence. Colonization shames people for their ethnicity, upholding white supremacy. Long ago, shame was used by the clergy to keep the poor from seeking a better station in life by calling it greed, which, coincidentally, ensured they remained in power.

Online, shame is driving the entire shape of society as we know it. Public shaming creates a spectacle that people can't resist. Some even join in, hoping that the shame machine will never turn its voracious hunger upon them. I just can't help but compare it to some kind of medieval public torture, albeit less bloody.

Shame is also extremely powerful in smaller-scale dynamics. A family might use shame to keep their children from following an alternative life path, or a boss might intentionally embarrass people to maintain control. Exerting shame directly onto another person through consistent bullying has long-term traumatic effects on the victim that can follow them for life.

It seems that human beings have always known about the power of shame instinctively. It gives some people pleasure to see it inflicted upon others and can always be counted on to be effective in marginalizing a person or group.

This ritual is a means of locating the shame, tearing it out, and destroying it, leaving empowerment in its place. Chances are you didn't create this shame. It was inflicted upon you, most likely when you were vulnerable. It's not yours. Send it back to the person(s) or institution who gave it to you, for they deserve to carry the pain they have created.

Before you begin, spend some time considering your sense of shame and where it stems from. Sometimes it's easy to immediately name the source because it's a specific person or thing. Other times, it can be so deep-seated that it takes some soul-searching to figure it out. You might wish to journal this in your devil's book. Writing things down can be extremely therapeutic and lead to new realizations.

Choose an item that is a symbol of your shame. This can be almost any relevant object of reasonable size. Some examples are that if your ritual involves bodily shame, you could include an ad cut from a magazine. If you're targeting a specific person, use a photo of them or something small they have touched or worn. If it's a larger organization, their logo or associated symbols would work.

Do this ritual at your altar or any private space.

MATERIALS

Chosen representative item

Hammer or scissors (for destroying above item)

Devil's book (or pen and paper)

Sit quietly and look at the object you've chosen. Allow yourself to feel whatever comes up and make a concerted effort to transform it into anger. If you want, try writing down or speaking aloud all the ways that the person or thing has harmed you.

Pay attention to how your body feels and where your emotions are manifesting physically. Then, destroy the object. Put all your feelings into it. Go crazy. Smash it to bits. Rend it to smithereens with your bare hands until it hurts. Stomp on it. Obliterate it. Spit on it. The physical act of destroying the object should be satisfying and give vent to your building rage, which will be released through the breakage of the object.

Do this until you feel your anger start to ebb.

Gather the remains. You can either throw them away to symbolically toss your oppressor in the trash, or you can go a step further, if possible, by leaving it in their vicinity. (I do not mean trespassing or stalking! I mean in a garbage can in their city or in a place that, for some reason, reminds you of them.) Send all the shame their way. Say "Hail Satan" and walk away.

Shame doesn't go away overnight. It might take repeated work to feel a difference. Each time you feel it creeping in, remember the rage you felt during this ritual instead of that sinking, disempowering sense of shame.

Making a Pact

To make a pact with the devil is to make a pact with yourself. If you do not believe in an outside higher power and consider yourself your own god, this kind of promise is especially sacred.

People break promises to themselves all the time, probably more frequently than they do to others. We've all done it. It's easier to let ourselves down than someone else. Aligning your promise with the devil can replace the spiritual element of pacts or promises to gods. It creates a similar sense of obligation. The devil teaches us the importance of the self, and when you think of breaking your pact, you will be reminded of your reason for making it: to align with your satanic philosophy, your vow to reach your own version of apotheosis, or at the very least, to be the best person you possibly can.

Based on folkloric tales of pacts with the devil, this simple ritual is meant to help you achieve a state of being that is beneficial in whatever ways you currently need. It could be that you wish to stop drinking for a while, even just for a month, or that you want to dedicate more time to building a skill.

Part of this ritual is to be completed at a crossroads because based on folklore, this is a place where the devil can be summoned. The dramatic elements of the ritual, such as the location and tools, may not possess magical qualities for you but create an atmosphere with beneficial psychological effects.

First, you must think of an attainable goal. I say attainable because we are all limited by our circumstances to a certain degree, and these limitations require a step-by-step approach. For example, if you make a promise to yourself that in one year you will be a billionaire with a private jet when currently you're a struggling student who is barely making ends meet, this is highly unlikely to occur. There are so many steps to take between where you are now and where you'd like to be that it isn't possible. Be realistic in your goal and give it a reasonable time frame.

When you think of your goal, what are some of the smaller things that need to be addressed? It's tackling these small things that will lead you in the right direction. If your big goal is to find a loving relationship, consider some of the immediate things that might be preventing this. If it's because you are too shy to meet anyone in person or that you're lingering in an unsatisfying relationship, those are the realistic things you can tackle. If your will is to have more money, rather than swearing to become a billionaire, consider actionable things you can do right now, like applying for better or different jobs, committing to taking some courses, or simply just keeping your eyes open for opportunities.

And if a little part of you believes that the devil is real and will receive this pact you make, well, that only works in your favor.

First, create your pact. On some good quality paper, write out what you are promising and for how long you will uphold it. The example I'm going to use here is a pact to stop excessive inebriation, but you can modify it to suit your own needs. As with other rituals, you can add your blood to the ink you write with (see the safety information on page 215). Consider decorating the paper with devil imagery or symbols to further signify that this pact is part of your bigger journey toward the path of enlightenment and self-mastery.

Here is an example of a pact you can write, although feel free to get creative.

On this night I make a solemn pact with myself and with the devil. For one month, I will abstain from alcohol in exchange for health, personal growth, clarity, and power. In doing so, I dedicate my growth and success to Lucifer the light bringer, Satan the beast of self-empowerment, and the devil of earthly delights. In exchange for my efforts, I will be rewarded with the inner fire of inspiration, which pushes me onward toward greatness.

This pact is officially made and will not be broken.

Hail Satan.

(Your name)

Take your pact to a crossroads after dark, where the folkloric devil is so often said to be found. If this is unrealistic, you can use any liminal space, such as a doorway, gateway, or a spot where water meets land. Make a pentagram on the ground, if possible, by drawing it in the dirt, using chalk, or simply making the shape in the air with the pointer finger of your left hand. Stand within the pentagram and picture your version of the devil as if he were there in front of you. Imagine the goatlike smell of him, the earth caught in his fur, and the beastly ancient presence of death and creation. Read the pact aloud or just in your head. Leave a coin or something of value that you can part with at the crossroads.

Keep your pact hidden somewhere you can revisit daily to strengthen your resolve. As needed, imagine the devil as you saw him in your mind that night, to further encourage yourself. Most importantly, keep your pact! Please note, this ritual is not meant to take the place of professional help for addiction.

Here are some other ideas of reasonable pacts:

- I will read one page per day of this academic text to increase my knowledge until it is done.
- I will meditate for ten minutes each day for one week in pursuit of mental health.
- I will not unblock (person) for one month in the name of self-respect.
- I will go walk outdoors each day for 90 days for my health.

The periods of time stated are examples only. You should choose a timeframe that is reasonable for your goal. As you can see, your pact can be many things. Regardless of what you choose for your pact, if you stick to it, it will benefit you one way or another. It might be in a perfectly expected manner, like you break a bad habit, or it might be that you are led to the right people or places. This small step is one of many, setting you on the path of power.

Celebration of the Flesh

We are constantly bombarded by people, corporations, and systems that police our bodies, no matter what body we happen to be in. We are told what the ideal standard of beauty is and often that we don't measure up to it, creating hatred for our own amazing selves. People who wish to find peace through changing their bodies with cosmetic and corrective surgery are shamed for doing so and, in the case of gender-confirming surgery, subjected to violence. In many places, people are denied reproductive rights and are forced into unwanted pregnancies. In Satanism, bodily autonomy is our birthright. How we perceive, present, alter, and enjoy our bodies is our choice.

This ritual is to help nurture bodily autonomy. It can be done to refresh how we perceive our physical selves, reminding us it's our own choice: not our partner's, the law's, society's, or a god's. None of them have the right to determine our sense of worth.

For this ritual bath, you will include the most opulent elements that you can afford. If you like essential oils, choose your best, most expensive ones. If you're into bath bombs, use one selected especially for this occasion. Get candles and flower petals, or make an herbal mix to add to the water.

The purpose of this ritual is that you will enter the bath covered in the mental filth you've been poisoned with regarding your body and emerge with those attributions washed away.

Optional: Beforehand, create a sachet of the devil's plants using an empty teabag or bit of cheesecloth tied with thread. The idea is that the energy of the plants will be drawn into the warm water and into you, so be very careful that you don't choose poisonous ones! Use any of the following devil's plants:

- Apple seeds or dried apple bits because it is the devil's fruit
- Yarrow (devil's nettle) for its associations with love and its banishing properties. In this instance, it's banishing the control that others claim to have over your body.

- Parsley (devil's oatmeal) because it was superstitiously linked to the devil in so many ways and is very easy to find
- Thorns or the spines of a cactus for protection
- Jacob's ladder (devil's backbone) for strength
- Golden pothos (devil's ivy) for survival
- Devil's paintbrush to represent fire
- Twigs or roots of the elder tree to invite the devil into your ritual

If you can't find any of these ingredients, be creative and come up with your own, or find local plants with the same properties. Be sure to carefully research them to guard against allergic reactions and to find their magical meanings. There are many excellent books about the magical associations of plants to learn from.

Light some candles and put an image of the devil where you can see it from the tub. Fill the tub with warm water, add your oils or bath bombs and the sachet if you're using one, and immerse yourself in the bath. Sprinkle the top of the water with herbs or flowers of your choosing.

While you enjoy the warm water, envision the things that are impacting your body image. These could look like imaginary hooks in your skin or words stamped onto your flesh. Think about the bathwater slowly wearing them away, like thorns being eased from the skin and dissolving. Mindfully enjoy the sensations you've created: the scents, the soft candlelight, the warm bath, and the devil image. When you feel finished, drain the tub, and rinse off in the shower, getting rid of the last "hooks."

Now you are reborn. Use your most luxurious body care products and go into your day or night.

If you don't have a bathtub, you can do the same ritual in the shower. Do all the same things, using your best shower products and omitting the sachet.

Materialism

Many people are taught that pursuing money or material objects is a bad thing. Somehow, it's intrinsically selfish to want those cute but pricey shoes or to spend a night in a luxurious hotel. What makes it bad? If we really think deep and hard about it, I suppose one could say, "It's a gross display of consumerism" or "It's unfair when so many people are in need" or it's "Just trying to fill a void in your life—you can't buy happiness."

There's no denying that wealth distribution in this world is staggeringly foul. I'm not attempting to gloss over how many people simply do not have enough money, period. The intention here is to banish the guilt and shame associated with wanting something for yourself.

Connecting morality to material things is yet another attempt to demonize our natural instincts. It's perfectly normal to want beauty and pleasure in your life. Even crows collect shiny things! Yet there is a general attitude that anyone who does so is vapid and selfish. I think people with this opinion should consider the real reason they feel that way. Where did they learn it? Why was it taught to them, and who does it benefit? (Hint: it's not them.) If you and your loved ones were offered the material things you needed and wanted, would you reject them on moral principles?

This ritual is designed to banish the idea that you are undeserving of material things and to welcome prosperity into your life. It encourages dreaming, fantasy, and hope. These things are the first steps toward getting where you want to be. While often scorned as a waste of time, daydreaming is actually a big part of achieving goals. It increases creativity and programs the mind to unconsciously see opportunities.[374] It also boosts your overall mood.[375]

Besides, a little money magic won't do any harm.

For this ritual, consider your version of material happiness. This needs to resonate with you personally, not with what society tells you. Maybe luxury to you is being able to afford the more expensive art supplies, all the

---

374. Eric Klinger, "Goal Commitments and the Content of Thoughts and Dreams: Basic Principles," *Frontiers in Psychology* 4 (July 11, 2013): 415, https://doi.org/10.3389/fpsyg.2013.00415.

375. Jill Suttie, "What Daydreaming Does to Your Mind," Greater Good, University of California, Berkeley, July 5, 2021, https://greatergood.berkeley.edu/article/item/what_day dreaming_does_to_your_mind.

books you want, or a trip to somewhere warm. Maybe you wish you could get cosmetic surgery or live in the country. Nothing is off the table.

Once you've identified your desire, find an object or picture that represents it. This will be used to trigger daydreaming. Be sure the object or picture is associated only with feeling good and doesn't bring you down by reminding you of what you do not have.

I suggest, if possible, allowing yourself to indulge in the best materials for this ritual without guilt. Use that scented oil you've been saving and burn your prettiest candle. This is the first step in acting against the guilty feelings that surround materialism.

This ritual differs from other prosperity workings because it's not about survival. It's not asking for a better job, a raise, or food on the table (although you may need those too, but for now, let's focus on the fun stuff). It's about getting rid of guilt surrounding your wants.

MATERIALS
Your favorite scented oil

Green or gold candle with a holder

Dried plant material that you consider fancy. It might be a flower
   bought just for this ritual or any plant you deem precious.

Timer

Your symbolic object or picture

Choose a time when you won't be interrupted.

Rub the oil onto the candle. Inhale the scent and focus on the pure sensual joy of it. Put your candle in a holder and light it. Sprinkle the dried plants around its base. Take a moment to consider how beautiful your chosen ritual items are and how they make you feel.

Set a timer for 10 minutes. Look at the object or picture and imagine having it. How would it feel in your hands? Does it have a scent? If it's a place, what are the sounds? Let yourself dream for 10 whole minutes. Be as fantastical as you please; there is no judgment. No scenario is off-limits or too unrealistic. If you can't sit still, feel free to move around, play music, or sing, so long as it helps you daydream.

After 10 minutes, put the candle out. Repeat as often as possible.

This ritual serves two purposes. One, you challenge the guilt mindset by using materials you think are aesthetic and were maybe even purchased in protest of the guilt. Two, it implements the long-term positive psychological impact of daydreaming to change how you think.

While this ritual will not solve the world's problems, it might help you feel differently about your relationship with material things.

The Apple of Knowledge

What do you wish to learn?

This ritual can be performed for gaining knowledge of any kind. It might be that you're a student and want to do well in school, or it could be something deeper. Perhaps you seek emotional intelligence to understand the motivations of others. Maybe you want to be more informed about social issues. Perhaps you feel that information is being kept from you, and you want to uncover it. It can be anything you choose. The apple of knowledge ritual is meant to help with these things, but remember that just as in the myth, the knowledge you receive might be different than expected.

MATERIALS

Knife

1 apple

Inverted pentagram disk or an inverted pentagram
   drawn on a surface

Very carefully carve the shape of a star in the skin of the apple, to represent Lucifer the morning star, bringer of light and intellect. Leave the apple sitting on the inverted pentagram overnight. The inverted pentagram puts matter over spirit, which indicates the knowledge you seek will be factual and intelligent, not obscured by lies or delusion. The next day, the flesh of the apple will have turned brown where the star is. This is not a bad thing, but the unification of opposites: the apple is fresh and alive but decomposing at the same time, a mix of creation and destruction.

Take a bite from the apple. Bury the remainder in the earth if possible.

Go out into the world and find what you seek.

Tiny Fire and Brimstone

Sulfur, also known as brimstone, is associated with hell and the devil. It's said that Satan was cast into a lake of fire and brimstone, which is also a name for the wrath of God. When brimstone burns, it creates a horrible stench like rotten eggs. Supposedly, this is what hell smells like. In literal terms, sulfur is present all over the earth's surface and when exposed to heat, say from a volcano, it forms a stinky gas. A lightning bolt can also leave behind a whiff of sulfur.

Ordinary matches contain sulfur, and you've probably smelled it before: that slight tinge of rot beneath the scent of smoke.

This quick little ritual can symbolically light the fire within you while invoking the devil and the flames of hell, so to speak. It's suitable for when you're about to do a ritual, are in need of courage and conviction, or just want a mental pick-me-up.

Get a box or book of matches. Find a small image of the devil or Baphomet and glue it to the package. On the underside of the box lid or matchbook cover, write a powerful phrase, like *Hail Satan, Ave Satanas, Solve et Coagula,* or something similar.

Carry the matches with you if possible. Whenever you need a confidence boost, find a quiet spot. Look at the devil image on the box. Strike a match, and for the few seconds that it stays lit, feel the power of the flame, smell the brimstone, and remember your own worth. When it reaches your fingertips, blow it out and dispose of the remains.

That flash of fire, the whiff of brimstone, and the image on the package of matches act as a quick little spell of sorts, either asking the devil for assistance if you believe in him that way, or a symbolic act that brightens your mind and makes you feel powerful.

Try to do this outdoors where there is no wind or in a room where you know for certain it's okay to light a match, like at home. Do not light a match in a public bathroom, public indoor place, or most workplaces, because not only might others be annoyed by the scent, but you could trigger an alarm and sprinkler system, possibly with legal repercussions.

CONCLUSION

THE DEVIL'S IN THE DETAILS

At this point, you have learned that the devil is so much more than a horned beast on whom the world's ills can be blamed. He has helped shape Western culture, played a pivotal role in many societal shifts, and heralded the progress of civilization. Without him, we'd be in a very different place.

THE DEVIL IS AN ALLY

Women and especially feminists throughout time have been associated with evil. Whether it was daring to acknowledge a sexual appetite or a desire for education and personal freedom, it was chalked up to her devilish weakness. This was literally displayed in the witch hunts and later in literature when female characters were finally given some power, but only the evil kind. The devil was used to keep women under control. When powerful women embraced the devil as a symbol of freedom instead of fearing him, they essentially stole one of patriarchy's best weapons. The devil is not necessarily a "he," although many of us are accustomed to referring to him as such. Throughout history, he has taken on the form of women, men, all genders, and no gender. This is seen in famous artwork, folklore, and several strands of occultism.

THE DEVIL IS NEEDED

It's always been convenient to blame bad behavior on the devil instead of taking personal accountability. Satan is a vehicle for shifting fault away from ourselves and onto something else. In the *Malleus Maleficarum,* the devil was blamed for all the ills of men as he manifested through witches. It happened in the Old Testament when the sins of the entire community were placed onto a goat and cast out into the desert. During the satanic panic, several murders were committed by criminals who attributed their deeds to Satan and were genuinely believed. People need a scapegoat, which means they need a devil.

THE DEVIL IS POLITICAL

We learned from French creatives of the Romantic period that Satan is a vehicle for political change. He represents radical movements, usually ones that challenge the norm and shake the foundations of oppressive structures. Many modern Satanists continue to advocate for social justice. Satan represents the light that brings reason and change to society.

THE DEVIL IS A TRICKSTER

From Taxil to The Satanic Temple, the devil flips hypocrisy on its head in unexpected, clever, and often humorous ways. Taxil showed that the devil could be a tool to make a mockery out of the leaders of his time. In some folktales, the devil exploits a person's desires only to win their soul indefinitely. The devil could be a friend, but it came with a price. Satan, or at least his symbolism, tricks establishments into tripping over their own mistakes, making them into fools.

THE DEVIL IS A LEADER OF OUTSIDERS

In the Middle Ages, impoverished people turned to the folkloric devil for help, as they were on the fringes of a society that did not care about them. This is seen again in the witch trials, as outcasts were accused and killed. Today, this can be boiled down to those who can't or won't conform and are excluded from the group. Lucifer was ejected from heaven and cast down to hell, the ultimate story of ostracism for daring to give credence to his own feelings. This frequently happens to people who are different or who challenge tradition.

THE DEVIL IS INTELLIGENCE AND CREATIVITY

Lucifer shines light upon reason, critical thinking, and open-mindedness. Romantic writers and some occultists taught that the devil brings knowledge and inspiration. Some believed that "God" was not a being in the sky but our own creativity and imagination. The devil can open our eyes and our minds to our true potential.

THE DEVIL IS HERE

Many things that used to be considered evil are currently reframed in powerful terms. People who were once cast out or othered are celebrated now. The family scapegoat is called a cycle-breaker. The disobedient have been renamed as trailblazers and thought leaders. Empathy has become a well-known and valued characteristic, taking the place of cold-heartedly shunning anyone who is unique. The losers are quickly becoming the winners. When you look at it this way, I think we're entering a remarkably interesting era.

THE NECESSITY OF AN ANTAGONIST

When all is said and done, every story needs a bad guy. The antagonist is a guide for how to act (or more accurately, not act) and a means of deflecting attention away from our own shadows and shortcomings. Without an enemy, there would be no one to look down on and nowhere to dump blame.

An antagonist is necessary in every narrative from the vast stories of creation down to a small family dynamic. There must always be a villain so that the majority can feel righteous and safe.

Who is the antagonist in your story? Maybe you tell yourself they're evil, or dangerous. Maybe you ridicule them as a fool. Perhaps you paint them as morally corrupt, a liar, and a trickster. Your personal adversary is the reason for all your problems and difficulties. Who would you be without them? If they were removed from the narrative, would you be left gazing in the mirror?

A story without an antagonist is no story at all. There will always be an *other*, a shadow, or a monster because life demands one. Regardless of how religion evolves, how society shifts, or how science progresses, there will always be a bad guy.

There will always be a devil.

Ave Satanas.

RECOMMENDED READING

Here is a list of resources to explore. Each is educational in different ways. Some shed light on the subjects discussed in this book, and others are from the past, which helps explain the present.

Children of Lucifer: The Origins of Modern Religious Satanism
by Ruben van Luijk
This academic book is absolutely worth the time it takes to read. The author covers the origins of the devil and follows him through time into witchcraft, art, and modern practice. An excellent resource for anyone who wishes to thoroughly educate themselves about the devil and Satan.

The Devil's Dozen: Thirteen Craft Rites of the Old One
by Gemma Gary
For those interested in the folkloric devil of traditional witchcraft, this book supplies insight and ritual unlike any other book available. Gary evokes a deeply mysterious, ancient being that is the consort of witches and the embodiment of magic.

The Devil's Tome: A Book of Modern Satanic Ritual by **Shiva Honey**
This book thoroughly explains modern nontheistic Satanism. It includes beautiful rituals and ideas for building your own practice and details the author's hands-on, personal experiences as a Satanist in today's world.

The Dictionary of Demons: Names of the Damned by M. Belanger
Name any demon and it's in this book. This tome contains information on hundreds of demons, interspersed with interesting facts, folklore, and history about demonology and the devil. It is almost 500 pages of useful information that you will return to repeatedly.

The God of the Witches by Margaret Murray
Reading this book is sort of a history lesson, showing you firsthand where the mythology of the underground witch cult came from. Although written in an old-fashioned style, it contains many recognizable bits and pieces of modern-day witchcraft practices.

The Horned God of the Witches by Jason Mankey
This book is a deep dive into the history of the horned gods paired with Mankey's personal experiences working with these deities. You will learn all about Pan, Cernunnos, the Green Man, and more. It has instructions for rituals, divination, and magic.

The Little Book of Satanism: A Guide to Satanic History, Culture, and Wisdom by La Carmina
This little book is a succinct run-down of the history of modern Satanism. It's an excellent read for those who want a quick explanation of Satan past and present. It's also a perfect resource to share with those who have misconceptions about Satanism.

Lights, Camera, Witchcraft: A Critical History of Witches in American Film and Television by Heather Greene
If you love witchy films, this book covers them all. Greene analyzes witch films throughout the ages. The book explores how the witch archetypes in movies and TV mirror the views on women according to the era they were made in. You will want to watch every show and movie mentioned in this book.

Malleus Maleficarum **by Heinrich Kramer and James Sprenger,**
translated by Montague Summers
Many people have heard of the *Malleus Maleficarum* but never actually examined the contents. You will be truly horrified by the violence, misogyny, and bizarre "science" you find inside. The scariest part is how literally it was taken and how far its readership spread. Reading this will give you insight into the history of witchcraft and the witch hunts.

Michelle Remembers **by Michelle Smith and Lawrence Pazder**
If you are wondering just how baffling and horrific the satanic panic of the 1980s was, look no further than this book. If you can get through it, it will give you a very clear picture of what was going on in people's minds during the time. Bear in mind while reading that many readers believed it was nonfiction.

Plants of the Devil **by Corinne Boyer**
This book sums up the devilish folklore behind a range of plants and trees. It is written in enchanting prose instead of list form and features stunning artwork. Those interested in plant lore and superstition will love it.

The Poison Path Herbal: Baneful Herbs, Medicinal Nightshades,
and Ritual Entheogens **by Coby Michael**
For those curious about poisonous and mind-altering plants for use in witchcraft, Coby Michael's book provides correspondences, instructions, and insight. Michael forges a link between plant allies, astrology, deities, and spirits and includes recipes and rituals.

The Satanic Bible **by Anton LaVey**
Although this book is older, it will teach you how the ideology of Satanism began, and you'll see the ways LaVey's philosophy informs some of today's satanic beliefs. If you were taking a course on Satanism, this would be required reading.

Satanic Feminism: Lucifer as the Liberator of Woman in Nineteenth-Century Culture **by Per Faxneld**

If you're fascinated by the relationship between women and the devil, this book explains the complex history in detail. Faxneld covers witches, art, literature, and feminism, all in relation to Satan.

Season of the Witch: How the Occult Saved Rock and Roll **by Peter Bebergal**

Rock fans with a witchy streak will love this book. Bebergal covers the overlap between music and the supernatural, with facts about famous bands and their esoteric doings. The amount of influence that the occult has had on music is genuinely astounding no matter what your taste.

Speak of the Devil: How The Satanic Temple Is Changing the Way We Talk about Religion **by Joseph P. Laycock**

Speak of the Devil details the humble beginnings and subsequent growth of The Satanic Temple from the inside. Main members and key participants are quoted throughout, providing a fascinating glimpse into the formation of this organization.

The Witches' Sabbath: An Exploration of History, Folklore, and Modern Practice **by Kelden**

Kelden takes the infamous witches' sabbath and expands upon it with information I've never read elsewhere. It contains history and folklore and goes deep into the details, such as flying ointments and familiars. It also provides modern rituals and recipes.

BIBLIOGRAPHY

"About Us." Satanic Temple. Accessed June 30, 2023. https://thesatanic temple.com/pages/about-us.

Afzal, Thahiya. "Iconic Dualism: Satan in Paradise Lost." VIT University, March 14, 2016. https://www.academia.edu/23260187/Iconic _Dualism_Satan_in_Paradise_Lost.

Albright, Mary Beth. "Michaelmas: The Day the Devil Spit on Your Blackberries." *National Geographic*, September 28, 2015. https://www .nationalgeographic.com/culture/article/michaelmas-the-day-the -devil-spit-on-your-blackberries.

"Alphabet of Ben Sira 78: Lilith." Jewish Women's Archive. Accessed June 16, 2023. https://jwa.org/media/alphabet-of-ben-sira-78-lilith.

Artisson, Robin. *The Clovenstone Workings: A Manual of Early Modern Witchcraft*. Hancock County, ME: Black Malkin Press, 2020.

Bailey, Michael D. *Origins of the Witches' Sabbath*. Magic in History Sourcebook Series. University Park: Pennsylvania State University Press, 2021.

———. "Witchcraft and Reform in the Late Middle Ages." In *The Witch-craft Reader*, edited by Darren Oldridge, 37–42. 2nd ed. New York: Routledge, 2008. https://archive.org/details/witchcraftreader0000 unse/.

Barret, Francis. *The Magus: A Complete System of Occult Philosophy.* New York: Carol Publishing Group, 1989. https://archive.org/details /magus0000barr/mode/2up.

Barton, Blanche. *The Secret Life of a Satanist: The Authorized Biography of Anton Szandor LaVey.* Rev. ed. 1980. Reprint, Port Townsend, WA: Feral House, 2014.

Bebergal, Peter. *Season of the Witch: How the Occult Saved Rock and Roll.* New York: Jeremy P. Tarcher/Penguin, 2014.

Belanger, M. *The Dictionary of Demons: Names of the Damned.* Rev. ed. Woodbury, MN: Llewellyn Publications, 2021.

Benner, Jeff A. "Definition of Hebrew Names: Satan." Ancient Hebrew Research Center. Accessed May 28, 2023. https://www.ancient -hebrew.org/names/Satan.htm.

Black, Jeremy, and Anthony Green. *Gods, Demons, and Symbols of Ancient Mesopotamia: An Illustrated Dictionary.* 2nd ed. 1998. Reprint, London: The British Museum Press, 2004. https://archive .org/details/gods-demons-and-symbols-of-ancient-mesopotamia -an-illustrated-dictionary_202012/.

Blair, Judit M. *De-Demonising the Old Testament: An Investigation of Azazel, Lilith, Deber, Qeteb and Reshef in the Hebrew Bible.* Tübingen, Germany: Mohr Siebeck, 2009. https://archive.org/details /dedemonisingoldt0000blai/.

Blake, William. *The Marriage of Heaven and Hell.* Boston, MA: John W. Luce and Company, 1906. https://archive.org/details/marriageof heaven00blak/.

Blauvelt, Christian. "'Paul Is Dead': A Beatles Secret Message in an Album Cover?" BBC Culture. February 24, 2022. https://www.bbc .com/culture/article/20180807-paul-is-dead-a-beatles-secret -message-in-an-album-cover.

Blavatsky, Helena P. *The Secret Doctrine: The Synthesis of Science, Religion, and Philosophy.* Vol. 1, *Cosmogenesis.* London: Theological

Publishing House, 1893. https://archive.org/details/thesecret doctrin54824gut/.

Blavatsky, Helena P., and Mabel Collins, eds. *Lucifer: A Theosophical Magazine* 1, nos. 1–6 (1887–88). Project Gutenberg, 2019. https://www.gutenberg.org/files/60852/60852-h/60852-h.htm.

Blumberg, Jess. "A Brief History of the Salem Witch Trials." *Smithsonian Magazine*, last modified October 24, 2022. https://www.smithsonian mag.com/history/a-brief-history-of-the-salem-witch-trials -175162489.

Bolinger, Hope. "Why Is Satan Depicted as a Goat in Scripture?" Cross-walk. October 12, 2020. https://www.crosswalk.com/faith/bible-study /why-satan-shows-up-as-a-goat-in-scripture.html.

Boyer, Corinne. *Plants of the Devil*. 2017. Reprint, Hercules, CA: Three Hands Press, 2021.

Bradley, Ed. "Dungeons & Dragons." *60 Minutes*. CBS News, 1985. You-Tube video, 15:01. https://www.youtube.com/watch?v=YFq5aci6CHA.

Brown, Katie. "Salvation and Scapegoating: What Caused the Early Modern Witch Hunts?" TheCollector. April 20, 2023. https://www .thecollector.com/early-modern-witch-hunts/.

"Burial with Black Mass Alleged." *Birmingham Daily Gazette*, April 2, 1948. https://www.100thmonkeypress.com/biblio/acrowley/articles /1948_04_02_birmingham_gazette.pdf.

Burkert, Walter. *Greek Religion: Archaic and Classical*. Translated by John Raffan. Malden, MA: Blackwell Publishing, 1985. https://archive.org /details/greekreligionarc0000burk/page/n5/.

Burks, Raychelle. "The Dead of Aconite." Chemistry World. October 22, 2021. https://www.chemistryworld.com/opinion/the-dead-of-aconite /4014423.article.

Burr, George Lincoln, ed. *Narratives of the Witchcraft Cases 1648–1706*. New York: Charles Scribner's Sons, 1914. https://archive.org/details /narrativesofwit00burr/page/5/2up.

"A Cannibal at Large." *John Bull*, April 10, 1923. https://www.100th
monkeypress.com/biblio/acrowley/articles/1923_03_24_john_bull
.pdf.

Churton, Tobias. *Aleister Crowley: The Biography*. Oxford, UK: Watkins
Publishing, 2011.

Cohut, Maria. "The Controversy of 'Female Hysteria.'" Medical News
Today. October 13, 2020. https://www.medicalnewstoday.com
/articles/the-controversy-of-female-hysteria.

Conybeare, F. C. "The Testament of Solomon." *The Jewish Quarterly
Review* 11, no. 1 (October 1898): 1–45. https://doi.org/10.2307
/1450398.

Crowley, Aleister. *The Book of the Law*. Berlin: Ordo Templi Orientis,
1938. Reprint, York Beach, ME: Weiser Books, 1976. https://archive
.org/details/bookoflawtechnic00crow/.

Dear, William. *The Dungeon Master: The Disappearance of James Dallas
Egbert III*. Boston, MA: Houghton Mifflin Company, 1984. https://
archive.org/details/dungeonmasterdis0000dear/.

"Death Rate for Homicide in the U.S. 1950–2019." Statista. Accessed
June 30, 2023. https://www.statista.com/statistics/187592/death-rate
-from-homicide-in-the-us-since-1950/.

De Jong, Albert. *Traditions of the Magi: Zoroastrianism in Greek and
Latin Literature*. Religions in the Graeco-Roman World 133. Leiden,
Netherlands: Brill, 1997. https://archive.org/details/traditionsof
magi0000jong/.

De La Forge, Louis. *Traitté de l'esprit de l'homme: De ses facultez et
fonctions, et de son union avec le corps*. Paris: Michel Bobin & Nicholas le Gras, 1666. https://archive.org/details/bub_gb_AqQ6kEP-vFcC.

Del Rabina, Antonio. *The Grand Grimoire*. 1752. https://archive.org
/details/grand-grimoire/.

"Devil Worship: Exposing Satan's Underground." IMDb. Accessed October 13, 2023. https://www.imdb.com/title/tt1136645/mediaviewer
/rm365130240/?ref_=tt_ov_i.

Dickson, EJ. "We Asked Satanists What They Think of the New Lil Nas X Video." *Rolling Stone*, March 29, 2021. https://www.rollingstone.com /culture/culture-news/lil-nas-x-montero-call-me-by-your-name -video-church-of-satan-1147634/.

Di Placido, Dani. "Sam Smith's Grammys Performance Criticized By Conservatives and Satanists." *Forbes*, February 10, 2023. https://www .forbes.com/sites/danidiplacido/2023/02/10/sam-smiths-grammys -performance-criticized-by-conservatives-and-satanists/?sh= 5d875aff30b1.

"Dissociative Identity Disorder (Multiple Personality Disorder)." *Psychology Today*. Last modified September 21, 2021. https://www .psychologytoday.com/ca/conditions/dissociative-identity -disorder-multiple-personality-disorder.

"Do Jews Believe in Satan?" My Jewish Learning. January 3, 2022. https://www.myjewishlearning.com/article/satan-the-adversary/.

Dorsey, Lilith. *Voodoo and African Traditional Religion*. New Orleans, LA: Warlock Press, 2021. Kindle.

Dyrendal, Asbjørn, James D. Lewis, and Jesper Petersen. *The Invention of Satanism*. New York: Oxford University Press, 2016.

Editors of Merriam-Webster. "The Left Hand of (Supposed) Darkness." Merriam-Webster. Accessed November 3, 2023. https://www.merriam -webster.com/wordplay/sinister-left-dexter-right-history.

Ehrenreich, Barbara, and Deidre English. *Witches, Midwives and Nurses: A History of Women Healers*. 2nd ed. Old Westbury, NY: The Feminist Press, 1973. https://archive.org/details/witchesmidwivesn00ehre/.

Eldridge, Alison. "Inside Jonestown: How Jim Jones Trapped Followers and Forced 'Suicides'." History. November 13, 2018. https://www .history.com/news/jonestown-jim-jones-mass-murder-suicide.

Encyclopaedia Britannica. S.v. "Salem witch trials." By Jeff Wallenfeldt. Last modified August 16, 2023. https://www.britannica.com/event /Salem-witch-trials.

Encyclopaedia Britannica. Vol. 23, vase to zygote. Chicago, IL: Encyclopaedia Britannica, 1947. https://archive.org/details/dli.ernet.14918/.

EvilG. "Ronnie James Dio." Metal-Rules.com. September 14, 2006. https://www.metal-rules.com/2006/09/14/ronnie-james-dio-2/.

Faxneld, Per. *Satanic Feminism: Lucifer as the Liberator of Woman in Nineteenth-Century Culture*. Oxford Studies in Western Esotericism. New York: Oxford University Press, 2017.

———. "In Communication with the Powers of Darkness: Satanism in Turn-of-the-Century Denmark, and Its Use as a Legitimating Divide in Present-Day Esotericism." In *Occultism in a Global Perspective*, edited by Henrik Bogdan and Gordan Djurdjevic, 57–78. New York: Routledge, 2014.

Folkard, Richard. *Plant Lore, Legends and Lyrics: Embracing the Myths, Traditions, Superstitions, and Folk-Lore of the Plant Kingdom*. London, 1884. https://archive.org/details/cu31924067949028/.

Forbes, Bruce C. *Christmas: A Candid History*. Los Angeles: University of California Press, 2007.

Ford, Michael W. *Apotheosis: The Ultimate Beginner's Guide to Luciferianism & the Left-Hand Path*. Houston, TX: Succubus Productions, 2019.

———. *Necrominon: Egyptian Sethanic Magick*. Houston, TX: Succubus Productions, 2013. Kindle.

Fox, Robin Lane. *Pagans and Christians*. New York: Alfred A. Knopf, 1986.

Frothingham, Mia Belle. "Moral Panic and Folk Devils." Simply Psychology. Last modified August 31, 2023. https://simplypsychology.org/folk-devils-and-moral-panics-cohen-1972.html.

Furniss, J. *The Sight of Hell*. Books for Children and Young Persons 10. Dublin, Ireland: James Duffy and Co., 1874. https://archive.org/details/sightofhell661furn/.

Gage, Matilda Joslyn. *Woman, Church and State.* Classics in Women's Studies. Amherst, NY: Humanity Books, 2002. https://archive.org /details/womanchurchstate00gage/.

Gardner, Gerald B. *Witchcraft Today.* 1954. Reprint, New York: Magickal Childe, 1982. https://archive.org/details/witchcrafttoday00gard/.

Garland, Emma. "Throwing the 'Metal Horns' Is the Same as Calling Someone a Cuck." *Vice*, February 2, 2018. https://www.vice.com/en /article/a34wk8/throwing-the-metal-horns-is-the-same-as-calling -someone-a-cuck.

Garofalo, Robert, dir. *In Search of the Great Beast 666: Aleister Crowley, the Wickedest Man in the World.* Classic Pictures Productions, 2007. YouTube video, 2:05:23. https://www.youtube.com/watch?v=BEI _L35BzDU.

Geanous, Jacob. "Hundreds of Protesters Swarm Sold-Out SatanCon in Boston: 'Hellfire Awaits!'" *New York Post*, May 17, 2023. https:// nypost.com/2023/04/29/hundreds-of-protesters-swarm-sold-out -satancon-in-boston/.

Gilmore, Peter H. "Anton Szandor LaVey." Church of Satan, 2003, https://www.churchofsatan.com/history-anton-szandor-lavey/.

Goethe, Johann Wolfgang von. *Faust: Parts One and Two.* Translated by George Madison Priest. Great Books of the Western World 47. Chicago: University of Chicago and Encyclopaedia Britannica, 1952. https://archive.org/details/faust100goet/mode/2up.

Goldman, Russell. "Satanists Perform 'Gay Ritual' at Westboro Gravesite." ABC News. July 18, 2013. https://abcnews.go.com/blogs /headlines/2013/07/satanists-perform-gay-ritual-at-westboro -gravesite.

Göranssan, Niklas. "Black Funeral Interview." *Bardo Methodology*, May 29, 2019. http://www.bardomethodology.com/articles/2019/05/29 /black-funeral-interview/.

Gorney, Cynthia. "The Terrible Puzzle of McMartin Preschool." *Washington Post*, May 17, 1988. https://www.washingtonpost.com

/archive/lifestyle/1988/05/17/the-terrible-puzzle-of-mcmartin
-preschool/067b38f3-eff0-4548-a094-cf6bd955803f/.

Grabenstein, Hannah. "Satanic Temple Unveils Baphomet Statue at Arkansas Capitol." *Associated Press*, August 16, 2018. https://apnews .com/article/religion-arkansas-state-governments -1dfef6715487416eadfd08f36c7dbb4b.

Graves, Robert. *The White Goddess: A Historical Grammar of Poetic Myth*. New York: Farrar, Straus & Cudahy, 1948. Reprint, New York: Vintage Books, 1958. https://archive.org/details/bwb_W7-DDE-215/.

Greene, Heather. *Lights, Camera, Witchcraft: A Critical History of Witches in American Film and Television*. Woodbury, MN: Llewellyn Publications, 2021.

Griffiths, Jack. "Wellington: Does Waterloo's Iron Duke Deserve His Reputation?" All About History. May 20, 2015. https://www.history answers.co.uk/people-politics/wellington-the-iron-duke/.

Grimm, Jacob, and Wilhelm Grimm. *Grimm's Household Tales*. Translated by Margaret Hunt. Vol. 2. London: George Bell and Sons, 1884.

Grow, Kory. "PMRC's 'Filthy 15': Where Are They Now?" *Rolling Stone*, September 19, 2020. https://www.rollingstone.com/music/music-lists /pmrcs-filthy-15-where-are-they-now-60601/.

Guaita, Stanislas. *Le Serpent de La Genese: La Clef de La Magie Noir (Livre II)*. 1897. Reprint, Paris: Henri Durville, 1920. https://archive .org/details/LaClefDeLaMagieNoire/mode/2up.

Guazzo, Francesco Maria. *Compendium Maleficarum: The Montague Summers Edition*. Translated by E. A. Ashwin. Mineola, NY: Dover Publications, 1988. Kindle.

Guiley, Rosemary. *The Encyclopedia of Demons and Demonology*. New York: Facts on File, 2009.

Hanson-Baiden, Joelle. "The Debate on Repressed Memories." News-Medical.net. Last modified December 23, 2021. https://www .news-medical.net/health/The-Debate-on-Repressed-Memories.aspx.

HarpWeek. "The Bewitching Brokers—Women on Change." *Harper's Weekly*, March 5, 1870. https://www.harpweek.com/09cartoon /BrowseByDateCartoon.asp?Month=March&Date=5.

Holmes, Clive. "Women, Witches and Witnesses." In *The Witchcraft Reader*, edited by Darren Oldridge, 267–86. 2nd ed. New York: Routledge, 2008.

The Holy Bible. King James Version. Pure Cambridge Edition, n.d. https://archive.org/details/king-james-bible-pure-cambridge-edition -pdf/.

Huber, Chris. "The Four Led Zeppelin Symbols, Explained." Extra Chill. March 21, 2021. https://extrachill.com/led-zeppelin-symbols -meaning.

Hughes, Michael M. *Magic for the Resistance: Rituals and Spells for Change*. Woodbury, MN: Llewellyn Publications, 2018. Kindle.

Hunt, Garry. "Why Venus Is Called the Morning Star or the Evening Star." *BBC Sky at Night Magazine*, February 2, 2023. https://www .skyatnightmagazine.com/space-science/venus-morning-star -evening-star/.

Huysmans, J. K., and Robert Irwin. *Là-Bas (Lower Depths)*. France, 1891. Reprint, London: Dedalus, 1986. https://archive.org/details/labas lowerdepths0000huys/mode/2up?view=theater.

Jackson, Gabrielle. "The Female Problem: How Male Bias in Medical Trials Ruined Women's Health." *Guardian*, November 2, 2020. https:// www.theguardian.com/lifeandstyle/2019/nov/13/the-female -problem-male-bias-in-medical-trials.

James I, King of England. *Daemonologie: In Forme of a Dialogie*. Scotland: Robert Walde-graue, 1597. Project Gutenberg, 2008. https:// www.gutenberg.org/cache/epub/25929/pg25929-images.html.

James, Robert, dir. "Devil Worship: Exposing Satan's Underground." *The Geraldo Rivera Special*. Tribune Entertainment Company and Investigative News Group, October 22, 1988. YouTube video, 1:31:50. https:// www.youtube.com/watch?v=MjVpqMHrRpU.

Janisse, Kier-La, and Paul Corupe. *Satanic Panic: Pop-Cultural Paranoia in the 1980s.* Surrey, UK: Fab Press, 2016.

"Judas Priest: The Lawsuit Over Better By You, Better Than Me That Shook The Metal World." Rock N' Roll True Stories, June 24, 2022. YouTube video, 13:48. https://www.youtube.com/watch?v=gHOFI 5UNNck.

"Judgement for Defendants in Black Magic." *The Evening News*, April 13, 1934. https://www.100thmonkeypress.com/biblio/acrowley/articles /1934_04_13_evening_news.pdf.

Jung, Carl G. *The Archetypes and the Collective Unconscious.* The Collected Works of C. G. Jung, vol. 9. Translated by R. F. C. Hull. Edited by Herbert Read, Michael Fordham, and Gerhard Adler. London: Routledge and Kegan Paul, 1959. https://archive.org/details /archetypescollec0009_part1/.

Kelden. *The Witches' Sabbath: An Exploration of History, Folklore & Modern Practice.* Woodbury, MN: Llewellyn Publications, 2022.

Klinger, Eric. "Goal Commitments and the Content of Thoughts and Dreams: Basic Principles." *Frontiers in Psychology* 4 (July 11, 2013): 415. doi:10.3389/fpsyg.2013.00415.

Kramer, Heinrich, and James Sprenger. *The Malleus Maleficarum of Heinrich Kramer and James Sprenger.* Translated by Montague Summers. New York: Dover, 1971. https://archive.org/details/malleus maleficar00inst.

La Carmina. *The Little Book Of Satanism: A Guide to Satanic History, Culture & Wisdom.* Berkeley, CA: Ulysses Press, 2022.

Lane, Penny, dir. *Hail Satan?* Hard Working Movies. Magnolia Pictures, 2019. 95 minutes.

Lachman, Gary. *Madame Blavatsky: The Mother of Modern Spirituality.* New York: Penguin, 2012.

Lamar, Cyriaque. "When Geraldo Rivera Took on Satanism (and a Very Confused Ozzy Osbourne)." Gizmodo. August 9, 2011. https://

gizmodo.com/when-geraldo-rivera-took-on-satanism-and-a-very
-confus-5829171.

LaVey, Anton. *The Devil's Notebook*. Port Townsend, WA: Feral House,
1992.

———. "The Eleven Satanic Rules of the Earth." Church of Satan.
Accessed June 30, 2023. https://www.churchofsatan.com/eleven
-rules-of-earth/.

———. "The Nine Satanic Statements." Church of Satan. Accessed June
30, 2023. https://www.churchofsatan.com/nine-satanic-statements/.

———. *The Satanic Bible*. New York: Avon Books, 1969.

Lawrence, Richard, trans. *The Book of Enoch*. Oxford, UK: John Henry
Parker, 1838. https://books.google.com/books?id=O-0QAQAAIAAJ.

Laycock, Joseph P. *Speak of the Devil: How the Satanic Temple Is Changing the Way We Talk about Religion*. New York: Oxford University
Press, 2020.

Leeser, Isaac, trans. *Twenty-Four Books of the Holy Scriptures: Carefully
Translated After the Best Jewish Authorities*. New York: Hebrew Pub-
lishing Company, 1853. https://archive.org/details/ENGTHB_DBS
_HS/.

Leeson, Peter T., and Jacob W. Russ. "Witch Trials." *The Economic Journal* 128, no. 613 (August 2018): 2066–105. https://doi.org/10.1111
/ecoj.12498.

Leland, Charles G. *Aradia, or The Gospel of Witches*. 1899. Reprint,
Custer, WA: Phoenix Publishing, 1996. https://archive.org/details
/aradia00char/.

Lessis, Rebecca. "Lilith." Jewish Women's Archive. December 31, 1999.
https://jwa.org/encyclopedia/article/lilith.

Lévi, Éliphas. *The Doctrine and Ritual of High Magic: A New Translation*.
Translated by Mark Anthony Mikituk. New York: TarcherPerigree,
2017.

———. *The Mysteries of Magic: A Digest of the Writings of Éliphas Lévi*. Edited by Arthur Edward Waite. 2nd ed. London: Kegan Paul, Trench, Trübner & Co., 1897. https://archive.org/details/mysteriesofmagic 00levi/.

———. *Transcendental Magic: Its Doctrine and Ritual*. Translated by Arthur Edward Waite. London: Rider and Co., 1896. https://archive .org/details/in.ernet.dli.2015.219124/.

Luck, Georg. *Arcana Mundi: Magic and Occult in the Greek and Roman Worlds*. Baltimore, MD: Johns Hopkins University Press, 1985. https://archive.org/details/arcanamundimagic0000unse/.

Mankey, Jason. *The Horned God of the Witches*. Woodbury, MN: Llewellyn Publications, 2021.

Manley, Brooks. "Why Was the Book of Enoch Removed from the Bible?" Understanding the Bible. Accessed July 10, 2023. https:// understandingthebible.org/why-was-book-of-enoch-removed-from -bible/.

"March 26, 1997: Heaven's Gate Cult Members Found Dead." History. Last modified September 26, 2023. https://www.history.com/this-day -in-history/heavens-gate-cult-members-found-dead.

Marlowe, Christopher. *Doctor Faustus*. Edited by Sylvan Barnet. New York: Signet Classic, 1969. https://archive.org/details/doctorfaustus sig00chri/.

Martin, Sean. *The Knights Templar: The History and Myths of the Legendary Military Order*. Harpenden, UK: Pocket Essentials, 2004. https:// archive.org/details/MartinSTheKnightsTemplar/.

Mathers, S. L. MacGregor, and Aleister Crowley. *The Lesser Key of Solomon: Goetia, The Book of Evil Spirits, Lemegeton-Clavicula Salimonis Regis*. Fairhope, AL: Mockingbird Press, 2016. https://archive.org /details/lesserkeyofsolom0000math/.

McKeown, Robert E., Steven P. Cuffe, and Richard Schulz. "US Suicide Rates by Age Group, 1970–2002: An Examination of Recent Trends."

American Journal of Public Health 96, no. 10 (October 2006): 1744–51. https://doi.org/10.2105/ajph.2005.066951.

Meiji, Deli. "Esu Is Not the Devil: How a Yoruba Deity Got Rebranded." OkayAfrica. December 15, 2017. https://www.okayafrica.com /yoruba-esu-is-not-the-devil/.

Michelet, Jules. *Satanism and Witchcraft: A Study in Medieval Superstition*. Translated by A. R. Allinson. 5th ed. New York: Citadel Press, 1965. https://archive.org/details/satanismwitchcra0000mich/.

Milton, John. *Paradise Lost*. Edited by James Robert Boyd. New York: Baker and Scribner, 1851. https://archive.org/details/paradiselost 00miltgoog/mode/2up.

Murray, Margaret A. *The God of the Witches*. New York: Oxford University Press, 1970. Reprint, 1981. https://archive.org/details/godof witches0000murr/mode/2up.

———. *The Witch-Cult in Western Europe*. London: Oxford University Press, 1963. https://archive.org/details/in.ernet.dli.2015.24123/.

Nast, Thomas. "'Get Thee Behind Me, (Mrs.) Satan!' / Th. Nast." *Harper's Weekly* 16, February 17, 1872, 40. https://www.loc.gov/item /95512460/.

Newell, Venetia. *An Egg at Easter: A Folklore Study*. London: Routledge & Keagan Paul, 1971. https://archive.org/details/eggateasterfolk l00newa/.

"New Milestone: Over 700,000 Members!" Satanic Temple Accessed October 6, 2023. https://thesatanictemple.com/blogs/news/new-mile stone-over-700-000-members.

Nobel, Carmen. "The Power of Rituals in Life, Death, and Business." Harvard Business School. June 3, 2013. https://hbswk.hbs.edu/item /the-power-of-rituals-in-life-death-and-business.

Noll, Richard. "Speak, Memory." *Psychiatric Times*, March 19, 2014. https://www.psychiatrictimes.com/view/speak-memory.

O'Donnell, James J. *Pagans: The End of Traditional Religion and the Rise of Christianity*. New York: Ecco, 2016.

Pliny. *Natural History, Volume IV, Books XII–XVI*. Loeb Classical Library 370. Edited by H. Rackham. 1945. Reprint, Cambridge, MA: Harvard University Press, 1960. https://archive.org/details/L370PlinyNatural HistoryIV1216/.

Peterson, Joseph H., trans. *Grimorium Verum: A Handbook of Black Magic*. Scotts Valley, CA: self-published, CreateSpace Publishing, 2007.

Phillips, Phil. *Saturday Morning Mind Control*. Nashville, TN: Oliver-Nelson Books, 1991.

———. *Turmoil in the Toybox*. Lancaster, PA: Starburst Publishers, 1986.

Pohlsander, Hans A. *The Emperor Constantine*. 2nd ed. New York: Routledge, 2004.

"Protest and Prayer Fill Air Outside Greater Church of Lucifer." ABC13 Houston. October 31, 2015. https://abc13.com/church-of-lucifer -spring-protesters-protest/1060363/.

Pulling, Pat, and Kathy Cawthon. *The Devil's Web: Who Is Stalking Your Children for Satan?* Lafayette, LA: Huntington House, 1989. https:// archive.org/details/devilswebwhoisst00pull/.

Richard RemembersJoePyne. "Anton LaVey Interviewed by Joe Pyne 1966 or 1967." October 13, 2009. YouTube video, 4:45. https://www .youtube.com/watch?v=8m3hHYtdegw.

Roehl, Thomas. "#059 *Tremella mesenterica*, Witch's Butter." Fungus Fact Friday. Last modified October 20, 2017. https://www.fungusfactfriday .com/059-tremella-mesenterica/.

Romano, Aja. "Why Satanic Panic Never Really Ended." Vox. March 31, 2021. https://www.vox.com/culture/22358153/satanic-panic-ritual -abuse-history-conspiracy-theories-explained.

Russell, Jeffrey Burton. *Lucifer: The Devil in the Middle Ages*. Ithaca, NY: Cornell University Press, 1984.

———. *Witchcraft in the Middle Ages*. Ithaca, NY: Cornell University Press, 1972. https://archive.org/details/witchcraftinmidd0000russ _c5b1/.

Schlosser, S. E. "Garlic: Superstitions, Folklore and Fact." American Folklore. Last modified August 28, 2022. https://americanfolklore.net /folklore/2010/10/garlic_superstitions_folklore.html.

Shachat, Emma. "The Antisemitic History of Witches." Hey Alma. October 29, 2020. https://www.heyalma.com/the-antisemitic-history-of -witches/.

Sibley, W. G. *The Story of Freemasonry*. 3rd ed. Gallipolis, OH: The Lion's Paw Club, 1913. https://archive.org/details/The_Story_Of _Freemasonry_-_W_G_Sibley/.

Siegle, Steve. "The Art of Kindness." Mayo Clinic Health System. August 17, 2023. https://www.mayoclinichealthsystem.org/hometown-health /speaking-of-health/the-art-of-kindness.

Skinner, Charles M. *Myths and Legends of Flowers, Trees, Fruits, and Plants in All Ages and in All Climes*. Philadelphia, PA: J. B. Lippincott Company, 1911. https://archive.org/details/mythslegendsoffl00skin/.

Smith, Michelle, and Lawrence Pazder. *Michelle Remembers*. New York: Pocket Books, 1980.

"Sojourner Truth." Library of Congress. December 9, 1998. https://www .loc.gov/exhibits/odyssey/educate/truth.html.

"Sojourner Truth." National Park Service. Last modified September 2, 2017. https://www.nps.gov/wori/learn/historyculture/sojourner-truth .htm.

Somerset, Anne. *The Affair of the Poisons: Murder, Infanticide, and Satanism at the Court of Louis XIV*. New York: St. Martin's Press, 2014.

Stephen, Thomas. *The History of the Church of Scotland: From the Reformation to the Modern Time*. Vol. 2. London: Longman, Brown, Green, and Longmans, 1848. https://books.google.com/books?id=eQR MAAAAYAAJ.

Sulaiman al-Ashqar, Umar. *The World of the Jinn and Devils*. Translate by Jamaal al-Din M. Zarabozo. Denver, CO: Al-Basheer Publications and Translations, 1998. https://archive.org/details/en_The-world-of-jinn -and-devils.

Summers, Montague. *The History of Witchcraft and Demonology*. London: Kegan Paul, Trench, Trubner & Co., 1926. https://archive.org /details/in.ernet.dli.2015.173667/.

Suttie, Jill. "What Daydreaming Does to Your Mind." Greater Good. University of California, Berkeley. July 5, 2021. https://greatergood .berkeley.edu/article/item/what_daydreaming_does_to_your_mind.

Taqi-ud-Din al-Hilali, Muhammad, and Muhammad Muhsin Khan, trans. *Translations of the Meaning of the Noble Qur'an in the English Language*. Madina, Saudi Arabia: King Fahd Complex for the Printing of the Holy Qur'an, 2017. https://archive.org/details/english __qu46977976946974679n__translation/mode/2up.

The Torah: The Five Books of Moses. Philadelphia, PA: The Jewish Publication Society of America, 1962. https://archive.org/details/torahfive booksof0000jewi/.

"The Occult Revival: A Substitute Faith." *Time*, June 19, 1972. Accessed June 30, 2023. https://content.time.com/time/subscriber/article /0,33009,877779-1,00.html.

Van Luijk, Ruben. *Children of Lucifer: The Origins of Modern Religious Satanism*. Oxford Studies in Western Esotericism. New York: Oxford University Press, 2016.

Vernor, E. R. *Lilith: The Mother of All Dark Creatures*. Fort Wayne, IN: Dark Moon Press, 2015.

Waite, Arthur Edward. *Devil-Worship in France or The Question of Lucifer: A Record of Things Seen and Heard in the Secret Societies According to the Evidence of Initiates*. London: George Redway, 1896. Project Gutenberg, 2007. https://www.gutenberg.org/cache/epub/21258/pg21258-images.html.

Watts, D.C. *Dictionary of Plant Lore*. San Diego, CA: Elsevier, 2007.

"When Was the Bible Written?" Biblica. Accessed May 26, 2023. https://www.biblica.com/resources/bible-faqs/when-was-the-bible-written/.

"The Wickedest Man in the World." *John Bull*, March 24, 1923. Accessed March 29, 2023. https://www.100thmonkeypress.com/biblio/acrowley/articles/1923_03_24_john_bull.pdf

Wiederhorn, Jon. "36 Years Ago: Ozzy Osbourne Exonerated in 'Suicide Solution' Fan Death Lawsuit." Loudwire. Last modified August 7, 2022. https://loudwire.com/ozzy-osbourne-exonerated-suicide-solution-fan-death-lawsuit-anniversary/.

Wilde, Jane. *Ancient Legends, Mystic Charms, and Superstitions of Ireland*. Vol. 1. Boston, MA: Ticknore and Co., 1887. https://archive.org/details/ancientlegendsm00wildgoog/.

Wing, Nick. "Phoenix City Council Votes to End Prayer Rather Than Let Satanists Lead It." HuffPost. February 5, 2016. https://www.huffpost.com/entry/phoenix-satanists_n_56b4e2b2e4b04f9b57d9639f.

Zimmerman, Frank, trans. *The Book of Tobit*. New York: Harper & Brothers, 1958. https://archive.org/details/bookoftobitengli0000fran/.